sex again

sex again

Recharging Your Libido—Ancient Wisdom *for* Modern Couples

JILL BLAKEWAY, LAc

with COLLEEN KAPKLEIN

WORKMAN PUBLISHING
NEW YORK

As with any adjustment to your diet or exercise regimen, consult your doctor before implementing changes. If you have a medical issue that you are concerned about, consult your health care practitioner. Workman will not be liable for any complications, injuries, loss, or other medical problems arising from or in connection with using this book.

 Published simultaneously in Canada by Thomas Allen & Son Limited.

Library of Congress Cataloging-in-Publication Data is available.

ISBN 978-0-7611-7169-0

Design by Sarah Smith

Workman books are available at special discounts when purchased in bulk for premiums and sales promotions as well as for fund-raising or educational use. Special editions or book excerpts can also be created to specification. For details, contact the Special Sales Director at the address below, or send an email to specialmarkets@workman.com.

Workman Publishing Company, Inc.
225 Varick Street
New York, NY 10014-4381
workman.com

Printed in the United States of America
First printing December 2012
10 9 8 7 6 5 4 3 2 1

For my husband, Noah.

Acknowledgments

Thank you to everyone who has worked so hard on this book as well as the family, colleagues, and friends who have supported me as I completed it.

I am grateful to writer Colleen Kapklein, who worked tirelessly on this project and whose talent is evident on every page. Thank you also to Suzie Bolotin and Mary Ellen O'Neill at Workman Publishing for wise advice and careful editing and the whole Workman team, who brought a wealth of experience and hard work to the finished book. I tell everyone who'll listen what a great literary agent I have, so once again thank you to Daniel Greenberg, who had faith in me when my confidence wavered.

My husband, Noah, is my rock. His strength has bolstered me during rough times and his humor has made the good times even better. Like many marriages, ours has been a long and complex journey that has taught me so much. Noah, you truly are my best friend and I thank God each day for your warmth and kindness. Emma, our daughter, has grown into a loving, quirky, funny, and smart woman and I'm looking forward to seeing what she does next. Emma, I know it's not easy when your Mum writes a book about sex, so thank you for being so patient and supportive.

The inspiration for this book came from my work as the founder of the YinOva Center in New York City. In my wildest dreams I never thought we would be able to assemble the team who currently work at the YinOva Center. It seems almost mystical that when the center grew and I could no longer run it on my own, some of the most capable, sensible people I've ever met marched into my life. Our acupuncturists are not only a talented, experienced, and hard-working team but they are also some of the nicest people I know. You bring warmth, a sense of fun, and great compassion to our center, which make it a lovely place to work and a healing place to be a patient. All of our administrative staff are an essential part of our healing team and work tirelessly to ensure our center runs smoothly. We are a better practice because of each and every one of you and I thank you from the bottom of my heart. Nicole Kruck is our wonderful YinOva massage therapist and I drew heavily on her experience when writing the massage sections of this book. Thanks for sharing your knowledge so freely, Nicole.

Neale Donald Walsch was a source of wise counsel during the time I was working on this book. In fact, the title was Neale's idea and I thank him for sharing his time and talent so generously. If you haven't read *Conversations with God,* I cannot recommend it highly enough.

Lastly I'd like to thank my patients. Thousands of people have trusted me with their health care, which is an honor I take very seriously. Thank you for sharing your stories with me and for allowing me to support you. This book is for you.

contents

part **one**

Why Don't We Do It?

part **two**

Renewing Your Sexual Self

part **three**

Balance and Connect

part **four**
Troubleshooting

part **one**

Why Don't We Do It?

1

Sexual Healing

For Women Who Want to Want To

Americans have sex eighty-five times a year, on average, or once every 4.3 days. That's according to an extensive survey by condom maker Durex, which also reported that this is less sex than people have pretty much anywhere else in the world. As I read these results, all I could think was, *where on earth did they find people having that much sex?* Clearly Durex hadn't asked the women I treat or otherwise discuss such matters with. That is, women primarily in their thirties and forties, as well as moving into the menopausal years, in lasting primary relationships. If you talk to those women—or if you *are* one of those women—you get a much different picture of Americans' sex lives than you do from a peddler of prophylactics. But many of those women do indeed feel they are having less sex than anyone else in the world!

I am an acupuncturist and clinical herbalist, and what I hear in my office, as well as from my friends, is that a lot of couples can only dream of the weekly sex just over half of Durex's respondents report. And plenty don't even have the energy to dream it. So as much as Durex's numbers puzzled me, I was not surprised to find that, according to the American Medical Association (AMA), forty million adult Americans are not having sex with their partners at all. Nor was I startled by a study published in the

Journal of the American Medical Association that documented that about one in three American women report a lack of interest in sex. In any survey of sexual problems, low libido always tops the list—and by a wide margin.

It may seem almost inevitable that any sexual spark is so often muted in our fast-paced, highly competitive, multitasking, me-first, stressed-out world. Your friends probably agree that it seems as if everyone is *not* doing it, and that's just the way things are. Well, that's not the way it has to be. You may be out of touch with your own desire, but that doesn't mean it's not there. The trick is to reconnect to it.

You may be out of touch with your own desire, but that doesn't mean it's not there.

So although you may well be one of the women not much in the mood, I'm betting you don't like it that way. I'm betting you are like the women I see in my office every day who aren't having much sex—but *want* to. Not women looking for someone to have sex with—that's outside my purview as a health care practitioner, I'm pleased to say—but women with long-term partners. Women, in other words, with plenty of opportunity—but little desire. Women who are too stressed for sex. Women who are too tired for sex. Women who somehow don't feel they are sexy enough for sex. (I hear these complaints from single women, too, whether or not they are in the market for a partner, and from women in newer or less formalized relationships—the ones we old-marrieds might imagine are in that honeymoon stage.)

This book is for those women. Women who aren't having much sex, don't feel much like having sex—but want to want to. Those who may have gotten a bit out of practice but are ready for sex again.

Just Do It

If you want to want to have sex, but haven't been really feeling it, my single best piece of advice is to do it anyway. Pretend you are in a sneaker commercial and *just do it.*

I don't mean to be flip about this. This is actually a piece of the ancient Chinese philosophy this program is built on. Which is why it sounds like a bit of a departure from how we are used to approaching things in the Western therapeutic mind-set, especially when it comes to "psychological" issues. Chinese medicine aims to get you back in your body; we are more used to living more in our heads. We are accustomed to working on issues ahead of time, and when it comes to sex advice, that plays out as strategies for fixing the relationship, improving communication, uncovering emotional issues, and so on. And often, *talking, talking, talking* about all of it. Chinese medicine doesn't make a distinction between issues of the body and issues of the mind, and takes on what Western medicine considers psychological all of a piece with what is physical. In Chinese medicine, too, you can improve sex by improving the relationship. But you can also improve the relationship by improving the sex. And the key way you improve the sex is by having sex. Not if it is truly damaging, of course, but in almost every other case, it's highly recommended.

Still, I realize "just do it" may be easier said than done, and the rest of this book is about *how* you can feel like having sex again, including how and why and when you should (and sometimes shouldn't) just do it. One important part of the journey is making it for yourself. It may also be good for your partner, and for your relationship. But most of all, this is about *you*.

Another important factor is making the sex you have better. You can't wait around, hoping great sex will somehow happen to you. You can't wait until it will be perfect before you have sex. It will *never* be perfect. To have better sex, to want more sex—you have to have sex. You have to start where you are. And if right now that means humdrum sex, that's OK. It won't stay that way for long, not if you follow the Sex in Six plan. After about six weeks you'll be back to wanting sex, and so presumably having sex. More sex. And better sex. In fact, how much sex you have is not what really matters most: Quality trumps quantity.

But the fact remains that to have sex again you need to . . . have sex. Right now you might be stuck in a negative loop—lack of desire breeding lack of sex, and though you might not realize it, lack of sex breeding lack of desire—but soon you'll be experiencing the positive flip side of that cycle: The more sex you have, the more sex you'll want. The more you enjoy sex, the more satisfying it is, and the more you will want to have it.

To be clear I do *not* think you should "just do it" if "it" is painful or otherwise harmful. I don't think you should "just do it" only because you feel like you *have* to for your partner. I don't think you should "just do it" if you resent doing it, and resentment is building up in your relationship. But do keep in mind much of your attitude about sex is under your control. You don't have to be excited about it (at first) to go ahead and give it a whirl. If you are thinking actively negative thoughts about sex (*Ugh, I* really *don't want to do this* or *let's get this over with!*), you are not going to gain what you might if you consciously decided to keep a more open mind. In choosing this book, you've already made a shift in the way you think about sex. And many of the strategies in this book will serve to support and extend that new approach.

This program is built of practices found in two-thousand-year-old Chinese texts written by ancient Taoist sages and honed by my clinical experience treating thousands of patients by drawing on that ancient wisdom in a very modern way. The "sexercises" range from simple deep breathing, or just thinking about sex for five minutes, to thrusting techniques and strategies for intensifying orgasm. They are layered on top of advice about the best ways to eat, exercise, and otherwise optimize your health (both physical and mental)—which are also the best things to do for your sexual health—all customized for your particular situation. I recommend herbal formulas when they apply—all are available over the counter and very safe for use on your own. (See Appendix 1 for advice on buying high-quality herbs.) For those who are interested and have access to it, acupuncture can also be useful (though it isn't necessary). Once your own house is in order, there is guidance on seeing to the health of your relationship as well.

But the sexercises are the heart of the Sex in Six plan. They are accessible to everyone—nothing aerobic, acrobatic, or pornographic required, I promise. Not all involve actually having intercourse, or even any sexual contact at all. Some are done with all your clothes *on*. Some are designed to be done without a partner. And some of them may inspire you to go ahead and get naked before you finish reading the relevant passage. Don't say I didn't warn you!

Sex Is Good for You

Let me urge anyone who thinks that they are pretty much OK with not caring much about sex these days to think again. You *should* want to have sex. Your sexuality is an integral part of what makes you *you*. And sex is an integral part of what makes a couple a couple.

> ***Having sex makes people—and their relationships—healthier and happier. Having sex literally makes love.***

Sex is a great invention. It's free. It's fun. It feels terrific. And it's good for you. Really, really good for you. Having sex makes people—and their relationships—healthier and happier. *Good* sex does, anyway. And there's research to prove it! Sex reduces heart rate, lowers blood pressure, increases immunity, and provides a wide range of other health benefits. Sex reduces the perception of pain. It burns calories and increases energy levels. It's one of the best stress-busters I know. Sex improves your mood, too. It clears the mind and brightens your outlook. It's relaxing and calming. It's a great release for emotional as well as physical tension. Sex promotes a positive psychological state and emotional security.

Furthermore, sex helps create and maintain a strong relationship. Sex is, in fact, *key* to a relationship. Without sex, you are just roommates. I was going to say "just glorified roommates." But really, without the sex, where's the glory? Sex helps create the strongest bond to someone, particularly over the long haul. Sex—independent of its use for procreation—helps create stability in a relationship. Having sex literally makes love.

Any kind of positive touching, including nonsexual touching, is good for you, your body, your mood, your relationship, and your overall sense of well-being. But sex, assuming it is a full-body, skin-to-skin experience of intimacy, and perhaps an aerobic workout as well, brings the maximum payoff. The best of the best is sex with a partner you love and trust, in a strong relationship. (Sex-for-one will give you most of these same benefits, however, so don't let lack of the immediate availability of a partner hold you back!) It is not necessary to have an orgasm to experience the

Do I Have to Have Acupuncture?

Almost all of the patients you will meet in these pages received acupuncture as part of their treatment. I am, after all, an acupuncturist—acupuncture is what most of my patients come to see me for. And acupuncture can be very useful in treating a variety of sexual issues—and the physical and emotional issues leading to or compounding them.

But acupuncture is not the kind of thing you can do on your own—and this book is designed as a DIY project. That's why I don't usually mention it when I describe cases.

I want to assure you that you can get results without acupuncture. The exercises in this book work along much the same lines as acupuncture does when it comes to moving and balancing energy in your body, so you can use them instead. Add in the herbs and lifestyle adjustments most applicable to your situation—just as I recommend to my patients—and you'll be well on your way. (True, I customize prescription herbs for most patients, and a professional could do the same for you, specific to you and your circumstances, for optimal results—but the high-quality over-the-counter formulas I recommend will do the trick in almost every case.)

If you do choose to seek out acupuncture, you may find results come more quickly, easily, or clearly. But no one *has* to have acupuncture in order to want sex again.

good sex can do, but when you *do* orgasm you add a whole other layer of benefits.

The positive effects of sex appear not just in the immediate aftermath but also, if you have reasonably regular sex, over the long term as well. "Afterglow" lasts much longer than most people realize. It can follow us for hours, even days, after sex.

One more thing: *Having sex increases libido*. Having sex is the single best thing to do about lack of desire. If you want a robust libido, you have to take it out and drive it around frequently. If you leave it parked in the driveway all the time, then it's going to get rusty and be hard to start. You *can* start it up again, though, no matter how long it has been, what age you are, or what your attitude is right now. You really can want to have sex again, and you really will have good sex, if you believe you can and truly give the program in here an honest and invested effort.

Energy and Balance

There can be many different factors underlying loss of interest in sex. There may be something going on in your body. Or your mood. Or your relationship. Or some combination of the above. Chinese medicine addresses all these areas at once, without making a distinction between body and mind. It targets symptoms, and the underlying problems that cause them, as a path to restoring libido. But part of what I love about Chinese medicine is that it also works the other way around: Restoring libido can be a way to alleviate symptoms and address those underlying problems.

You might not be having sex because you are tired, or stressed-out, or sick, or upset, or in a fight. But you also might be tired or stressed or sick or upset or fighting *because* you aren't having sex. When you look at it this way, the Chinese medicine way, you are no longer limited to working on the body or mind or relationship as a means of improving the sex. It's just as valid to work on the sex as a means of improving the body, mind, or relationship. In many cases that's bound to be not only quicker, but also much more enjoyable. And perhaps even more effective.

Chinese medicine places a lot of importance on energy and balance. If you have negative symptoms, they indicate a lack of energy, or imbalance. Fixing the problem can restore energy and/or balance—or you can fix the problem by building up energy and improving balance. That's true in pretty much all areas of life, but never more true than with sex. The Sex in Six program helps you restore your energy levels, rebalance your self and your relationship, and recharge your sex drive. In any order!

Not too many of my patients place low libido at the top of their list of things they want to deal with. (Though many of my patients experiencing menopause do!) Either way, more often than not, when I ask about sex as part of my standard initial interview, women mention they are not interested like they used to be and don't have sex very often. Usually they sound pretty wistful.

What *does* happen all the time is that women who come in for any number of reasons find that as their other concerns resolve, their libido also improves. Even if they weren't fully aware they had an issue going on in that area. And even if they were aware they had a problem, but unaware there was a relatively simple solution, as is often the case with women in menopause. That's because Chinese medicine always works along the same pathways: building, moving, and balancing energy. The effects are not limited to just the targeted condition. Your whole body—in fact, your whole life—might experience changes. Balanced energy knows no boundaries.

FOR THE GUYS: This Book Is for You, Too. (Just Maybe Not the *Whole* Book)

My name is Noah Rubinstein, and I am the clinic director, and an acupuncturist, at the YinOva Center. I am also Jill's husband. Our culture presents essentially one idea about couples not having much sex: men who want more and women who want less. That might well be the basic story for many couples, but here at the Center we see just as many men struggling with low libido as we do women. Trust me when I say your manhood is *not* defined by your ability to get an erection or to thrust away all night like a porn star—or your desire to do such things. If you really want to "man up," what you need to do is *own* your issue, whatever it is, and take the necessary action to address it.

So while the main thread of this book addresses women as individuals, and as part of couples, much of the information and advice applies to men as well. The topics of interest primarily to men I've gathered into "For the Guys" sections, just like this one, throughout the book. So if you scan through, looking for these sections—or read them when your partner passes you the book—you will get most of what you need to know to get a handle on your own sex drive.

I think you'll find, however, that the more you read along with your partner, the more you both will get out of it. When it comes to relationships, no one goes it alone. And your sex life isn't about just you; it's about you two. Even more important than the reading is the doing. Here's my promise, man to man: Do this program with your partner and you will feel better physically and mentally. You will strengthen your relationship. And you will want—and have—more (and better!) sex.

Our experience at the Center has shown that good communication—verbal and otherwise—holds the key to getting the spark back in the bedroom. This means understanding ourselves as well as our partners. This all may take a little work on your part, and may require getting out of your regular routine—even outside your comfort zone. But the rewards (did I mention more and better sex?) will be worth it!

Balance and Connect

Sex doesn't have to be perfect to be good or beneficial. It won't be, because it never is. It doesn't have to set off fireworks, or mend all the little weak spots in your relationship, or reclaim your youth, or provide a spiritual experience. It doesn't even have to be with a partner.

Over time, sex might do or be any or all of those things. *But not if you don't have any.* It all starts with your desire. No matter how long it's been since you felt it, or how deeply you have it buried, you can rediscover and recharge it.

If you commit to the process. Think of it like you would going on a diet, or following any other plan to make a change in your life. You have to put in the effort to reap the reward. Only unlike a diet, this is about *eliminating* deprivation rather than instituting it. With *Sex Again* the stuff that feels good and the stuff that's good for you are the same stuff. If it were a diet, it would tell you to eat more chocolate.

Your journey starts here. You've already taken the first steps: recognizing something is out of whack and deciding to take action to address it. Now you'll learn how to identify and balance the energy patterns in your body, and in your relationship. And how to connect both to your own sexual self and to your partner. You'll add a plethora of sexercises to your repertoire, from meditation to masturbation. You'll uncover any specific problems that are creating roadblocks—along with strategies for removing or surmounting them. And in about six weeks you'll be fully recharged, and ready for sex again.

Good Sex

We often have no real idea of what "good" sex is. The sexual imagery that saturates our society leaves a lot of us holding ourselves up to extremely unrealistic models—models that don't have anything to do with really good sex anyway. We tend to aspire to the kind of "mind-blowing" sex between physically perfect people promoted by Hollywood and Madison Avenue, not to mention the pornography industry. Then we either judge our real-life experiences as somehow falling short, or we expend lots of energy trying to mimic that impossible standard. Or we give it up as impossible. Either way we miss out on the more profound pleasures of truly good sex.

The sexual imagery that saturates our society is unrealistic and unrelated to really good sex.

There is no one technique that guarantees good sex, no set of instructions that makes it a sure thing. That's because good sex is not about what-goes-where or who-licks-what. Good sex is not gymnastic, or rose-petal romantic, or *Cosmo* (or cosmo) inspired. (At least, not necessarily!) Good sex has nothing to do with how old you are or how much you weigh. Good sex is not about how often you do it or how long you last or how hard you come.

Good sex *is* about connection between two people. It is about the mutual flow of energy between partners, with both people giving and receiving it. Good sex comes from and/or takes you toward a state of balanced energy. You can get up to whatever exotic high jinks you like, but without the exchange of energy between partners, sex will never be deeply satisfying. Energetic connection is crucial not just to the sexual experience, but also, ultimately, to the relationship itself.

All the other characteristics of good sex play into these. The exact same act could constitute good or bad sex, depending on whether or not it creates connection. You can have good sex without having an orgasm. (Though you increase the benefits when you do orgasm!) You can also orgasm without having good sex. You can create connection without having intercourse. It's all about that sense of union, that two-becomes-one feeling, occurring on multiple levels—anatomically, of course, but also psychologically, emotionally, even spiritually.

When your desire for sex is MIA, it is often because this sense of connection is missing. Luckily, mutual energetic exchange is a simple thing to ensure. The main requirements are a little time and attention. Anyone can feel the kind of energy I'm talking about—it isn't esoteric or mysterious or for-sages-only. Anyone can learn to tap into it. Repair or rebuild that essential connection, and you will rediscover desire and reignite your sex life.

Last but not least, connected sex is a gateway to spiritual growth. This was the heart of the ancient Taoists' plan, the ultimate point of all their techniques: channeling and transforming of sexual energy into spiritual energy. Some of you may be thinking this really isn't your cup of tea. Fine. I'm not trying to sell you on any kind of bedroom metaphysical experience, though that is indeed what some devotees of these practices are looking for—and finding. There's a simpler way to look at it: The connection good sex creates is more than physical. You can feel it between the two of you. And for many people, that feeling extends outward further still, tapping into a feeling of—pardon the corniness, but there's really no other way to put it—oneness-with-the-universe. The bit of connection between two people gives many people a relatively concrete experience of the idea that we are *all* connected. Sex is spiritual when the feeling of union, of communion, expands to include not just two people but the world around them as well, and they feel as one with all of *life*. The way the Taoists understood it, the energy you balance and exchange with your partner connects you not just to each other but also to the universal energy. Sex is many things to many people; to the Taoists one of them is a portal to experiencing the energy of the universe.

Good Sex Again

Good sex—connected sex—is a recipe with a lot of ingredients. Leave one out and you could end up with a whole different dish. But it is also a forgiving recipe, and one that anyone can whip up with a little practice. You do have to make sure the pantry is stocked with everything you need (see below), and there are a few basic techniques you'll need to really get cooking (conveniently located throughout this book).

Good sex involves **love.** That's why the best sex is often sex between long-term partners. You might have good sex early on in a relationship, too, because when you are doing it right, having sex is actually *making* love. Good sex both inspires and builds love. It expresses love. And in the moment-to-moment experience of it, good sex is lov*ing.*

Good sex is **an exchange.** It's mutual. Cooperative. It's giving and receiving—for both partners. It's shared energy, flowing in both directions. Good sex is selfless. It's not about *you.* It's about *us.*

Good sex is **energizing.** And energy-balancing. Good sex only adds to your stores of energy; it never drains them.

Good sex is **committed.** In a stable, long-term relationship you can draw on the most profound and powerful benefits of sex. Casual sex isn't necessarily bad sex, and it most certainly can be fun, or so many of us wouldn't be reminiscing about it. But it tends to be energy depleting—you give away energy and you don't really get it back. Because casual sex is not typically truly connected sex, there's no pathway for energy to get back to you.

Good sex means both partners are **present**—present with each other, present in the moment. For sex to be good, you have to have your head in the game. Your attention needs to be on what you are doing and who you are doing it with. Both of you really need to engage, or you won't get everything out of the experience you could.

Good sex is **pleasurable.**

Good sex is **satisfying.** Physically and emotionally. For both of you. Orgasm is a big part of that, but it's not the be-all and end-all of satisfaction. Exactly what counts as satisfying will vary from person to person, couple to couple, and even from time to time.

Good sex is a **total body experience**. There's a lot to be said for the genitals when it comes to sex, of course, but that's just one item on a much longer menu. There are a few variations on this theme: Good sex uses **all five senses.** And good sex involves **heart, mind, and body.**

Good sex is a form of **communication**—some of it verbal. But like music, or dance, or art, the point is: Expression is often beyond mere words.

Good sex is **meaningful.**

Good sex is also generous, warm, enjoyable, joyful, tender, sincere, sharing, supportive, responsible, open, compassionate, empathetic, energetic, genuine, and passionate—sometimes all at once. Sometimes not!

Good sex is **a whole greater than the sum of the parts.**

Bad Sex

Another great thing about good sex is that by having it, you avoid the pitfalls of having *bad* sex as well as the pitfalls of having no sex! Bad (or nonexistent) sex can generate negative emotions and alienate partners. It can leave you feeling the relationship is incomplete. It wastes or otherwise misuses your sexual energy, and your partner's, leaving you both drained rather than revitalized. So don't do it!

Nothing good will ever come of sex that is exploitative, abusive, coerced, or violent. But sex doesn't have to be as bad as all that to be bad sex. Bad sex is any sex that leaves you sad or depressed or otherwise empty. Or that is disconnected or devoid of emotion. Or that is frustrating. Or monotonous. Or exhausting. Bad sex is sex with an inappropriate partner or in inappropriate circumstances. Sex that is a power struggle. Sex that is goal oriented or merely mechanical. Sex that is *only* about relieving stress, or *only* about having an orgasm. Sex that leaves you physically or emotionally unsatisfied. Sex that is too rushed. Sex that focuses on performance. Sex that does not involve an exchange of energy.

None of that will do you any good. And to the degree it creates physical or emotional pain, it can even *create* problems in physical or mental health, or in the relationship. Bad sex depletes energy instead of generating it, endangering your sex drive. And—you guessed it—depleted energy is a pathway to (more) bad sex.

Fantasy Versus Fantastic Sex

Fantasy is a part of many people's sex lives, and there's nothing wrong with that. Fantasy can help awaken sexual awareness. It might be useful in getting you in the mood, or taking you over the top. But if it is the *only* way you can get going, that should be a wake-up call. There are better ways to arouse or stimulate yourself, or trigger orgasm. If fantasy is always your go-to, you will miss out.

Fantasy is all about being in your head, and the best sex is all about being in your body. Fantasy is anywhere-but-here; the best sex is be-here-now. When you are fantasizing, you can't give all your attention and energy to your partner, or your own body for that matter, because you are diverting attention and energy to your fantasy. If you learn one new attitude from your experience with this book, I hope it will be to be *present*, with your partner, and in your own body, during sex. That's what really will enhance your sexual experience. Fantasy just distracts from it, sabotaging the energetic connection between partners, and draining your energy to boot. Over time, reliance on fantasy can create distance between partners and diminish love.

DON'T Have Sex

Don't have sex is not something you will hear me say that often. But you do want to set yourself up for success (good sex) by not having sex when conditions are conspiring against you:

- *Don't* have sex if you are feeling really lousy, or are totally drained.
- *Don't* have sex if you are seriously exhausted. Like just-getting-over-the-flu exhausted, or just-ran-a-half-marathon exhausted. (When your fatigue is not linked to a specific, limited cause like that, having sex every now and then won't hurt you. And sex can *give* you energy, so it might even be just the ticket to lifting you out of milder fatigue.)

- *Don't* have sex if having sex itself is draining or exhausting. (DO take it as a sign you need to shift something about the way you are having sex.)
- *Don't* have sex when you are in the grip of a lot of negative emotion (anger, sadness, fear . . .) or otherwise highly emotional.
- *Don't* use sex as an escape from anger, boredom, concerns about the relationship, or anything else you should really be dealing with. Sex can help you experience and express emotions, and it can take the edge off negative emotions. But you are abusing its power if you use it to avoid dealing with your problems.

A Little More Conversation

To have good sex, you're going to have to talk about it. Open and honest communication is key to connecting, sexually and otherwise. Good communication is important to your relationship, which is important to your sex life. Good communication is also important *during* sex—in fact, sex itself is one big act of communication. But for right now I want to focus specifically on talking *about* sex. For many of my patients, this is the missing ingredient in their sex lives—and I hear from them over and over again (usually with surprise in their voices) how a little talk can be all it takes to get everything on the right track. Couples who have been together for years are often stuck in a rut, and no one ever says "Hey, how about trying . . .? or "You know what I'd like even more . . . ?"

Start with all the things that are working for you in your current sexual experience. Be specific, sincere, and enthusiastic. A little lavish praise never hurt anyone's sex life.

If you want to *be* a good sexual partner, you are going to have to figure out what your partner needs and wants, likes and dislikes. And if you want your partner to know what *you* need and want, like and dislike, you're going to have to tell him. I also recommend showing him. In fact, I encourage learning all you can by trial and error! But you won't get complete information unless you also talk about those things.

No matter how much he loves you, your partner cannot be relied upon to guess what floats your boat. By all means, when he does manage it, let him know in no uncertain terms (talking permitted, but not required). But the same thing isn't going to do it for you every time, or for the whole time every time, and since you are the one inside your body you are going to know sooner than anybody else what would feel really good right about now.

Many couples find the prospect of a conversation like this daunting. Many of us have way more trouble talking about such intimate matters than we do *doing* them. Most of the time, though, it turns out to be easier than you think it will be. Most couples want to please each other, so once the topic is up for discussion, they can roll with it. And in most cases patients report that having such a talk, even if they have concerns about it in advance, produces very positive results that make any anticipatory jitters—and any effort necessary to overcome them—more than worth it. So I'm going to give you the same advice about talking about sex as I do about having sex: Just *do* it!

Begin by finding a time you can talk when you are *not* having sex or about to have sex. The best way to begin this conversation is with everybody fully clothed. Beyond that, the best circumstances for a talk like this are going to vary from couple to couple. Some of my patients tell me they wait for a quiet moment when they can look their partner in the eye. Some prefer to talk in the car—the classic setup for non–eye-contact discussions. Setting a warm, romantic tone, talking over dinner, or a glass of wine, or in the Jacuzzi are all lovely ideas and may well kick-start things, but setting a romantic tone is not essential. What *is* essential is taking the initial risk, and speaking up, with love and honesty.

It's a good idea to start with all the things that are working for you in your current sexual experience. Be specific, sincere, and enthusiastic. A little lavish praise never hurt anyone's sex life.

Then ask your partner what he likes, what he'd like more of, and what he might like to try. You can ask what he fantasizes about, or if there's anything he'd like you to know. But the trick to this isn't in asking just the right question, or rehearsing the best opening gambit, or setting the stage perfectly, or turning the discussion into a seduction. The important thing is to create a safe space for a full and free discussion for both of you. So: Be honest. Be patient. Stay present—in the sense of being fully engaged in the moment and the conversation. But don't dredge up the past. If your partner feels that you are speaking earnestly and lovingly—not to mention that your goal is to give him pleasure—he's going to be more able to tell you what you want to know.

And when he does: Listen carefully. That's one way to show him you really want to know—and encourage him to share more. Equally important: This is valuable information, and you are going to want to act on it. Let your partner know the things that sound good to you, too. Try not to reject anything out of hand. You shouldn't agree to anything you seriously object to, but in general you'll be better off with a don't-knock-it-'til-you-try-it attitude. If you try it and find you don't care for it after all—well then, no need to keep at it. But you might also discover something enjoyable you hadn't thought of by yourself.

It is then your turn to share with your partner the things *you'd* like more of, and the things *you'd* like to try. (If he's particularly reticent, you can always go first.) In many cases it is a good idea to start off slowly, perhaps with a simple request that's easy for your partner to accomplish: "Honey, I love when you ______. Can you do that more often?" If *you* are particularly reticent, you might try writing some things down. Or, backing up a step or two, you might set the stage for a conversation with a note or email that includes some specifics to get you started. Via love note or out loud, nothing is too large or too small to mention. If you have a secret hankering, now's a good time to speak up. If you'd like to bring back the days of just plain kissing for a while before you go further, say that. If you've been doing one of the meditations in this book and would like to do it with your partner, let him know. If there's an area of your body you'd really like a little more attention paid to, point it out.

When I am encouraging my patients to take on a conversation like this, many of them complain that they wouldn't even really know what to ask for. It is not surprising, really, that a woman dealing with low libido has fallen out of touch with her own sexuality. But no worries: The program at the end of the "Do It Yourself" chapter (Chapter 9) is designed to help you hone back in on it—and so fully prepare you to make a good case to your partner.

When you are ready to make your case, if you want your partner to be able to really hear what you are saying, choose your phrasing carefully. *Don't* criticize what he has been doing, but *do* say what you would like. Don't force an idea on him that obviously doesn't appeal. But don't self-censor either—give your partner a chance to give something the thumbs-up or thumbs-down.

Word of warning: Sometimes these conversations can get a little . . . shall we say sidetracked? Perhaps there was a little something that was easier to demonstrate than to explain? If you find yourselves suddenly practicing what you had been preaching . . . well then, that was a very successful bit of communication. Just be sure to go back and finish the conversation at some other time, to be sure you both get your say.

On the other hand, you might meet some resistance when broaching this topic. Defensiveness, perhaps. Or embarrassment or nervousness. Or, jokes—probably reflecting any or all of the previously mentioned issues. As a way of dealing with discomfort, joking around is not necessarily bad. Truth be told, a lot of people and relationships could use some lightening up around the subject of sex. So if this is the response you get, one option is to run with it. When it comes to sex, playful is good. But if the talk is always and only jokey about sex, it may be there is something un-silly you are avoiding talking about, and you may want to look at that. Or, just for a change of pace, agree to try out not being so jokey, and see if you have a different experience. One more important point: This is not a conversation to have once and then never again. Check in with each other every once in a while as you move forward.

TO DO (IT) LIST: Getting to Good Sex

Specific techniques for having good sex are to come, but you'll get much of the way there with a few underlying strategies:

➜ **Be a generous lover.** The more you give, the more you'll get.

➜ **Have your mind on the matter at hand.** Be there, be engaged, be with your partner.

➜ **Hold the intention** of fully sharing in the experience and exchanging energy.

➜ **Honor your body and your sexuality**—and your partner's.

➜ **Aim for variety,** creativity, and surprise. Get your whole body involved.

➜ **Take care of your well-being**—physically and emotionally—as well as the well-being of your partner and your relationship.

➜ **Have a spiritual or meditative practice.** Activities like qi gong, tai chi, meditation, yoga, and even just devotion to virtuous living will enhance your sexual practices as well, mostly by giving you easier access to connecting at a deeper level.

➜ **Know yourself.** You're going to be able to truly connect with someone else only to the degree that you connect with *you*—your body and your self.

➜ **Know you won't form a more perfect union each and every time;** it's the total effect over time that really counts anyway.

➜ **Remember sex can be transcendent**—but don't wait to have it until you're sure that's what you're going to get. It won't be that way every single time; the key is just to be open to it when and if it should occur.

➜ **Focus on the sex, not on the orgasm.** You want to avoid being goal oriented in any way when it comes to sex. Peak orgasmic intensity is not going to happen every time you have sex anyway—nor, for some people, is an average, everyday orgasm. Seeking solely for that will lead to imbalance. Plus you will miss all the other good stuff.

➜ **Choose regular sex over occasional but explosive sex.** Intensity will vary from time to time. There's no point in waiting around for the absolute most perfect conditions. Sometimes a couple simply needs to have some sex—even sex that's just OK. Then later they can fine-tune how well they do so. Once you are having really good sex, you might be satisfied with fewer but deeper encounters. And quality is far more important than quantity. But as the sex gets better and better, you may well want more of it. And under the law of practice-makes-perfect, the more sex you have, the better at it you will be.

➜ **Experience the emotion** of a sexual encounter, rather than focusing solely on the physical aspects of it. But don't put all your attention on the emotional or spiritual parts at the expense of physical pleasure, either. Like so much else, it's a matter of striving for balance.

➜ **Live a passionate life** in general, and some of that passion will flow into your sex life. Make time for the stuff you love—activities or people or places—and pause to take stock of all that you are grateful for. Passionate sex will send passion into your life as well. Passion must be created and nourished by devoting attention, energy, and skill to the matter, whether in your sex life or just your *life.*

➜ **Value the connection.** Don't rely on sex to create some kind of magical connection between you and your partner. But honor the bond created and renewed by having sex.

2

I'm Too Stressed for Sex

How Libido Goes with the Flow—of Qi

It's just the two of you, alone at last. Cell phones are off. No laptop, no TV. No clothes! The bed beckons, but neither of you is thinking about sleeping. You felt your body begin to respond even as you dimmed the lights and rearranged the pillows, and now each touch is speeding the process along. It's not long before you're wanting more, yet there's no need to rush. The union of your bodies is familiar, but the rush of feeling is still powerful. You are focusing on your sensations and *letting yourself be carried away, and soon you peak. You linger in an embrace afterward, just feeling each other's hearts beat . . .*

That—or something like that—is how it goes when you, your partner, and your relationship are healthy and happy, calm and strong. When, as Chinese medicine might put it, your "qi" is robust and flowing. And while it's probably not how it's going for you now, it can be—and in just six weeks, when you devote yourself to the Sex in Six program.

Lackluster bedroom experiences may ultimately be traced back to a few different sources, but for many, many people, and a good deal of my patients, the main blame for lack of sex and lack of desire for sex can be summed up in just one word: stress. Chinese medicine would choose a different term: qi stagnation. Qi (pronounced "chee") is the life force, or energy, that moves throughout the human body. Trouble crops up when there's not enough qi, or when qi isn't flowing freely—trouble that will surely include loss of libido. "Stress" or "stuck qi" are the same thing: Stress stagnates qi, and stuck qi causes stress.

Without moving qi, your bedroom scenario may look like this:

It's just the two of you. Alone at last. The bed beckons, and you are thinking about nothing but sleep. If *you can even get to sleep, that is, with all that is on your mind. In fact, you're still pretty stressed-out about how little sleep you got* last *night. If your partner so much as looks at you the wrong way, much less* that *way, you are going to lose it.*

Yeah, nobody's getting any tonight.

Or maybe it is more like this:

You've managed to find the time to have sex with your partner. And even the energy. As you get down to business, you notice you are turned-on. You're having a pretty good time. For a while.

Quite a while.

And by now you've been at it for a pretty long time, you sense your partner's had about enough, your mind is wandering a bit... and still you seem to be getting nowhere. Finally you just say you've had enough. Or you fake it. Anything to wrap this up, since it's clear orgasm isn't in the picture for you. Or maybe you double down, pull any kind of trick you can think of, determined to come no matter how long it takes and who gets what kind of cramp in the effort.

No wonder you don't feel like doing this very often.

One more common story looks like this:

You agree to have sex with your partner, but orgasm is the least of your worries, because you just can't get going. You thought you wanted to, it seemed like a good idea, but your body apparently hasn't gotten the memo. Maybe you get "wet" eventually, or wet enough, anyway. Or maybe you proceed without waiting for that—since how long is this supposed to take, anyway?—but then intercourse is uncomfortable, even painful, because you still aren't properly lubricated.

Like I said: No wonder you aren't eager to do it all over again anytime soon.

DO IT NOW: Take a Breath

The most basic way to combat stress is to take a deep breath. Breathing is also the simplest way to start your sexual energy moving. Breathing circulates qi. A deep breath sends qi downward, where it energizes the pelvic area. And purposeful breathing keeps you in your body and out of your head, making you more attuned to pure physical sensation, which will increase your sexual responsiveness.

You don't need to do anything fancy to reap most of the benefits of breathing. It's as simple as sitting, standing, or lying quietly, and taking some slow, deep breaths. We tend to breathe in a shallow way, so even one minute of gently using more of our lung capacity can make a big difference.

Variation: Let your exhale take the form of a big sigh. That's going to mean you make some noise, but don't be shy. Take a few more regular deep, slow breaths, then sigh out again. Repeat as many times as you like. You should feel a noticeable difference in your body after just a few breaths.

If any of these is more familiar than the opening scenario, your qi—your life force, or energy—is not flowing fully through you. In Chinese medicine, we say it is stuck, or stagnant. And when that happens, your libido takes a hit. And stress is probably to blame. Almost all of my patients who talk with me about lagging sex drive have stuck qi—and are totally stressed-out. That's not to say there's nothing else going on with them, because there usually is. But in nearly every case, getting a grip on stress and getting qi moving is the place to start recharging someone's sex life. Fortunately, it's usually not hard to do.

Sexual energy is one form of qi. Freely moving qi ensures healthy, active sexual energy. Free-flowing qi is considered crucial to health and well-being—not least because of what it does for your sex life.

Nothing stops the flow of qi faster than stress. The tensed muscles, the unquiet mind, the aching stomach, the shallow breathing—they all trap qi and keep it from moving smoothly through you as it should. Given no outlet, stress tends to build up inside people with stuck qi—until capacity is maxed out and some kind of explosion is inevitable. Stress and stagnant qi can cause a host of physical, emotional, and relationship problems. Starting with—you won't feel like having sex. If qi isn't flowing, neither energy nor blood moves as it should to or in the genitals. That's bad not only for arousal, but also for orgasm.

In a classic catch-22, having sex is an efficient way to boost qi, or get it unstuck. (Also the most enjoyable!) Sex generates qi and invigorates its flow. That's one of the reasons it feels so good. Another is: Sex is a great stress buster. Furthermore, lack of sex can *cause* stagnant or stuck qi, and lack of sexual energy. And seriously stress you out.

Sex in Real Life: Delphine

Delphine complained that she didn't often feel like having sex: It was hard for her to get turned on, and she had trouble reaching orgasm. These are typical signs of stuck qi, but so were Delphine's many other symptoms. Most notably, she was stressed-out, to the point where her body was sending up all kinds of signal flares: She had frequent headaches, a "nervous stomach," high blood pressure, poor circulation, and muscle tightness and aches, especially in her back, neck, and shoulders. Delphine regularly demonstrated another famous symptom of stuck qi: irritability. Which she mostly directed at her husband, which, frankly, was doing nothing for her sex life.

Delphine also struggled with hormone imbalances, with symptoms tending to show up at times of hormonal transition, like just before her period. Both arousal and orgasm rely on a precisely choreographed dance of hormones, and Delphine's were definitely out of step. She brought work stress home and right into the bedroom. She found it very hard to "switch off" at the end of the day. On the infrequent occasions when she and her husband had sex, she was distracted and not completely present. She had a lot on her mind and felt overwhelmed, which made focusing difficult, which made orgasm difficult.

Like a lot of people with stuck qi, Delphine was a type A achiever. She was generally lively, interesting, proactive, and innovative . . . but also tightly wound, tense, quick to anger, and highly critical of herself and others. She often felt overwhelmed.

> ***Both arousal and orgasm rely on a precisely choreographed dance of hormones, and Delphine's were definitely out of step.***

Delphine, as is typical in cases of stuck qi, was living life with all cylinders firing at once. She was at the peak of her career, making more money than she'd ever dreamed of, putting in long hours to keep that up, but also raising two teenagers with her husband (who had his own very demanding career). Oh, and did I mention that she was slowly but surely needing to be more involved in her elderly parents' lives? Like a lot of people with stuck qi, Delphine *felt* stuck, as if she was trapped underneath her life circumstances.

Western medicine looks at a patient like Delphine and sees hormonal problems, or perhaps stress, or some combination of the two—hormonal patterns disrupted by stress—but probably wouldn't have a lot to offer in the way of treatment. Generally speaking, Western medicine excels in black-and-white cases where you need to bring out the big guns. A situation like Delphine's is more subtle. Fortunately, correcting hormones that are subtly out of sync is one of the things Chinese medicine is really, really good at. The holistic approach is crucial.

Although stagnant qi is the most common thing I see in patients with libido complaints, it is also the easiest thing to fix. Barring additional complicating factors, I know I can get patients unstuck in a matter of weeks, with stress management techniques, a few lifestyle tweaks, an herbal formula, and some sexercises like the ones throughout this book—starting with Take a Breath (page 25). Not that it doesn't take effort to get unstuck. But when patients do make that effort, most quickly regain their sexual vitality. And once they start having sex again, they soon see for themselves that sex creates more sex.

Are You Avoiding Something?

In my practice I have seen over and over again women who are stuck because they have been raised to think that sex is immoral, dirty, or wrong—or have painful or degrading sexual experiences in their past. Those negative, or simply unpleasant, attitudes and experiences—anything from sexual abuse to just a really bad "first time"—can make a body shut down. Being stuck is a way of avoiding what we don't want to deal with, whether it's a relationship issue or a traumatic memory. If things get stuck in your life, or your relationship, or your *head,* they will get stuck in your body as well. And vice versa.

It isn't always easy, but finding a way to deal with those experiences that may be holding you back is one way to restore the free flow of qi—and with it, your libido. Sometimes just identifying and understanding the link can help break it. If that doesn't happen for you on your own, or in discussion with a trusted friend, or your partner, therapy might be a good choice.

The Qi Checklist

If what you've read so far resonates with you, you might already recognize whether or not your qi is stagnant. But if you want a more definitive identification, the following list can help. If you prefer, you can complete it online at sexagainprogram.com.

It's easy enough to do here, too. Simply tick off each item that often applies to you. That doesn't mean it happens all the time, or every time—but experiencing a thing once doesn't make it "you" either. Choose what tends to describe you. Tally up your check marks to determine your score. (See scoring at the end of the quiz.)

MY SEXUALITY

☐ I lose interest during sex and start to think about other things.

☐ I have trouble reaching orgasm.

☐ I experience dyspareunia/pain during sex.

MY RELATIONSHIP

☐ There are things I don't say or things I keep back from my partner.

☐ I sometimes feel disconnected from my partner.

☐ I can be controlling toward my partner.

☐ I sometimes feel aggressive toward my partner.

MY EMOTIONS

☐ I am undergoing emotional upheaval.

☐ When I am stressed, I get irritable, or depressed.

☐ I am often irritable.

☐ I feel tense, overwhelmed, blocked, or just generally stuck.

☐ I am stressed-out.

☐ I don't want to talk about it.

☐ In the face of stress, I withdraw.

☐ I bring work stress home and have trouble switching it off.

☐ I am prone to outbursts/overreactions.

☐ I can be quite volatile.

☐ I change my mind a lot.

MY BODY

☐ My stress shows up as physical symptoms (headaches, digestive troubles, etc.) or various vague aches and pains.

☐ My ribs or flanks are painful.

☐ I feel better or have more energy if I exercise.

☐ When I am stressed, I like to have a drink to relax.

☐ My bowel movements are thin and long like a ribbon.

☐ My bowel movements are like small pebbles.

☐ I have alternating bouts of constipation and diarrhea.

☐ I sigh a lot.

☐ I grind my teeth at night.

☐ I sleep poorly.

☐ I have tense muscles.

☐ I have poor circulation.

☐ I have a nervous stomach or get diarrhea when I'm stressed.

☐ I have cold hands and feet.

☐ I have fibrocystic breasts, fibroids, or endometriosis.

MY MENSTRUAL CYCLE

☐ I am menopausal and experience frequent bloating, irritability, and sluggishness. (If you are menopausal, skip the remaining points in this section.)

☐ I have PMS. My breasts are sore premenstrually and sometimes midcycle. I have mood swings and/or irritability, and digestive disturbances, especially right before my period.

☐ I have discomfort, cramps, or pain with my period.

☐ I have an irregular menstrual cycle.

☐ My period stops and starts.

☐ My menstrual blood is clotted and/or dark red or brown rather than bright red.

☐ I have a very heavy period.

A score of eighteen or more indicates stagnation for women not yet in menopause.

A score of fifteen or more indicates stagnation for women in menopause.

The higher your score, the more stuck you are.

♂ FOR THE GUYS: Qi Checklist for Men

Men can use the qi checklist to evaluate whether or not their qi is stuck—just skip over the menstrual cycle questions and add the items below.

- ☐ I have erectile dysfunction (ED).
- ☐ I ejaculate prematurely.
- ☐ I take a long time to ejaculate.

A score of sixteen or more indicates stagnant qi. The higher your score, the more stuck you are.

Sex and Stress

The relationship between sex and stress goes deep. Sex often becomes just one more thing on the to-do list, one more chore, one more occasion to be under pressure to perform. Physiologically, stress triggers a hormonal chain reaction that ultimately suppresses libido. Stress also causes a wide range of other physical ailments. And anything that dents your health is likely to dampen your sex life as well. Furthermore, sex is a great pressure release, and when we skimp on that we also deprive ourselves of one of the best ways we have of dealing with stress—and create a new stressor to boot.

Everyone can feel stress, of course, but it tends to show up somewhat differently in women than it does in men. The familiar "fight or flight" response to stress is really more of a male paradigm. Women under stress are more likely to go into "tend and befriend" mode under duress. Instead of running away or violently confronting a threat, women generally respond first by protecting offspring ("tending") and joining together in groups for mutual defense ("befriending"). Once upon a time, this might have meant that when a saber-toothed tiger appeared, women rounded up the children and banded together to keep them all safe. In today's world, the female response is more likely to involve reaching out to a friend for support and focusing on caring for others. Of course, generalizations are not going apply to every single individual, but to many.

By this point you may be wondering if stress wouldn't be rather *good* for your sex life, if you're going to respond with all that reaching out, and coming together, etc. But there's a hormonal catch. The tending and befriending is driven by a rise in oxytocin, which is triggered by stress. Estrogen enhances the effects of oxytocin, which accounts for the stronger showing of this strategy in women than in men. As oxytocin rises, however, so does a protein called sex hormone binding globulin (SHBG). SHBG binds to testosterone in the cells, reinforcing a less aggressive reaction to stress—and leaving less testosterone available for the body to use for other things. Like libido.

With stress and without moving qi, your ability to enjoy sex will be undermined, which will push sex even further down your list of priorities, causing strain on your relationship, thereby creating guilt and even more stress—and even less sex.

That, in a nutshell, is Western medicine's understanding of the stress response in women as it affects libido. Chinese medicine tells a different tale based on similar observations. The basic view is that stress throws off the body's energetic balance, and/or blocks the flow of qi. It works the other way around, too: An imbalance of energy and qi that isn't moving causes stress. And either way, a variety of symptoms result, with loss of libido prime among them. With stress and without moving qi, your ability to enjoy sex will be undermined, which will push sex even further down your list of priorities, causing strain on your relationship, thereby creating guilt and even more stress—and even less sex.

FOR THE GUYS: Man Stress

When under stress, men tend to fall back on the familiar "fight or flight" response, ready to run or violently confront a given (or perceived) threat. Once upon a time, this might have meant that when a saber-toothed tiger came to call, most of us would take up arms—or flee. And I think those are probably both excellent options when faced with a predator larger than you are. But it is a less effective response to, say, deadline pressure at work, a chaotic dinner hour with the kids, or a holiday with the in-laws.

The "fight or flight" response to stress shoots adrenaline, noradrenaline, and cortisol into the body, putting it in a heightened state of arousal—of the sort that would let you outrun that saber-toothed tiger. Meanwhile, the sort of arousal that has you hoping the kids fall asleep on the early side tonight falls to the very bottom of the body's list of priorities, while it focuses only on the things needed to keep you alive right now. Digestion and other nonessentials like blood circulation to some parts of the body slow up or shut down, for example. Testosterone, too, is not on the list of things you need for immediate survival, so it decreases with stress—and takes libido down with it. And that's all fine—when dealing with a life-or-death situation. Otherwise, not so much.

Perhaps you think you have mastery over natural tendencies such as these—after all, you hardly ever find yourself in combat or a full-out run. Let me point out, however, just on the off chance that it sounds more familiar, that in today's world "fight or flight" often looks more like avoidance, such as withdrawing from others, or self-medicating.

Qi Stagnation and Hormones—and Stress

There's an intricate relationship among stagnation, hormonal imbalance, and stress. Each can be the cause of *or* the result of the other two. For example, being stuck can create difficulty during hormonal transitions—like ovulation, menstruation, perimenopause, menopause—and if you weren't stressed already then the symptoms from wonky hormones may well get you there. Or tricky hormonal shifts can make you stuck (and probably stressed). For many women, the symptoms of stress, stagnation, and hormonal imbalance are very similar.

Stagnation interferes with hormonal transitions by making you feel like you are going over a cliff rather than rolling smoothly into the next

DO IT NOW: Think About It

Where your mind goes, your qi follows. That's a guiding principle of Chinese medicine—and the whole point of this simple yet powerful meditation exercise. This exercise is about as easy as it gets: All you do is spend just several minutes thinking about sex. If you have a partner, think specifically about having sex with your partner. The only rule is: Good thoughts only. Run over a previous encounter in your mind. Plan a future encounter. Imagine (finally) telling your partner exactly what you really want—and getting it!

You can do this in traditional meditation fashion, say, while sitting quietly with eyes closed. But you can also do it while working out on the treadmill, or stuck in traffic, or walking down the street. As long as you spend a few minutes with positive thoughts of your sex life front and center, you're doing it right.

phase. This generally happens in a couple of typical patterns. Sometimes stuck qi leads to high progesterone. But most typically, women with stuck qi are prone to having high estrogen or low progesterone levels—or estrogen levels that are high in relation to progesterone levels, a condition known as estrogen dominance. Often this happens thanks to the stress hormone cortisol. When the body is under stress cortisol levels increase, which decreases progesterone, which then increases estrogen. (See Chapter 4 for more on estrogen dominance and yang deficiency.)

So PMS is typical of both estrogen dominance and stuck qi. It can play out in three different ways:

1. You get through the month reasonably well, facing the menu of daily stresses we all order from, but then, when you are most vulnerable, as your hormones shift dramatically, the wheels come off. You experience the symptoms of PMS (and stagnation) for a few days.

2. Your life is really out of whack, your stress levels are through the roof, and you end up in a state that's like being premenstrual throughout the entire month. You have full-time qi stagnation.

3. You acknowledge your tendency toward stuck qi and have taken steps to keep it in check; you've learned how to channel your stress so it doesn't overwhelm you (and how to avoid what stress you can); you practice lifestyle habits that support optimal health for you. You can handle even the steepest hormonal transition without symptoms, which means your qi is flowing freely.

I recommend option three. So I want to underline for you that even if option one or two is more familiar to you, you *can* get to a place where you transition with ease. Learning to move your qi, as with the To Do (It) List at the end of this chapter, is the key.

Stagnant qi can also be associated with elevated testosterone levels in women. Other signs of too much testosterone include acne, irritability, and the growth of excess, unwanted body hair. Too much testosterone can be the result of a serious problem, so you should have your doctor thoroughly check you out if you have this cluster of symptoms.

FOR THE GUYS: Men and Stagnation and Hormones

Stagnation and stress throw men's hormones off balance, too—sometimes in the form of elevated testosterone levels. (*Low* testosterone levels are actually more common in stressed men with qi stagnation, and there's more about that in Chapter 4, on yang deficiency.) Too much testosterone can exaggerate sexual desire and create abnormally aggressive behavior. Not a good combination! Excessive testosterone may also cause or intensify acne, baldness, infertility, or enlarged prostate. It also increases the risk of prostate cancer. In other words, if you have excessive testosterone it's important that you deal with it and consult your physician.

Chinese medicine has a lot to offer men, too, when it comes to rebalancing hormones. Unlike with women, Chinese herbs prescribed for men with high or low testosterone don't provide hormones directly, so you can use them in tandem with taking hormones—but you need the supervision of an herbalist and the cooperation of your doctor. Sometimes Chinese medicine will be sufficient, and you won't need to take hormones.

You can help balance hormones on your own at home, too. Try cutting back on meat and saturated fats in your diet (aim to keep meat to no more than three servings a week—preferably less), and eat more vegetable sources of protein, such as legumes, beans, tempeh, and tofu.

Sex Again in Real Life: Amy

Amy came into the office for help with PMS complaints—irritability and lumpy breasts—but it wasn't long into our interview before she was talking about how hard it was for her to achieve orgasm. She said that when she and her partner tried and tried she could climax, but that they both usually got bored long before that point and gave it up as a bad job. "It's like I never really got the hang of having an orgasm," she told me. Most of the time she preferred to have sex without orgasm, she said. That way she could enjoy the intimacy and connection, and not work so hard that the sex began to seem like a chore. "But still, I feel I'm missing out," she confessed.

Classic stuck qi.

I suggested she get more aerobic exercise to move qi, and prescribed an herbal formula that would help rebalance her hormones as well as move her qi—a version of the one available over the counter as Xiao Yao Wan (Relaxed Wanderer).

In addition, I suggested massage. If Amy could spare the time and handle the expense of professional massage, that would be fine, but I actually thought partner massage (as described on page 132, Chapter 7) was more to the point. I told Amy to use either kind of massage as a time to practice focusing on her body and its sensations, as a way of staying "present"—just what she needed to do during sex with her partner to reach orgasm.

Ancient Taoist sexology texts explain that the purpose of foreplay is to relieve stagnation and encourage the energy flow necessary to enhance sexual pleasure. So I suggested she and her partner look at the way they used (or didn't use) foreplay, with the goal being to get Amy much further along the path to orgasm before they ever started to actually try to achieve the orgasm itself.

Listening to Amy, I suspected that she might be harboring a buildup of resentments and fears, and that the stagnating of these emotions, along with her qi, could be causing her whole body to tighten up. That would block sexual feelings and make orgasm difficult. So we also talked about how she might explore those areas within herself. If she could answer for herself when and where she shut down, she might be able to identify a pattern she could then disrupt.

Amy saw results quickly. Within two weeks she was feeling more relaxed when having sex—more relaxed in general, in fact—and felt herself getting close to orgasm without really thinking about it. And her PMS symptoms let up as well. Within another two weeks, she was having actual orgasms with the same lack of extraordinary effort. And she and her husband had had

Qi Sexuali-Tea

The herbs in this qi-moving, caffeine-free tea particularly target the reproductive organs. This recipe lets you mix up a batch to keep on hand for any time you want a cup—just combine all the ingredients and store in a resealable container. All these ingredients should be available at your health food store. Check the herb, spice, supplement, and tea sections.

1 cup dried mint leaves

¼ cup oat straw tea leaves

½ cup red raspberry leaf tea leaves

2 teaspoons dried orange peel

To make one cup, place 2 teaspoons of the mixture in a cup. Fill cup with boiling water, cover, and steep for 10 minutes. Strain and serve.

What Stagnates Qi?

The most common things getting your qi stuck are:

* Stress
* Lack of exercise
* Too much fatty, rich food
* Negative sexual experiences
* Injuries that result in chronic pain
* Unfulfilled desires
* Repressed emotions
* Unexpressed frustration and anger
* Ignoring signals to change or evolve

sex more times over that month than they had in the last six months put together, she guessed. Amy was pleased to tell me *she'd* been the one to initiate, at least some of the time—for the first time in years.

FOR THE GUYS: Steve Was Stuck

Men can have stuck qi, too, of course, and, it's often related to some kind of emotional disturbance and stress. Reproductive hormones aren't usually involved for us, though being sexually frustrated, anxious, or overwrought can be, in a way that it generally isn't true for women.

For men, the most likely manifestations of stuck qi are an odd trio: erectile dysfunction (ED), premature ejaculation (PE), and taking a really long time to ejaculate. When qi isn't flowing, it can lead to blood not flowing properly to or in the genitals, and that can lead to ED. When qi is stuck, it is also hard to get sexual energy started, or keep it flowing, and premature ejaculation is a possible result. When stagnation builds up it creates pressure and heat, which rises and then bursts: again, PE. Stuck qi can also create lack of sensation, which can lead to taking a long time to ejaculate. Men with stuck qi may have either a hyper or an erratic sex drive. Some experience pain in the testicles or penis during sex.

The unholy trifecta of ED, PE, and delayed ejaculation are also all manifestations of *performance anxiety.* For a lot of guys, the unique combination of feeling not only pressured but also physically exposed—which shows up pretty exclusively in the sack—just does them in.

Whether you think of them as caused by general "stuckness" or stress or performance anxiety, none of these conditions are any guy's favorite thing to admit to. Which is why Steve didn't mention until I'd already seen him for a few visits that he was often embarrassed by how quickly he ejaculated and was afraid his wife was not satisfied sexually.

Steve and his wife were having trouble conceiving, and he was understandably frustrated, disappointed, and sad about the situation. They were at the point where they would try anything to get pregnant, but she was also complaining that Steve was too demanding about sex, wanting it too often; when she demurred, he would withdraw and sulk. She was also concerned that Steve had become quite volatile, displaying a hair-trigger temper that had not been in evidence before.

For his part, Steve admitted that he often lost his cool, behaving in ways that he regretted later, but he felt out of control in the moment. That said, he didn't think he had any sexual problems—aside from a wife who wasn't as into it as he was. A lot of times men with stuck qi see their stress as being imposed on them by others, rather than being generated from within themselves. Steve didn't connect the dots that trying to get pregnant had ratcheted up his stress level beyond his ability to diffuse it, resulting in the outbursts his wife described—and the premature ejaculation.

My first step with Steve was to discuss that we needed to focus on stress, not on the timing of his ejaculation per se. For Steve, as for a lot of men in his situation, the pressure of sex on a schedule in order to conceive was the overriding stress in his life. It seemed to me he was, in a way, backing away from the whole experience to try to cut off that stress. What he really needed to do was exactly the opposite: Accept the process, get more involved in it, renew the partnership with his wife, develop better understanding of what they were both going through, and determine to deal with it as a team. All of that would take the edge off living through fertility issues—and lead to more fulfilling sex.

My other advice to Steve was that he get more exercise—to improve the circulation of both his qi and his blood, and to release tension in his whole body. In addition we discussed some techniques for delaying orgasm (like the ones on pages 230 through 232) which he seemed eager to try. I also prescribed an herbal formula to move qi, which is available over the counter as Si Ni San (Frigid Extremities Powder).

Within a couple of weeks, Steve felt more in control and less liable to have an outburst. After a month, he reported that he felt less sexually "hungry," and also that he was able to last longer, which he attributed to both the herbs and the specific delaying techniques. As a result, he was feeling more connected to his wife. His work paid off in another important way, too: A few months later, Steve called to tell me his wife was pregnant. They were both over the moon.

I've seen similar qi-moving strategies work for men with ED or "delayed ejaculation," too, especially when used along with the more specific advice on pages 124 and 255. In any case, the key is to admit *you've* got something going on sexually, and to recognize that you can do something about it. Nine times out of ten it has nothing to do with the equipment itself. Though, of course, if you have a real concern that there is a physical problem, please see a doctor. You don't have to be trying to conceive to go to a urologist to get checked out.

Qi for Two

In talking about qi and sex, you have to consider the qi both in the individuals, and in the relationship. When two people have sex they are sharing not just their bodies but also their qi. A continuous exchange of energy is the hallmark of good sex. It is what creates the feeling of "one-ness" between two people. And knowing how to tap into the feeling is the key to sustaining your sex drive and your sex life over the long term.

Without enough qi you may not be able to spark your own libido—much less charge the relationship between you and your partner, sexually or otherwise.

To the ancient Taoists energetic connection and exchange were pretty much the whole point of sex and why sex was considered healing, life extending—and spiritual. I'm not going to promise you that learning to swap qi with your partner will make you live longer. But I do think it will support longevity in your relationship and your sex life. (See Chapter 10, about energy balance in relationships.)

TO DO (IT) LIST: De-Stressing, and Moving Qi

Stuck qi is the easiest pattern to correct, but you have to take action to make it happen. One of the easiest and quickest means of increasing qi and getting it moving is to have sex. Sex is also a great stress-buster. While you're gearing up to "just do it," the suggestions below describe other ways of getting qi moving again, and keeping it moving:

➔ **Exercise.** Aerobic exercise is best, with yoga or tai chi a close second. Either way, you want to get your blood pumping.

➔ **Eat right for your sex life.** Qi moves best when you are eating a largely plant-based diet with lots of leafy greens, some lean protein, and a small amount of whole grains. Refined carbs (too much pasta and bread) will make you more stuck. So will using food (or alcohol or coffee) as a way to try to relieve stress.

➔ **Choose qi-moving foods,** including broccoli, kohlrabi, turnips, cauliflower, peppermint, radish, parsley, tomato, celery, asparagus, oranges, lemons, plums, strawberries, barley, buckwheat, rye, brown rice, sesame seeds, chicken, lima beans, fish, fava beans, chia seeds, pistachios, and yogurt.

➔ **Avoid caffeine.** That morning joe stagnates qi, which is why it is infamous for exacerbating PMS symptoms and fibrocystic breasts.

➔ **Avoid toxins** like processed foods or milk tainted with hormones and antibiotics.

➔ **Relax.** Experiment to find what works for you—a relaxation tape, a warm bath, massage, meditation—but your best bet, at least for starters, is probably basic progressive relaxation (page 108).

➔ **Manage stress.** Meditation, laughing, aerobic exercise, and sex (yes, even if you don't feel like it at first) are all excellent candidates. Combinations of movement and meditation are particularly effective, such as tai chi or yoga, or simply walking mindfully.

→ **Take a calcium supplement.** Your body uses calcium at a record pace when coping with stress, so you can optimize your ability to deal with stress by topping off the reserves. A supplement of 1,000 milligrams a day should cover you.

→ **Take B complex** to offset the effects of stress on the body and help you feel calm, zinc to calm the central nervous system, black current seed oil to help with hormonal transitions, and magnesium to relax muscles.

→ **Focus on your breath.** Even the simplest series of deep breaths will help reverse the effects of stagnation and get qi moving again.

→ **Get a massage.** It's a great way to relieve stagnation, thereby making energy available for sex.

→ **Choose sexercises that move qi.** You will learn more of them in upcoming chapters, and Appendix 2 gives you a quick reference to which of the exercises throughout this book are best for improving the flow of qi.

→ **Consider acupuncture.** It's very good for moving qi and it's great for any stage of life—while planning pregnancy, postpartum and new parenthood, peri- and menopause.

→ **Take Xiao Yao Wan (Relaxed Wanderer)** herbal formula (available over the counter) to move qi, rebalance hormones, and relieve stress. It is especially good if you are frequently irritable.

→ **OR take Suan Zao Ren Tang (Sour Jujube Decoction),** which is good if you have anxiety.

→ **Add Yu Jin (Curcumin) and/or Dan Shen (Salvia)** to either of the above if you are dealing with pain as well as stuck qi. They are also good for the heart and can reduce inflammation. But *do not* take these herbs if you are taking a blood thinner.

3

I'm Not Sexy Enough for Sex

How (and Why) to Nourish Yin

There was a time when Yvette didn't think much about sex . . . because she was having it pretty regularly. And it always happened—always worked—in ways that simply didn't require much thought. The mood would strike her, or her partner, and there'd be that *look* between them. A little kissing here, a little caressing there, and they'd be off to the races. She always enjoyed it, and it was never long before the mood would strike again.

Those days are gone.

Now, Yvette doesn't think much about sex . . . period. It's hard for her to sort out whether she really doesn't have much desire, or if she just tunes out those impulses because she associates them with uncomfortable encounters. When she looks in the mirror these days, she just sees "old." Which already feels to her like the opposite of sexy. She feels as if she is so old she is drying up. In fact her whole body seems to lack "juice" now—she has dry skin, dry hair, dry nails, dry eyes. And she doesn't have much vaginal moisture and has very little discharge. She supposes this is all to be expected with menopause, but the signs of yin deficiency are much the same at any age.

All in all, Yvette finds it difficult to become aroused. And when she does have sex, it is often painful, due to lack of lubrication. So Yvette often avoids sex. Lately she has begun to realize she is also turning her back on a lot of nonsexual touching and loving in the process.

Yvette fits into another major pattern of Chinese medicine—lack of yin (another form of energy in the body). Without enough yin, the body becomes very dry—including a telltale lack of the moisture (lubrication) that signals sexual arousal. Another typical sign is a lack of self-nurturing, which often shows up as some form of negative self-image. Increasing yin improves self-acceptance, including positive body image, which is a boon to sexual desire.

Sufficient yin is key to optimal performance in all areas of life, and that's just what Yvette had during the time she now looks back upon as her sexual peak. By learning to better nourish and balance her yin, Yvette can reclaim the sexual part of herself she fears is lost.

Looking at Yin and Yang

If you know anything about Chinese medicine or philosophy, you may have heard about the idea of yin and yang. Yin yang theory is about five thousand years old, though it was first written down only around 700 BCE. Yin yang theory is a way of thinking about the nature of life and the universe in which all objects, all beings, all phenomena contain energetic forces within them. These forces move along a continuum, with yin at one end and yang at the other. There is a perfect balance point somewhere in between, though that point is constantly on the move. Everything in existence contains both yin and yang energy, in varying (and ever-changing) proportions. Yin and yang are *not* two types of energy, as one common misinterpretation has it, but rather different aspects of one energetic force: qi. Yin and yang are like different charges, the way an atom's energy can be negative or positive.

In the Chinese language pictogram, yin represents the shady side of a mountain, while yang is the sunny side. As the sun moves along its daily path, it will eventually light what had been shaded—and what was bright will slide into shadow. It is this idea of yin and yang gradually but continually trading places with each other—as the sun comes around again, light and shadow will shift once more—that carries over into the more

> ***The familiar Taoist* taijitu *diagram is a profound illustration of a key philosophical principle. And really good sex advice.***

metaphorical way "yin and yang"' is used today.

Back before it was a tattoo, a dorm room poster, or a necklace charm, the familiar Taoist *taijitu* diagram was not so much a visual cliché as a profound illustration of a key philosophical principle. Not to mention really good sex advice.

So let's take a look at the symbol with fresh eyes. At the most basic level, it is two equal parts—white and black, representing yin and yang—joined together into a greater whole. The image is half black and half white, but there is no dividing line down the middle, yin over here and yang over there. The white flows into the black and the black flows into the white. Just as one is reaching its peak, it begins to transform into the other. The yin and yang give rise to each other. There's a small circle of white within the black, and a small circle of black within the white—what is yang always contains some yin, and what is yin always contains some yang. Yin and yang are opposites but are not opposing. They are complementary. They are interconnected and interdependent. They need each other to exist—without both black and white, there is no circle. Yin and yang play off each other. You can't separate them. And you can't pin them down; they are always shifting in relation to each other, searching for balance. Hence, the Chinese *yin yang* translates as "dynamic balance."

What Do Yin and Yang Look Like?

Taoist philosophy identifies pretty much *everything* as predominantly yin or predominantly yang. For our purposes, however, we're going to look at just things that are important to sex and relationships. In the box on page 48 you'll see those key qualities of yin and yang listed. You'll notice they are in pairs, which is typical. Each word in a pair represents one end of a continuum of expressions of that quality: One end is yin, the other yang.

Everyone has a combination of yin traits and yang traits. And in any given pair of traits, you won't always fall on one side and never on the other—or be all the way to one extreme. Rather, you have a tendency toward one or the other at any given moment. You are *not,* for example, 100 percent "accepting" and zero percent "initiating" (or vice versa). But you probably fall somewhere more toward one end of the field or the other, rather than maintaining a permanent seat on the fifty-yard line. Which one describes you more often, or more intensely, or under more conditions? That's your dominant trait. And the other one is your nondominant trait—and probably where you are showing a deficiency. Or, to look at it another way, if you are deficient in either yin or yang, then you are likely to have an abundance—or overabundance—of the other, and that one is your dominant trait. For example, if you are low in yin, you are yang dominant.

> ***You have to find your sweet spot in between, even if you have to step away from what comes naturally to reach toward what will serve you better.***

Identifying symptoms of deficiency is often the most straightforward way to determine the patterns of yin and yang. However, it is much more important to find the balance between yin and yang than it is to precisely identify a deficiency. And to do that, you're going to want to see how yin and yang are expressed in your emotional life, mood, and relationship as well as in your body. And determine just how far away from balance you are. And what kind of energy you are running on—and possibly burning up.

Qualities of Yin and Yang

Please note: There's nothing exclusively sexual about any of these yin and yang traits. Though once you start looking at them from that angle, it gets difficult to think of "wet," "hot," "yielding," "hard," "slow," or "passionate" any other way! It reminds me of the game where everyone reads out the slip of paper from their fortune cookie, adding the phrase "in bed" at the end. In the yin yang version, it goes something like, You are "creative" and "loud" . . . in bed!

Yin	Yang
Receptive	Giving
Nurturing	Creating
Slow	Fast
Withholding	Expressing
Accepting	Initiating
Substance	Energy
Descending	Rising
Below	Above
Cool	Hot
Moist	Dry
Passive	Active
Including	Excluding
Introspective	Outgoing
Calming	Stimulating
Listening	Speaking
Home	Away
Reacting	Acting
Quiet	Loud
Soft	Hard
Dark	Light
Heavy	Light
Sedating	Energizing
Negative	Positive
Feminine	Masculine

And you are going to want to see where you are *strong* as well as where you need shoring up.

The qualities in both columns are positive, or sometimes neutral. There is no such thing as one "right" place to be on this scale. But taken to an extreme, any of these qualities will become problematic. If you are too yin, you run the risk of being *too* passive and *too* quiet; too much yang and you may end up *too* active and *too* loud. You have to find your sweet spot in between, even though sometimes that may mean you need to push yourself a bit, stepping away from what comes most naturally to you to reach toward what will serve you better. Not everything works equally well all the time and under all circumstances. Your yin and yang can—and should—shift in relation to each other, depending on what you are doing, your situation, and the relationship you are in. Check back when circumstances change—as circumstances always do—and you'll see that how you rate yourself on any of these qualities may well have shifted. Just like sunshine sliding over a mountain.

My Yin and Yang: The Scale

The rating scales on the following pages are designed to help you discover if your yin and yang are out of balance. For most people, the answer is yes—at least some of the time—so these scales help you identify in which direction you've fallen out of balance (are you lower in yin, or in yang?) and therefore what you should reinforce to regain your balance.

Mark the line between each pair of statements below, indicating which one you have experienced most often over the last three months. (Be sure to answer according to your current situation—without thinking about anything that "used to" be true for you. This is especially important if you are in menopause.) If neither of the statements applies to you (for example, it is a question about your period, and you no longer have a period), just leave that line unmarked. If you want to get a little fancy, you can make your mark closer to the center or closer to the end of the line depending on how frequent or intense these symptoms are for you. But all you really need to know is which side of center most often applies to you. If your marks cluster to the left of center, you have low yin—and the To Do

(It) List on page 71, on yin deficiency, will be the most important one for you. If your marks cluster to the right of center, you have low yang—and Chapter 4, on yang deficiency, will be more your territory.

Everyone will have marks on both sides of these scales—but one side will predominate.

There are thirty-six items, so if you have nineteen or more marks on one side or the other, that's the way in which you tend to fall out of balance.

The more marks you have on one side, the more out of balance you are at the moment.

You can complete this scale online at sexagainprogram.com.

low yin	**MY SEXUALITY**	*low yang*
I feel restless during sex	——————+——————	I switch off during sex
I have trouble staying connected during sex	——————+——————	I have trouble initiating sex or feel tired during sex
I have difficulty getting aroused/lubricated during sex	——————+——————	I don't have much interest in sex
I rush through sex	——————+——————	It takes me a while to get going sexually

low yin	**MY RELATIONSHIP**	*low yang*
I find it hard to commit to my relationship	——————+——————	I find it hard to make changes in my relationship
I can easily feel as if I don't have the support I need	——————+——————	I have trouble supporting my partner
I feel needy in my relationship	——————+——————	I have trouble expressing my emotions to my partner
I feel neglected by my partner	——————+——————	I neglect my own needs
I can be stubborn and inflexible in my relationship	——————+——————	I give too much

low yin	**MY EMOTIONS**	*low yang*
I can easily get anxious	——————+——————	I can easily feel overwhelmed
I sometimes feel jumpy or jittery	——————+——————	I tend to worry or overthink
When I am stressed I can accomplish a lot	——————+——————	When I am stressed I get tired and shut down
When I have trouble concentrating it is because my mind is racing	——————+——————	When I have trouble concentrating it is because my mind feels cloudy
I often neglect my own needs	——————+——————	I often neglect the needs of others
I am scattered	——————+——————	I can be unmotivated
I want someone to take care of me	——————+——————	I have trouble standing up for myself
When irritated I am likely to snap at people	——————+——————	When irritated I'm likely to brood
I get easily frustrated	——————+——————	I can easily feel hopeless or gloomy
I have vivid dreams	——————+——————	I don't tend to remember my dreams
I find my partner's touch irritating or overwhelming	——————+——————	I feel as if I need a lot of touching from my partner

low yin	**MY BODY**	*low yang*
I tend to feel warm	——————+——————	I tend to feel cold
When I get tired I feel "wired"	——————+——————	When I get tired I feel lethargic
I am often thirsty	——————+——————	I don't drink much or am seldom thirsty
My face gets flushed easily	——————+——————	I am pale
I crave salty foods	——————+——————	I crave carbohydrates and sweets
I tend to get constipated	——————+——————	I tend to have loose stool
I have restless sleep and wake up during the night	——————+——————	I sleep a lot or need a lot of sleep

My skin and/or nails are dry	———————+———————	I bruise easily
My hands and feet get hot or sweaty	———————+———————	My hands and feet are often cold
I am thin and tend to be underweight or lose weight easily	———————+———————	My metabolism is sluggish and I tend to gain weight easily
I don't tend to urinate frequently or my urination is scanty	———————+———————	I urinate frequently and often in copious amounts
I sweat more when I am sleeping	———————+———————	I tend to sweat during the day with no exertion

low yin	**MY MENSTRUAL CYCLE**	*low yang*
My vagina often feels dry or unlubricated	———————+———————	I have profuse vaginal discharge
My menstrual cycle is short	———————+———————	My menstrual cycle is long
My periods are light	———————+———————	My periods are heavy
I get constipated during or before my period	———————+———————	I get loose stool during or before my period

FOR THE GUYS: Yin and Yang Scale for Men

Men can use the scale above to begin assessing their relative levels of yin and yang. Just skip the questions on sexuality and menstrual cycle, and add in the items below.

There are thirty-six items, so if you have nineteen or more marks on one side or the other, that's the way in which you tend to fall out of balance.

low yin	**FOR MEN**	*low yang*
I have a strong sex drive	——————+——————	I don't have much of a sex drive
I am easily aroused but can lose my erection	——————+——————	I have trouble getting an erection

I prefer quick sex, with little or no foreplay	——————+——————	I take a long time to get aroused
I have trouble staying connected during sex	——————+——————	I have trouble initiating sex or feel tired during sex
I sometimes ejaculate prematurely	——————+——————	I sometimes take a long time to ejaculate
I have been diagnosed with a low sperm count	——————+——————	I have been diagnosed with poor sperm motility
My ejaculate is scanty and/or concentrated	——————+——————	My ejaculate is very thin and watery
My ears sometimes ring after I ejaculate	——————+——————	I feel exhausted after I ejaculate

Yin and Balance

Yin (and the lack thereof) manifests in your body and your life in many ways, including physical and psychological/emotional signs. Here's how it relates to your sex life: The state of your health, both physical and emotional, depends on the balance of yin and yang within you; the health of your relationship depends on the balance of yin and yang between you and your partner. And your sex life depends on both the state of your overall health and the state of your relationship.

If there's an imbalance anywhere, it will show in your health, your psychological well-being, your relationship—and your sex drive. In fact, lack of libido is one big flashing sign that something has fallen out of balance.

Chinese medicine and philosophy attribute a long list of characteristics to yin and to yang. These characteristics generally come in pairs, seeming opposites. To take just one particularly relevant example, yin is considered moist, while yang is considered dry. Lack of yin creates lack of moisture. Or: Lack of moisture reveals lack of yin.

It might also be said that lack of moisture reveals too much yang—too much dryness. That's what it means to have a constantly shifting relationship between yin and yang. If it's less moist, it's more dry. If it's less yin, it's more yang. These are opposite ends of a spectrum, not entirely separate camps. In general, most Chinese medicine treatments for libido seek to build up what you are low on as the way to restore balance, so I've chosen to identify the pattern by the lack rather than the oversupply.

TRY THIS TONIGHT: Opening the Senses

This exercise is a favorite of massage therapist Nicole Kruck, LMT. I sometimes call it "the chocolate bite meditation," though it can be done just as well with a piece of fresh ripe fruit. It is a classic practice of mindfulness. The point here is to tune into all your senses with the goal of intensifying pleasure—an excellent skill to employ when having sex!

Choose a small piece of chocolate, and sit quietly with it for a few minutes. Take a good look at the chocolate. Describe it to yourself. Light or dark? Smooth or rough? Even or uneven? Now close your eyes. Hold the chocolate, touch it, and notice how it feels—the texture and shape. Bring it to your nose and notice how it smells. You can even *listen* to the chocolate as you break or bite off a piece.

Bring the chocolate to your lips and slowly take a small bite. Allow the chocolate to linger on your tongue, blossoming in your mouth, before swallowing or taking another bite. Notice not only the taste and the smell but also the feeling in your mouth as the texture shifts. Let your senses speak to you.

Throughout this meditation, check in periodically to notice if you are feeling any sensations in parts of your body not directly involved with the chocolate. Bring awareness specifically to your pelvis. Are you feeling any sensations there? There are chemical components in chocolate that make a good case for it being an aphrodisiac. Even so, for our purposes the more powerful effect of chocolate in this exercise is the way it awakens your senses, which opens you to sensual experience in general.

Sex Again in Real Life: Yvette

Yvette, whom you met in this chapter's opening, was not only dry but also hot—and *not* in the sexy sense. She was generally overheated, and often felt hot when no one else around her did. This is also the result of a lack of yin; yin is considered cooling, with yang being heating. Without enough yin, Yvette was sliding too far toward the yang end of the scale. She felt especially hot at night, and she'd begun to have night sweats, so she was driving her partner nuts by kicking off all the bedcovers and opening windows even in cold weather. (Let's just say *that* wasn't doing her sex life any favors, either.)

Yvette was not only dry but also hot—and not in the sexy sense.

Yvette was quite thin, no matter what she ate and whether or not she was exercising. She tended to eat poorly (she especially loved anything salty) and to eat on the run, and she exercised in bursts, infrequently.

Yvette was very giving and affectionate, and put a lot of energy into her relationship—into all her relationships—when she was in balance. When she fell out of balance, as she was now, she tended toward overreaction. Her relationships, particularly the one with her husband, suffered.

Yvette had a pretty low tolerance for stress. She was often anxious, and seemed agitated or unsettled. The more tired she got, the more wound up she felt. She had trouble sleeping. But she seemed bent on getting by with as little sleep as she possibly could anyway, between working long hours and managing a very full calendar of social engagements. (Burnout is a common cause of yin depletion, and can also be a result of it.)

Yet when she was alone with her husband, Yvette wasn't that social at all. For women, physical arousal is very yin: It's all about lubrication and receptivity. A lot of arousal happens in the mind: You have to think sexy, and think of yourself as sexy. To feel sexy you also need to be in touch with your femininity—another yin thing. Without enough yin, Yvette was running into trouble in a lot of ways.

Sex Never Gets Old. Neither Does Sexy.

Sexual desire is not something anyone ages out of—and certainly not in your thirties or forties. (Menopause tends to make things more complicated, but it does *not* kill sex drive.) But almost every woman dealing with low libido struggles with how to think about sex and her body as she gets older.

Make that almost every woman, period. That's because, as Chinese medicine has it, all women experience decreasing yin with increasing age. As that happens, receptivity to sex—in all sorts of ways—changes. That doesn't mean it goes away, however. But it does mean you may have to make some changes yourself to maintain a healthy sex life. Some of those changes address the physical realities of an aging body. But the bigger shifts have to occur in our attitudes.

As we age, our bodies don't look (or work) like they used to. Those are the facts, and the sooner we learn not to fight them, the better. The ancient Chinese offer an alternative stance you can still see in contemporary Chinese culture that all of us would benefit by adopting. The philosophy of Chinese medicine holds that when women stop having menstrual periods as they age, the blood goes instead to nourish the heart, building wisdom and compassion. We should recognize and honor that wisdom and compassion in ourselves—the kind you gain only through the experience of years, even if you haven't made it all the way to menopause as yet—rather than dwell on wrinkles or lost litheness. In other words: Look to what you gain over time, rather than bemoan what falls away.

That's easier said than done in a society that reveres young toned bodies, so we tend to worry about the sagging here and there, and fret because we don't have the same stamina we did in our twenties.

Those young bodies, however, are decades away from reaching their full sexual potential. True sexual intimacy and deep connection require experience and maturity. This potential is what we gain as we grow older. The price may be a little less energy and a little more wrinkly skin, but still that's a pretty darn good deal. Many people report having the best sex of their lives in their fifties and sixties.

When we are young, pure physical attraction gets our motors running. We can decide who to have sex with on the basis of whether we like what we see. We can decide if *we* feel sexual, based on how we think *we* look. But if you stay dependent on this most basic drive to get you going, then sex will tend to drop off as you age. (And sometimes take relationships right along with it.) You can't go just with what feels good, what directly stimulates you the most, either—as we age both men and women need more genital stimulation to experience arousal and orgasm.

If we are going to keep having sex with the same person over the long term, we *have* to replace physical attraction and stimulation as our main motivators for having sex. That's not to say those things are gone or no longer matter at all. But they inevitably dim. And it's a good thing, too, because something richer is waiting to take their place.

Physical attraction and stimulation inevitably dim. And it's a good thing, too, because something richer is waiting to take their place.

In a long-term relationship, we have to shift more toward the substantive connections we have with a partner—our thoughts and emotions—to keep the flame lit. It's easy to shut down sexually when we start to feel less responsive in the old, familiar ways. But the most sexually successful couples (which are usually the most successful couples in general) set aside expectations about those biologically based desires and embrace deep emotional and energetic connection instead. They tap their maturity and experience to let themselves open up to and be vulnerable with each other. That reinforces a bond like nothing else. Couples that navigate this transition together often report the most meaningful sex—and the most powerful orgasms—of their lives, even long after they've gone gray. Now *that's* sexy.

Body Image

And yet: Many of us simply don't feel good naked. My patients, of all ages, give me long lists of things that are "wrong" with their bodies. Among the many I-don't-like-how-I-look variations: Too wrinkly.

Too fat. Too thin. Breasts too large. Breasts too small. Lack of muscle. Cellulite. Flabby stomach. "That jiggly bit under my arm." The list goes on—including a whole subcategory of issues with the look, smell, and feel of our genitalia.

This is one of the major issues my patients mention when complaining about their sex lives, and it reflects a lack of yin regardless of whether yin is declining with age. As you work to increase yin, you will soften your own view of yourself and your body, which will go a long way to reconnecting you to your desire.

Most important of all, you can't be fully present if you are worrying about your body when you have sex, and you can't create an intense sexual connection without being fully present.

Weight

Of all the many ways I hear that women negatively judge their bodies, the most popular has to be their weight. The best sex advice remains self-acceptance. While putting on weight is primarily associated with people deficient in yang (see Chapter 4), not accepting your body as it is is a sign of yin deficiency. So if you want to lose weight, following the suggestions in the next chapter's To Do (It) List is a good idea. For feeling sexy regardless of a number on the scale, nurturing yin is the way to go.

I do want to point out that being overweight (and *not* by just five or ten pounds) can cause problems with your sex life, beyond self-consciousness or embarrassment. Excess weight, I don't have to tell you, is a health risk, and poor health will negatively impact your sex drive. And research shows that overweight people report being far less sexually satisfied than the rest of the population—for women even more so than men—and that the scope of sexual problems increases with weight.

So I do recommend managing your weight, so long as you can find sensible ways to do so. You will reap some benefits in the bedroom. But please, don't put your sex life on hold for some future day when you will somehow achieve your ideal weight.

There's another way sex and weight are interconnected: For many people, food becomes a kind of substitute for sex. People feeling sexually

frustrated (whether from lack of sex or lack of sexual desire) may turn to food for another kind of physical gratification. People eat for all kinds of emotional reasons, and that often means unhealthy choices about what or how much you eat. So weight problems are often mixed up with the other issues, including sexuality. Ask yourself: What are you hungry for? The true answer may be a little alone time with your partner (or any other pursuit of sexual satisfaction).

I *do* recommend a certain amount of body-consciousness, in that practicing basic good hygiene is *way* sexier than not. You have to decide for yourself what that means, in terms of what exactly you routinely shave, or wash, or deodorize, or brush. (Though I think we can all agree clean teeth and fresh breath are better for kissing.) I think as a society, however, we tend to overdo it with the grooming, reflecting one big body image problem. Can we really all smell so bad that we require whole drugstore aisles devoted to perfumes and deodorants and soaps and perfumed deodorant soaps? Let's agree to keep ourselves reasonably tidy but not go crazy with it, shall we?

FOR THE GUYS: Does This Poor Body Image Make Me Look Fat?

Men get tripped up by weight and body image issues too. But as a group we tend to be a bit bipolar about it. Some of us are sucked into the whirlwind of cultural messages and images proving we can never be thin enough, or fit enough, or good-looking enough in general, where we learn to feel bad about ourselves and our bodies. And some of us appear not to give two figs about how we present ourselves physically. Of course for many of us, it's a mixed bag: Maybe we give up on our appearance because we feel it can never measure up anyway.

My main concern here is how all this will affect your sex life and your libido. So let me urge you to find and walk that fine line between letting your weight and your body get you down—and letting it get out of control. It's a good idea to get or keep to a healthy weight for all kinds of health reasons—including, as you'll see in detail in the last chapter, a number of them that affect your libido. But you *must* approach this in a measured way or you are bound to fail—and make yourself feel worse in the process. Which would probably adversely affect your weight, as well.

At the same time, you need to love your body as it is if you are going to find your inner Sex Machine. You might look at it this way: Love it enough to take care of it—including *not stressing* about taking care of it. You do this in the same ways recommended to women: Positive body image is positive body image, whether that body is male or female. You also get the same advice she does about basic hygiene: way sexier than the alternative, so keep yourself reasonably tidy. I'm not talking about waxing your back hair or sporting a manicure or even anything specific at all. You can decide for yourself what your regular personal grooming routine will consist of—as long as you have one. Although both your partner and I do absolutely insist that you regularly brush your teeth.

Self-Esteem

Feeling good about ourselves and believing others see us in a positive light can improve sexual experience and boost libido. But people plagued by self-doubt, and worries about how they are perceived (physically or otherwise), will be self-conscious and tentative lovers. That's already passion-killing. Go far enough down this path and you're likely to come to inability to orgasm. Followed by nose-diving sex drive.

In all forms, low self-esteem indicates that we are not centered enough. And when we are not centered enough, we cannot have an honest, energetic connection with a partner. Good sex involves not only vulnerability but also the willingness to be open about who we are at a very deep level. Which we can't do if we don't value ourselves as we are.

Healthy self-esteem changes the equation dramatically. With a positive view of oneself, sex becomes something to enjoy personally, and to share willingly with a partner for their enjoyment as well. We no longer feel we need to play roles to gain the acceptance of others. Sex is no longer transactional, undertaken in the hopes of getting something from the other

DO IT NOW: The Loop

The Loop is a powerful way to nourish yin and rebalance yin and yang. It can also help you tap into or cultivate your sexual energy.

Sit comfortably with your eyes closed. Imagine a shallow bowl nestled inside your pelvis—a bowl filled with warm oil. Now imagine a tube or straw running along your spine. Inhale, and as you do, imagine the warm oil coursing up through the tube, as if led by your breath, moving from your pelvic area up to the very top of your head. Hold your breath in for a count of three (or five, as you get more experienced). Then exhale, imagining the warm oil flowing down, along a line in the center of the front of your body, from your head through your mouth, across your chest, down through your abdomen, and back into the bowl in your pelvis. Hold your breath out as the bowl finishes filling, then after three to five seconds begin again with an inhale. The idea is to create a continuous loop—and run through it about six times.

As the energy/oil arrives at your head, notice what that feels like. You may get a little "buzz," or a tingly feeling, or a sensation of warmth. Imagine circulating the energy around inside your head as you are holding your breath.

This should all be done with ease—if you are straining, or uncoordinated with the breathing, or if your attention has strayed—simply pause for a moment, then begin again.

The oil is an image to help you focus, but water or light could also work. Some people just think about moving their attention in this pattern, rather than picturing anything. The way Chinese medicine sees it, you are moving qi, and if that resonates with you, you can skip an image and just concentrate on moving energy up your spine and down the front of your chest.

person. Solid self-esteem also allows you to value your own body and your own sexuality, which can encourage you, for example, to choose compatible partners and practice safer sex—and to do so for yourself, as well as for the benefit of the relationship. With a positive sense of self, sex adds to the intimacy of a relationship but isn't the only source of closeness.

Yin is important to supporting solid self-esteem. Yin allows self-love and self-nurturing. Yin is also needed to receive love—to open up to someone else. Addressing yin deficiency can redress low self-esteem.

Yin and Yang and Hormones

Chinese medicine views the stages of intercourse as governed by an interplay of yin and yang energy. It is yang energy from either partner that initiates sexual intimacy. It is yin energy from the other partner, then, that receives that initiation and reciprocates, transforming a solo act into something mutual. An erection is from yang energy; sexual receptivity, vaginal lubrication, for example, is yin. In this way of thinking, intercourse is about giving and receiving, creation and transformation, initiation and reciprocation. If the energy is a little off here or there, the whole system can run into trouble. But when it is in relative balance, everything runs smoothly.

Western medicine views sexual response as part of a similarly tricky balance—but of hormones, rather than energy. The feeling of sexual desire begins with a hormonal push—and starts a cascade of hormones contributing to arousal, sexual function, and orgasm, among other things. Hormones can go haywire in a variety of ways, ways that often involve interference with sexual desire or performance. In fact, hormone imbalance is the most common physical cause of sexual problems in women. How much you have of one hormone or another can be the culprit, but the most important thing is usually how much you have of one hormone in relation to the others.

Circling back to Chinese medicine: In the ancient view, hormonal balance relies on achieving a balance of yin and yang, and on good circulation of blood and qi. Imbalanced hormones will throw off the balance of yin and yang or impede the flow of qi; and, blocked qi or imbalance of yin and yang can throw off the balance of hormones and affect sexual function. Maintaining this balance gets trickier with age, as yin tends to dip in women; the symptoms of perimenopause and menopause are symptoms of yin deficiency. Stuck qi leads to poor circulation, which leads to poor hormonal transitions, which in turn leads to hormone imbalances.

Yin Deficiency and Hormone Imbalance

Many of the most common symptoms of lack of yin are due to the way yin deficiency knocks hormones out of balance. Low estrogen is often the result, and sometimes high or unstable progesterone levels. So you can use the symptoms listed below to help you figure out if you have a hormone imbalance and/or determine if you are low in yin.

Estrogen plays a specific and absolutely crucial role in women's sex lives: It is responsible for vaginal lubrication—the general everyday kind, but also for the increase during sexual activity. Balanced levels of estrogen provide an overall feeling of health and vitality—the best foundation for a strong libido.

You already know that estrogen decreases as women age. Chinese medicine says that yin naturally depletes over time as well. So women are more likely to have signs of low estrogen—and low yin—as they age. Or women might see those symptoms intensify. By menopause all women, by definition, have decreased estrogen. And most women have at least some yin deficiency.

Low estrogen levels can cause symptoms that lead to uncomfortable or even painful sex, particularly thin and dry vaginal tissue and lack of lubrication. The symptoms of menopause are symptoms of low estrogen. Low estrogen can cause hot flashes and/or night sweats, thereby earning you a diagnosis of perimenopause. Perimenopause symptoms are similar to menopause, but they tend to be milder, and to come and go more erratically. If you are forty-five or under, however, you are unlikely to be menopausal yet—though you may well be yin deficient. After many women have given birth they also experience the effects of low estrogen, which can last for about six months. In addition to yin deficiency, the signs of low estrogen include:

- Low libido
- Pain or discomfort with intercourse
- Vaginal dryness
- Fatigue
- Poor memory
- Insomnia
- Night sweats (especially premenstrually)
- Hot flashes (especially premenstrually)
- Heart palpitations
- Dry eyes
- Dry skin
- Short menstrual cycle with short, light periods *or* heavy periods with bright red blood and midcycle bleeding
- Perimenopause
- Menopause

Progesterone has a range of roles in a woman's body, including the way it works through the nervous system—in part, it functions to help relax both mind and muscles. As you probably know from experience, sex works much better when you are relaxed. In addition, a woman's body uses progesterone in making the testosterone it needs (see page 81).

High progesterone levels may manifest in a number of symptoms that will tend to squelch your sex life. Besides yin deficiency, signs that your progesterone may be elevated include:

- Mood swings
- Irritability
- Breast tenderness
- Headaches
- Drowsiness
- Weight gain
- Bloating
- Depression
- Hot flashes
- Acne

In most cases, though, the level of progesterone may not actually be that high; most likely it is high in relation to estrogen—and estrogen is low. This phenomenon often crops up in women with stagnant qi, as well (see page 34).

If you are experiencing clusters of the symptoms above, it may be worthwhile to get your hormone levels tested. Depending on your test results, your doctor may prescribe pills, patches, suppositories, creams, or gels. But few women take hormone therapy for libido issues alone. It is more common in cases where several symptoms are seriously interfering with a woman's daily life—and where restored libido is seen as a lucky by-product of treatment for these other things.

Chinese medicine is very often a better alternative—and women who are dealing primarily with sex drive are the most likely to respond to Chinese medicine. Hormone balance is one of the areas where its relative subtlety and holistic approach often outperforms what Western medicine can offer.

Sex Again in Real Life: Michelle

Michelle, thirty-nine, consulted me in hopes of revving up her low sex drive. She was concerned that it was hard for her to become aroused. Nothing seemed to flip her switch anymore. Nothing ever got her juices going; as a result, sex was quite uncomfortable, which certainly wasn't doing much to make her want sex. When she and her husband did have sex, Michelle found it difficult to really feel connected.

Michelle's skin and hair were also dry, and like a lot of people with low yin, she was always thirsty. She was extremely hot, too, and had hot flashes. Her doctor had suggested she was premenopausal, but I assured her she was too young for that. The pattern I saw was one of yin deficiency. She seemed restless and fidgety and, to complete the picture, had a slight, almost wiry build. And if I needed more evidence, Michelle was burnt-out and unhappy in her relationship with her husband.

"I feel totally sucked dry by my family," she told me, with a particularly apt choice of words. "We've got two kids, and I do pretty much everything to keep the family running, and no one even appreciates it, much less helps out." The resentment she was carrying around made her shut down emotionally with her husband, which effectively shut down their sexual connection as well. Michelle was caught in a trap common in people who fit this pattern: She was always doing for others while neglecting to nurture herself. With her yin low, she wasn't completely sure she really deserved the kind of support she yearned for. But she also didn't like the results of not asking for it.

I prescribed a Chinese herbal formula designed to nourish yin—a variation on a common over-the-counter formula called Liu Wei Di Huang Wan (Rehmannia Six). In addition, I taught her a meditative technique (see Inner Smile, page 112), a self- (and yin-) nurturing practice, and recommended The Loop (page 61). Michelle needed to reflect on her emotional life, develop insight into her own needs, and learn to understand the yin deficiency pattern within herself.

She wanted to rev up her sex drive, but nothing seemed to flip her switch anymore; nothing got her juices going.

In Chinese philosophy, one of the main characteristics associated with yin is *receptivity.* So for someone low in yin, taking what other people offer can be a challenge. Often they are more used to giving . . . and giving . . . and giving. Giving is considered yang, and doing it to excess can push a person right into yin deficiency. (Increasing amounts of yang decreases levels of yin.) Lack of yin also makes it hard to put up boundaries, so yin-deficient people may take on too much, or be vulnerable to being taken advantage of. Some adopt the role of martyr.

You can easily see the sexual issues you'll run into if you are not receptive of another person—for women, it can be quite literal. You can imagine the emotional roadblocks, too. For Michelle, though, the roots of the problem ran far out of the bedroom, right into the details of day-to-day living. To turn it around, Michelle decided to ask her family directly and specifically to help with chores around the house. When she did, she was surprised by their willingness to help.

The real trick for Michelle, as with many people with yin deficiency, was not only the asking, but also the ability to accept the help, once she'd finally thought to request it. Her kids *could* do their own laundry and pack their own lunches, she discovered. Her husband managed just fine with the scheduling and chauffeuring duties, given the chance. And if she had to occasionally bite her tongue about awkwardly scheduled dentist appointments, or sneak in to refold a few fitted sheets according to her preference . . . well, she was learning to do just that without reverting to taking the whole task on herself.

Within a few weeks of her new regime, Michelle was feeling less dry in general, and more receptive as well, both with her family and in her private time with her husband—and more clear within herself that she *should* have their input and support. After eight weeks, her hot flashes were much less frequent and much less intense. Around that time, Michelle realized she was harboring less resentment and cheerfully reported that her confidence was renewed enough that she had asked her husband for what she needed sexually. No longer worried that she was heading into menopause prematurely, she felt not only younger, but sexier.

Yin Sexuali-Tea

This herbal tea, drunk hot or cold, is moistening and anti-inflammatory, and used daily it can help with lubrication and painful sex. The quantities below will make enough for about a month's worth of tea, if you drink one cup daily. All these ingredients should be available at your health food store. Check the herb, spice, supplement, and tea sections.

- **1 cup chrysanthemum tea leaves**
- **2 tablespoons marshmallow root**
- **¼ cup stinging nettle tea leaves**
- **2 teaspoons anise**

Combine all ingredients and store in a resealable container. To make one cup, place 2 teaspoons of the mixture in a cup. Fill cup with boiling water, cover, and let steep for up to 10 minutes. Strain and serve.

Low Yin + Stuck Qi = . . . ?

Scratch the surface of someone with yin deficiency and you'll often find stagnated qi underneath. Yin/yang imbalance can also *cause* qi to stagnate.

The combination of stuck qi and low yin produces its own pattern, prominently featuring characteristics of each issue. People with the combination often have inflammation in their bodies, one sign of which may

What Depletes Yin?

Anything that leaves you feeling burnt-out is drawing down your supply of yin. The most common suspects include:

- Overwork or shift work
- Late nights
- Anxiety or worrying
- Depression
- Poor nutrition
- Use of stimulants, including caffeine and recreational drugs
- Alcohol
- Excessive nurturing of others without nurturing yourself
- Getting older
- Stagnant qi
- Carrying resentment

be red eyes. Women often have symptoms easily confused with menopausal signs, perhaps hot flashes and night sweats, especially at times of hormonal transitions, such as just before their periods. They may have other premenstrual symptoms as well, especially pimples. They may experience vaginal dryness, including lack of lubrication during sex, and painful intercourse—that's the yin deficiency—and also trouble reaching orgasm, thanks to the stagnant qi.

People with both stuck qi and low yin tend to irritability when they are out of balance—they may be quick to get snappy. Resentment is another common theme. They may feel claustrophobic or unfulfilled in their relationships. When they run into trouble with their sex lives, it's typically in the form of lack of desire and difficulty reaching orgasm. They tend not to have enough yin to be receptive to their partners' advances, or enough movement of qi to enjoy sex fully.

FOR THE GUYS: Dean

For men, arousal is more a yang thing, so men with too little yin—who actually have plenty of yang—tend to get aroused easily and often. They may have quite a strong sex drive—even excessive, sometimes. The most common male yin deficiency problems are difficulty *maintaining* an erection, and premature ejaculation. Men with yin deficiency may have strong libidos, but that sexual desire can burn out as quickly as it sparks up.

Some men with yin deficiency have wet dreams, even though they are decades past adolescence and are sexually active with a partner. They are sometimes diagnosed with erectile dysfunction, low sperm count, or high numbers of abnormal sperm.

Dean had recently been diagnosed with a low sperm count when he—rather reluctantly—came to see me. He and his wife were trying to conceive and his wife had read that acupuncture could help improve sperm count. And so here he was in my office.

In answering my questions, he explained that he had a very stressful job, worked long hours, and was always tired and often anxious. He had no complaints about his libido—he was easily and regularly aroused—but he was frustrated with his sex life. He said he either orgasmed too early, or had trouble maintaining his erection, all of which he chalked up to the stress he was under. When I asked if he noticed a ringing in his ears after ejaculation, he looked a bit surprised—but nodded.

This last bit is a classic Chinese medicine sign of yin deficiency, and Dean acknowledged many other symptoms that fit into the pattern as well. He often felt hot, especially later in the day, and when stressed. He admitted that one of the ways he chose to try to deal with his stress was occasional use of cocaine.

Dean also told me that his wife complained that he spent too much of his free time on his computer. This fit the pattern I've witnessed among yin-deficient men—withdrawing and being hard to reach even to those closest to them. Chinese medicine understands it as an effect of missing yin's receptivity.

I prescribed Dean the yin-nourishing Chinese herbal formula Zhi Bai Di Huang Wan (Anemarrhena, Phellodendron, and Rehmannia), which is available over the counter. And as a homework assignment I advised Dean to try masturbating. Very slowly. He looked at me like I was out of my mind when I suggested how slowly (taking fifteen minutes) but agreed to give it a try. And he knew without me even pressing the case that it was time to cut out the recreational drug taking. Among other things, cocaine is a very powerful stimulant, and stimulants deplete yin.

By his next visit two weeks later Dean already reported feeling less hot and anxious, though the external conditions causing him stress hadn't really changed. So he was happy to continue taking the herbs. I encouraged Dean to do some reflective things (very yin!) like reading or keeping a journal, and to cut out some of the things draining his yin, like always being on the go.

As the weeks went by, Dean's wife confirmed that he was spending more time with her, and after about six weeks of treatment they both agreed they were feeling more connected. They were both enjoying the massage exercise I'd suggested to them (see Exploring, page 129 in Chapter 7), which gave Dean a chance to experience being receptive, thus nourishing his yin. Two months in, Dean noticed his erections lasted longer and was happy to report that he was no longer ejaculating prematurely. (After six months of treatment he also had a normal sperm count, and three months after that his wife was pregnant.)

TO DO (IT) LIST: Nourishing Yin

Having sex is a great way to rebalance yin and yang. Regular sex also helps maintain estrogen levels—one of the reasons I can say "just do it" and know the advice will work. You can boost your production of sex hormones with any kind of sexual activity, so you don't even need a partner to reap the benefits. Even just thinking about sex until you feel aroused will do the trick. Even so, you may want to try some additional strategies for nourishing your yin:

➜ **Exercise.** Try something that promotes flexibility and freedom of movement, or that quiets your mind while working your body: yoga, tai chi, qi gong, swimming, or simply walking in nature. Get your aerobic workouts, for sure—but limit them to about thirty minutes at a time, three times a week.

➜ **Eat right.** Support your yin with a diet of whole foods that emphasizes vegetables, fruits, and whole grains, complemented with smaller servings of protein and healthy fats. That's a diet that's both densely nutritious and high in moisture content. To counter dryness within your body, you need fats as well as water. Cut out processed foods.

➜ **Eat less animal protein** if you have several of the symptoms of low estrogen. Especially avoid red meat—because too much will suppress production of estrogen. You might want to replace some of it with soy, which is naturally high in estrogenic compounds.

➜ **Choose yin-nourishing foods:** Seaweed, beets, flaxseeds, spinach, chard, cucumbers, string beans, grapes, blackberries, raspberries, blueberries, watermelon, lettuce, summer squash, eggplant, millet, whole wheat, amaranth, wild rice, eggs, dairy products, soy, mung beans, nuts, and sunflower seeds.

➜ **Choose estrogen-boosting foods** such as apples, lima beans, papayas, dates, plums, pomegranates, beets, tomatoes, yams, olives, potatoes, barley, rice, hops, oats, flaxseeds, chickpeas, garlic, parsley, split peas, sprouts, and licorice.

→ **Watch your weight.** Specifically: Be sure you weigh *enough*. When body fat dips too low, the body shuts down estrogen production. For example, competitive marathon runners can even cease having a period. But it's actually pretty common to experience a subtle but problematic hormonal imbalance as a result of just being very lean, or only slightly underweight. Women who are low in yin may be prone to this.

→ **Get plenty of potassium** because without enough of it your body can't make all the sex hormones it needs, including estrogen. Good food sources include whole grains, legumes, and fresh fruits and vegetables.

→ **Hydrate.** Drink at least eight eight-ounce glasses of water or other healthy fluids every day.

→ **Avoid alcohol.** It is dehydrating, as well as being a yin-depleting stimulant. One drink a day is generally fine, but from a libido perspective less is likely better.

→ **Avoid caffeine.** See above. On top of that, caffeine is a diuretic, which intensifies the loss of moisture.

→ **Avoid smoking and recreational drug use.** Cigarettes and drugs are yin-depleting and particularly likely to throw you severely out of balance. Stopping smoking will improve your circulation—and thus your libido.

→ **Evaluate any medications** you take in terms of whether they may be causing libido-damaging side effects, particularly dryness. Usual suspects include antidepressants, allergy and cold medications, and antiestrogen medications; talk to your doctor about your options for changing medications or dosages to avoid sexual side effects.

→ **As much as you can, avoid getting overheated.** Saunas, steam rooms, hot tubs, and hot baths are not good choices for you.

→ **Get enough good-quality sleep.**

→ **Learn to manage your stress.**

→ **Take an essential fatty acid (EFA) supplement.** Good choices include black current seed oil, flaxseed oil, or fish oil. You'll reap health benefits galore, but most relevant to your sex life and estrogen levels is the fact that taking EFAs will help combat vaginal dryness.

→ **Take a calcium/magnesium supplement.** Besides the usually touted benefits, I'm recommending calcium and magnesium because they are good for your sex drive: Calcium is calming, and magnesium helps circulation.

→ **List your positive qualities.** I'm talking about making an actual list. Add to it often. Read it over even more frequently.

→ **Try vitamin E** vaginal suppositories for vaginal dryness and/or use **a natural personal lubricant,** to reduce friction and discomfort during intercourse. Choose one without parabens, glycerin, or propylene glycol, since those chemicals can affect hormone balance and are easily absorbed by vaginal tissue. Many of my clients like Sylk, which is made from an extract of the kiwifruit vine. Astroglide also comes in a glycerin- and paraben-free version. **You can also use natural oils** such as grape seed, sweet almond, sunflower, or apricot seed oil; apply just a dab after you take a bath or shower, in the interest of generally keeping things moist down there. Not all of the natural oils are appropriate with condom use, so don't use them as lubricants in that context.

→ **Use massage and masturbation** strategies (see Chapters 7 and 8) to help develop a positive self-image and appreciation for your body just as it is. That includes getting comfortable with your genitals—an important but often overlooked part of your view of yourself as a sexual person.

→ **Choose sexercises that nourish yin.** The two in this chapter (The Loop and Opening the Senses) are a great place to start, and you'll be learning more throughout the book; Appendix 2 gives you a quick reference to which exercises are good for yin.

→ **Consider acupuncture.** Almost all of my patients get it because it's a great way to rebalance yin and yang. You can get results without it, but you're likely to progress less efficiently.

→ **Take the yin-nourishing herbal formula Liu Wei Di Huang Wan (Rehmannia Six),** which is moistening. You can add other herbs to it, depending on your symptoms. Most common would be Wu Wei Zi (Schisandra) and Dang Gui (Tangkui) for vaginal dryness, or huang bai (phellodendron) and zhi mu (anemarrhena) for hot flashes.

4

I'm Too Tired for Sex

How (and Why) to Boost Yang

"I'd almost forgotten: I *like* to do this!" Darcy said, about two months into treatment with me. She was giddily reporting that she had initiated sex with her husband. "I decided to just try it," she told me. "No more waiting around for some perfect moment I'd be just dying to do it. And I'm glad I did. It was a slow start, but I really got into it after a while." Besides a certain gleam in her eye, I noticed a definite uptick in her energy level.

When Darcy first came to my office, her sex life wasn't the first thing on her mind. She just wasn't that interested in sex. And she was too tired for it in any case. It just seemed to require more energy than she had. She had to make a conscious effort to do it anyway to reconnect with the idea that sex was an important part of her life.

If any of that sounds familiar, then you, like Darcy, fall into the Chinese medicine pattern of yang deficiency. Yang is considered active, fast, stimulating, and energizing—while yin is passive, slow, calming, and sedating. Without enough yang, you slide *too* far to the "sedate" side of the scale. Yang deficiency is about being *tired.*

For a typical woman with yang deficiency, it isn't the "sedate" to "energized" scale that concerns her most, however. It is her bathroom scale, which she probably avoids as much as she can. She's probably convinced she has the world's slowest metabolism. She puts on weight easily, especially when under stress. Over the years, those extra pounds add up.

On top of that, a lot of women with yang deficiency have less than perfect diets (don't we all!). They might skip meals, sometimes complaining of no appetite, then replace them with junk food. They are often extremely sensitive to sugar—they crave it, can't resist it, and like the initial burst of energy but always end up with a "sugar crash" that leaves them more tired than ever.

Identifying your pattern is an important first step toward knowing how to find your way back to balance.

They also harbor a bit of a couch potato tendency. They may get out of breath easily or describe themselves as weak, or lethargic. They tend to be tired and low in energy, often to the point of feeling quite overwhelmed. They may need a lot of sleep, but even when they get it may not feel refreshed when they wake up. Dark circles under the eyes is a telltale sign. Fatigue is the biggest complaint from women with yang deficiency.

So is it any wonder they are often not up for sex? Without enough yang, women just don't have the physical, mental, or emotional energy for it. They may be exhausted from caring for young children—or aging parents. Or both. Or maybe their jobs are wiping them out. Or sometimes the fatigue is a sign of a particular physical condition (low thyroid being a common one). And sometimes they are just done in by the speeded-up pace of life in the twenty-first century. Add to all that a general "brain fog" (trouble concentrating, low motivation, and just a general feeling of dullness), prolonged headaches, occasional dizziness, and various aches and pains, especially in the knees and lower back, and you've got a recipe for . . . well, I don't know what, but definitely not for a lot of hot nights!

Hot isn't ever really the word to describe a yang-deficient woman, not in the temperature sense of the word anyway. She's likely to have poor circulation, so her hands and feet are often cold. She tends to feel chilly, in general, even in summer, or when everyone around her is comfortably warm. She feels overly sensitive to all kinds of cold—cold drinks, cold weather, cold drafts. Poor circulation can also reduce sensation, which can put quite a crimp in one's sex life.

Women with low yang also often contend with hormonal imbalances, digestive disturbances, and low immune function.

When everything is in balance, women who tend to get low yang are caring, nurturing, and levelheaded. When things get out of whack, though, they may get gloomy, or shut down, or become passive.

Once they overcome their fatigue and take action, people with yang deficiency can get themselves up and running again with a combination

What Depletes Yang?

Some people just tend to be low in yang by nature. Wherever your baseline, the most common things that draw down your yang include:

- Taking on too much responsibility combined with not getting enough rest
- Inactivity
- Overwork
- Eating too many cold or raw foods
- Irregular meals
- Lack of exercise
- Excessive unconnected sexual activity (for example, porn)
- Stress and excessive adrenaline
- Chronic illness
- Feeling like you must get *everything* done
- Getting older
- Stagnant qi

of lifestyle adjustments, stress management, and strategies for balancing yin and yang, including some sexercises and possible herbs and/or acupuncture. Boosting yang will restore balance and in so doing improve general energy levels—and revive libido.

TRY THIS TONIGHT: Buddha Belly

I've named this exercise after the idea that rubbing the belly of a Buddha statue is good luck. Only in this case the goodness comes from rubbing your own belly! This exercise generates energy, particularly yang energy, and can channel it into sexual energy or arousal.

For this exercise, you can be naked, or in minimal, loose clothing, or covered by a sheet. Sit or lie comfortably on your back, and close your eyes. Rub your hands together vigorously to warm them and bring up qi. Rest one hand on the upper abdomen and one hand on your lower abdomen. Feel your inhalations move your hands as your abdomen rises with incoming breath. Take several slow, deep breaths and allow yourself to relax. Let any tension, worries, or to-do lists melt away with each exhalation.

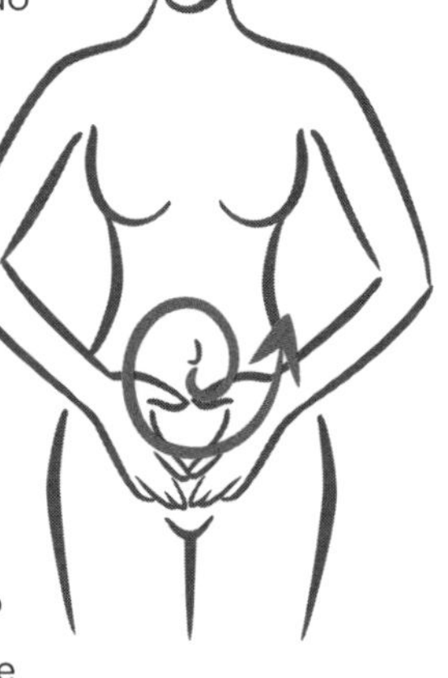

Now place both hands on the lower abdomen, still concentrating on your breath. Let your hands rest there gently, allowing their warmth and the breath to bring circulation to the area. When you are ready, spiral your hands out clockwise, moving slow and steady, with light pressure. Maintain the easy deep breathing. Let the circle cover your whole

If you recognize yourself in this portrait, chances are your yang is low—and that the scales in the previous chapter confirm that. Identifying your pattern is just the beginning of your journey—but it is an important first step toward knowing how to find your way back to balance.

Yang and Your Hormones

Many of the symptoms of yang deficiency link back to hormonal

belly, coming up under the ribs and down to just above the pubic bone. Continue for two or three minutes, then reverse the spiral for another few minutes.

Next, bring your hands to the inside of your thighs, as far as you can reach without having to lift your shoulders or upper body. Stroke up, using light pressure, as if you were applying lotion. Start on the inside of the thigh as far down as you can reach, and gradually shift your stroke outward and upward—toward the tops of your thighs. Then gradually shift outward farther still, continuing the upward strokes, until your hands reach the side of your hips. Then shift slowly up and over your thighs again, back inward to the groin. Repeat this pattern three times. Altogether you'll be spending at least a minute on your thighs—three minutes is even better.

Now finish the exercise by holding both hands still on your pelvis. Feel the warmth under them, and the movement of the qi, and particularly notice any sensations in your pelvis, but also anywhere else. Notice if you experienced any physical or emotional changes during this exercise. Does the area feel physically warmer? Tingly? Loose? Do you feel more relaxed?

imbalances. The reproductive hormones are likely to be out of whack—and messing with your sex life in the bargain—and there may also be imbalances in the thyroid, adrenal, and pituitary glands affecting metabolism and circulation. It is not uncommon for these to reach the level of clinical diagnosis (hypothyroidism or other metabolic disorders). Low thyroid is particularly associated with low yang—often the source of the weight gain and feeling cold typical of that deficiency.

Chinese medicine can recognize—*and treat*—subtler imbalances that may fly under the radar of Western medicine while nonetheless wreaking havoc on your health and your sex life. As Chinese medicine sees it, yang warms the body, so low yang can literally leave you cold. Progesterone is thought to be warming, too; low yang and low progesterone often go hand in hand. Yang is also thought to be responsible for transitions—including hormonal transitions such as the drop in estrogen at ovulation—or perimenopause/menopause. Yang is considered energizing, as are "male" hormones like testosterone; testosterone is often low in people with yang deficiency.

Chinese medicine can recognize and treat subtle imbalances in energy or hormones that may be wreaking havoc on your sex life.

The yang-hormone link also accounts for the way many symptoms of yang deficiency show up or are exacerbated during a woman's period, and/or about halfway through the cycle (at ovulation). Chalk up the fatigue, poor circulation, and digestive problems (especially loose stools) that come to the fore at those times to hormones, yang deficiency, or both.

Because of the way yang is tied up with your hormones, the characteristics of your menstrual cycle can also clue you in to yang deficiency. Signs include profuse vaginal discharge at times during the nonmenstrual phase of the cycle, menstrual cramps that are relieved by heat (like a heating pad or warm bath), or heavy but short periods. Or, in another version, long periods (more than five days). One thing you are less likely to see with yang deficiency is a typical twenty-eight-day cycle.

Estrogen, Progesterone, and Testosterone

Women with yang deficiency are prone to having high estrogen or low progesterone, and/or low testosterone. So the symptoms below can clue you in to what's going on with your hormones. They can also help you identify if you are low in yang. (If this list raises your suspicions, you can have your hormone levels checked by your doctor. But you can go ahead and follow the relevant advice even without lab results.)

Elevated estrogen can dampen sex drive. Besides yang deficiency, signs that your estrogen may be elevated include:

- Low sex drive
- Heavy periods
- Weight gain
- Fatigue
- Irritability
- PMS
- Water retention premenstrually—with your period, or just in general
- Bloating premenstrually—with your period, or just in general
- Mood swings premenstrually—with your period, or just in general

Low progesterone is often overlooked as a cause of low libido. Yang deficiency is one sign of low progesterone; others include:

- Feeling stressed-out
- Fibrocystic breasts
- Irregular or heavy periods
- Fluid retention and bloating
- Depression
- Weight gain
- Low body temperature
- Carbohydrate or sugar cravings
- Low libido

Sometimes symptoms that look like elevated estrogen levels are really the result of low progesterone levels. But it amounts to effectively the same thing—it's the relative levels of the two hormones that is important. This is called *estrogen dominance*. (Estrogen dominance is common in women with stagnant qi as well; see page 34.)

Low progesterone is sometimes mistaken for low testosterone in women complaining of diminished sex drive.

Testosterone, which in a woman's body is made from progesterone, boosts a woman's sex drive. It also has a direct effect on women's experience of pleasure during sex; without enough of it, enjoyment may be muted. Optimal levels of testosterone also provide a general sense of well-being.

Low testosterone often leads directly to low sex drive. Stress is often an underlying cause. Under stress, a woman's body converts progesterone into stress hormones (like cortisol), instead of sex hormones (namely, testosterone). When chronic stress is felt over time, this switcheroo results in lowered libido (and a host of other health issues). Birth control pills are another likely suspect here, because they inhibit the production of androgens ("male" hormones), including testosterone. In addition to yang deficiency, signs that your testosterone may be low include:

- Chronic stress
- Fatigue
- Poor memory
- Foggy mind
- Aching muscles
- Loss of stamina

FOR THE GUYS: Testosterone in Men

A man with low yang is also prone to low testosterone. Men's testosterone levels decline with stress, and with lack of sleep, drug and alcohol abuse, and some prescription medications—particularly statins (for high cholesterol)—among other things. Is it any wonder it is the most common hormonal imbalance in men?

Signs and symptoms of low testosterone—aside from the low yang—include:

- Loss of sexual desire
- General state of apathy (including, but not limited to, apathy about having sex)
- Erectile dysfunction
- Fatigue
- Disturbed sleep
- Depression
- Poor memory

It is not uncommon for men whose main issue is low libido to use supplemental testosterone. But hormones and their potential side effects are nothing to mess with, and taking them requires guidance by a specialist.

Sex Again in Real Life: Darcy

As part of her intake interview, Darcy admitted some concern about the fact that she had almost no interest in sex anymore. But she had come to see me because she had been gaining weight no matter how much or what she ate. She'd been to her regular doctor, complaining about her sluggish metabolism, but her thyroid hormone levels came back within "normal" range and the doctor had no other insight for her about why the scale kept showing higher and higher numbers. I suspected yang deficiency. She confirmed that she was always tired and cold. And she said she got enough sleep, but that she was still groggy in the morning—at least until the second cup of coffee.

I advised Darcy that she didn't need to focus too much on her weight *or* her sex drive. They would normalize, I knew, if she could get back in balance by boosting her yang energy. I got her started with exercises including Buddha Belly (page 78), The Loop (page 61), and The Squeeze (page 85), to help her generate energy, and specifically yang energy, and channel it toward arousal. I also suggested a Chinese herbal formula—Jin Gui Shen Qi Wan (Rehmannia Eight), which is available over the counter—to nourish her yang.

> ***She felt good about standing up for herself—and really good about her husband's response when she did.***

In addition, Darcy and I mapped out a series of lifestyle adjustments, including eating a diet with lots of whole grains, whose slow-release energy would replace the quick hits from sugar that she was used to. I recommended plenty of warming foods, too, such as soup, and using a hot water bottle on her low back every evening. Darcy also began to get aerobic exercise, starting out slowly and gradually increasing the length and intensity of her workout week by week. I also asked her to be sure to get enough rest during the day and plenty of sleep each night.

In addition, I talked with Darcy about working to assert herself in her relationship. I have noticed that women who are yang deficient often lack the assertiveness to ask for what they want, and that causes problems within their relationships. Darcy admitted she felt she had become a bit of a doormat with her husband, Dave. She then began to describe problems with her mother-in-law—"She is so critical of everything I do!"—that sounded to me more like a problem with her husband: "Dave never sticks up for me." When I asked if she had discussed this with Dave, she seemed surprised at the question. She shook her head no. She had just been continuing on, resentful of how she was being treated, and even more resentful that her husband wasn't doing anything about it, though she never said a word. Though she felt she wouldn't be able to get any better treatment anyway, she agreed to think about bringing it up with Dave.

After about three weeks, once her program had begun to take effect, Darcy was feeling less tired—and had started to drop some weight. Shedding a few pounds helped her body image and made her feel more sexual. At the same time, she was delighted to discover she had developed the confidence to explain to Dave about her issues with his mother, but in a calm and impersonal way. He, in turn, was able to establish appropriate boundaries with his mother, and the two women were getting along much better. Darcy felt good about standing up for herself—and really good about her husband's response when she did.

A little over a month later, we were at the point where our story began: After years of relying on her husband to initiate sex,

Yang Sexuali-Tea

This basic blend can spice up your sex life. The herbs, as well as the tea itself, are warming. Combine the dry ingredients below and store the mixture in a small resealable container; it's enough for about 30 cups.

1 cup black tea leaves

2 tablespoons ground allspice

2 tablespoons ground cardamom

Fresh ginger slices

To make one cup, place 2 teaspoons of the dry mixture in a cup, add two slices of fresh ginger, and fill cup with boiling water. Cover and let steep for 10 minutes. Strain and serve.

Darcy felt ready to take the leap herself and was happily reporting positive results at her appointments with me. More than once, they'd been alone together in the bedroom . . . and awake! "I didn't even miss having sex until I started to feel less tired," she explained. "I didn't really know what I was missing. Now I've realized getting that part of me back is the best part of my whole treatment."

Stuck Qi + Low Yang = ?

Because stuck qi nearly always leads to yin/yang imbalance, I often see patients who have both yang deficiency and stuck qi. They exhibit clusters of symptoms from both patterns. They tend to bottle up stresses, so they face ever-increasing pressure with no good release, while at

DO IT NOW: The Squeeze

The Squeeze improves yang energy in the body. Regular use of this exercise will boost response to sexual stimulation, increase sexual pleasure, and intensify orgasm—for everyone. And that's just for starters—which is why I recommend practicing it daily, and why you'll be hearing much more about it.

The full-length version of this exercise (see page 121) requires you to set aside a little private time devoted to it, but here you're going to start with just one key component of the exercise that you can do pretty much anytime, anywhere.

If you are familiar with Kegel exercises, you already know the essence of The Squeeze. All you do is tighten the muscles of your vagina and anus, as if you were trying to stop the flow of urine. When you do, you're giving your pubococcygeus (PC) muscles a workout. Just squeeze, hold for a count of ten, and release. Relax for another count of ten, then repeat the cycle for a total of ten times. If you can't hold it for ten seconds, no worries—just do what you can and gradually build up to the ten seconds as you get stronger.

the same time burning through yang like crazy, trying to get everything accomplished without getting much in the way of counterbalancing yin-building activities.

Women with the low yang/stuck qi combination are often reluctant to initiate sex and find it difficult to orgasm. Women who fit this pattern tend to have slow metabolisms and may well be overweight. Digestive issues are common, particularly at times of stress or with hormonal shifts.

Yang deficiency can also be the *cause* of qi stagnation, just as yin deficiency can. In the case of low yang and stuck qi, qi isn't flowing because there's not enough energy to power the flow, not enough "oomph" to keep things moving along.

FOR THE GUYS: Jonathan

Erections are all about yang, so without enough yang in relation to yin, a man may have a difficult time getting aroused and/or experience trouble getting an erection (or keeping one). He may contend with low sex drive, and diminished sensation.

The older a man gets, the more likely he is to have lower yang—as well as its symptoms. Overall levels of both yang and yin decrease with age, in both men and women. In men, the most likely outcome is an imbalance tipped toward relative lack of yang.

When Jonathan came into my office for the first time, he had a whole laundry list of things to tell me about, including weight gain, fatigue, back pain, feeling cold all the time, and frequent urination—but he seemed most concerned about his low sex drive and occasional erectile dysfunction. He complained that he was too tired for sex.

Jonathan worked long hours all week, and then his weekends were consumed with an extensive list of home improvement projects. Jonathan was proud of being both a good provider and a skilled handyman, but the dual demands left him feeling drained. His wife complained that he had no time or energy left for her—and he resented what he felt was a lack of appreciation for all he was doing. He found his wife's demands on him—such as regular date nights and taking walks together—unreasonable.

Jonathan's physical symptoms were familiar signs of yang deficiency. The issues in his marriage were typical for men who are relatively low in yang: retreating into a hobby or work or something else that feels safe, neglecting their relationships.

I suggested a gentle yang-building herbal formula for Jonathan—You Gui Wan (Restore the Right Pills), available over the counter. I also encouraged him to eat more warming foods, especially those that contained spices such as cinnamon, cayenne, and ginger.

Jonathan resolved to direct some of his energy into his relationship by doing one thing his wife wanted to do each week. I also gave him as a homework assignment a simple breathing exercise (Belly Breath, page 96) combined with the men's version of The Squeeze, to cultivate sexual energy. For men, The Squeeze involves focusing on contracting the muscles around the anus. Feel as if you are drawing them upward. Or squeeze as if you were trying to stop the flow of urination. Squeeze for ten seconds, working up to that time span if necessary, release, relax for ten seconds, and do it all over again nine more times. (A full version of The Squeeze appears on page 121 in the chapter on massage.) I also suggested he and his wife try out the Tiger position (see page 214 in the chapter on positions) to help activate his yang.

Diminished yang isn't just about not having energy—it's also about not directing the energy you do have toward the task at hand. That's why Jonathan complained of feeling scattered, and never quite *full on,* no matter what he was doing. Part of what the exercises did was help him focus where he wanted to focus—including on his relationship. Practically speaking, he also set out to be a better planner, so he'd know he had time set aside for his projects—and his wife.

Within a few weeks Jonathan started to have more energy and began experiencing improvements in his overall health. The first thing he noticed was feeling much less groggy when he woke in the morning. He was also pleased that he needed to pee less frequently, and never had to get up in the night to go to the bathroom anymore. He began to lose some weight and experienced a general sense of enthusiasm for life that he hadn't felt in years.

As Jonathan felt better, his sex life got better, too. With his yang reactivated, he began initiating sex more often, and found he was able to maintain an erection consistently. With that, his confidence increased—and so did his desire. He also discovered more interest in giving his wife pleasure—and not just by building new bookshelves or replacing all the faucets.

FOR THE GUYS: Yang To Do (It) List for Men

We go about raising yang in mostly the same ways women do such as the ones listed in the general To Do (It) List at the end of this chapter. But there are a few points men need to focus on if they are dealing with yang deficiency, starting with: Have sex. It'll stimulate your . . . testosterone production. This is one of the reasons the "just do it" approach to combating low libido works. Here's what else does:

- **Eat right for your sex life.** If you have low yang and/or low testosterone, your diet needs to be relatively high in protein, relatively low in carbohydrates, and moderate in fat.
- **Get plenty of essential fatty acids (EFAs),** especially if your testosterone is low. EFAs are important in the production of sex hormones in general and testosterone in particular. Good natural food sources include peanuts, avocados, fish, flaxseed oil, and olive oil. You can also take supplements.
- **Try Chinese herbs to boost testosterone.** In men You Gui Wan (Restore the Right Pills) is used to treat sexual dysfunction and infertility. You can expect good results

from that base formula, but if your testosterone is low you may want to tweak it a bit with one or more additions (even using all three would be perfectly fine):

- **Yin Yang Huo (Horny Goat Weed)** to increase testosterone. It also produces nitric oxide, a chemical that allows the blood vessels to expand enough during arousal to let in the increased blood flow that creates an erection. It also helps reduce stress and energize the whole body, thereby putting you more in the mood for sex.
- **Ginseng (Ren Shen)** is a popular tonic for many conditions and benefits sexual health in several ways, including promoting increased testosterone levels.
- **Bai Ji Li (Tribulus terrestris)** stimulates the pituitary gland to produce testosterone.

TO DO (IT) LIST: Boosting Yang

Having sex is just about the best way there is to rebalance yin and yang. But there are still many other ways to the same end, and they will, among other things, help you get more in the mood:

→ **Eat right for your sex life.** When yang is low, that means eating healthy carbs—especially whole grains aside from wheat—and small amounts of high-quality proteins, with very little dairy, wheat, fruit juice, or fried or fatty food. If your testosterone is low, you should use mostly animal proteins.

→ **Choose yang-building foods,** including carrots, parsnips, mushrooms, onions, leeks, sweet potatoes, winter squash, mustard greens, peppers, ginger, cherries, apples, bananas, oats, spelt, white rice, quinoa, chicken, salmon, lamb, kidney beans, lentils, black beans, peanuts, and walnuts. Cruciferous veggies (broccoli, cauliflower, kale, brussels sprouts, cabbage) are especially good if your testosterone is low.

→ **Choose testosterone-boosting foods** as necessary, including beef, eggs, garlic, oysters, radishes, and turnips.

→ **Eat low-fat yogurt** at least three times a week if you have low progesterone (or estrogen dominance). Yes, even though you should otherwise be steering clear of dairy. Yogurt is easier to digest, and in addition offers specific unique benefits. Read the label to make sure your yogurt has "live cultures" because those bacteria help the liver metabolize estrogen more efficiently, clearing it out of your system as necessary and preserving the balance with progesterone.

→ **Eat several small meals, slowly.** And eat them at regular times, spread out over the course of the day.

→ **Exercise.** Get thirty minutes of moderate aerobic exercise at least three times a week. Daily would be even better. Increasing exercise is especially important if testosterone is low.

→ **Avoid too much caffeine.** The boost you get is false energy and over time will make you feel even more run-down. Caffeine also impairs estrogen metabolism, which can raise estrogen levels in the body enough to overpower, rather than collaborate with, progesterone.

→ **Moderate your alcohol intake.** In excess, alcohol drains energy.

→ **Avoid excess salt,** especially if you are prone to retaining fluids.

→ **Manage stress,** sleep well, and get enough rest during the day. Learn to set limits; practice saying no.

→ **Keep warm.**

→ **Use chromium supplements** to boost metabolism by enhancing the action of insulin.

→ **Consult Appendix 2 for yang-boosting sexercises** to layer onto those you've already learned in this chapter (Buddha Belly and, of vital importance to your sex life, The Squeeze). Energy Meditation (page 114) is calming and relaxing and lays the groundwork for true connection with other people. The Mixing Bowl (page 127) circulates qi as well as building yang, which helps develop and spread sexual feelings.

→ **Consider acupuncture** to boost yang.

→ **Try Jin Gui Shen Qi Wan (Rehmannia Eight) herbal formula.**

→ **Try You Gui Wan (Restore the Right Pills) with Dang Gui** if your testosterone is low.

→ **Sip Gui Pi Tang (Restore the Spleen Tea)** to relieve stress and anxiety.

→ **Try Rou Gui (cinnamon bark)** to raise yang energy and increase libido.

part **two**

Renewing Your Sexual Self

5

You First

Finding Your Own Balance

You know the circus act where one person does all sorts of tricks while supported by a partner? Do you suppose the "flier" *learned* to do a handstand by doing one atop another person? She most certainly did not. She worked it out on her own before she ever involved the other person.

This is a strategy the Taoist sages—big fans of balance—would approve of. Get yourself in balance first, they teach, before attempting to balance with someone else. This isn't just an ancient or mystical idea. The Taoists who developed these ideas thousands of years ago would recognize a similar line of thinking in Western psychology, which holds that you must have a healthy relationship with yourself before you can form one with someone else. More technically, people need a strong sense of themselves as individuals (they need to be "differentiated") to form a successful relationship (or "attachment").

You will need to create balance between yourself and your partner, but true strength, stability, and flexibility—and sexuality—come from seeing to yourself first. And so we begin by learning to do our own handstands.

DO IT NOW: Belly Breath

I've done this exercise many times in yoga class—mainly for relaxation and general oxygenation. I'm totally OK with that, but simply breathing in and out also helps balance yin and yang. Breathing in is considered yin, while breathing out is yang, so abdominal breathing unites the two. It helps you find your center.

Doing belly breathing also brings breath and energy into the lower abdomen—the *dan tien,* the sexual center. Tuning in to sensations in that area is a great way to tap into your sexual energy and increase sexual response and satisfaction.

You can do this on your own, or alongside your partner. Make yourself comfortable in a chair with your feet flat on the ground, or lie on your back with your legs extended, or bent with the feet flat on the ground. At least at the beginning, rest your hands, fingertips touching one another, on your belly just under your belly button.

Inhale slowly through your nose, feeling your belly rise and swell beneath your hands, enough to separate the fingertips. Continue evenly inhaling, next feeling your chest expand as air continues to fill your lungs.

Now exhale through your nose, pulling your abdomen in toward your spine to firmly (but gently) push air out. Repeat a few times, then pause to take a few regular breaths before doing another set of belly breaths.

Both inhales and exhales must remain easy and smooth. If you are working too hard to move the air, dial it down a bit; being relaxed has to take priority over getting the absolute maximum volume of air into your lungs.

You can continue as long as you like. Start with at least a couple of minutes, and build up to as many as ten minutes at a time.

Variation: At the end of your inhale, hold your breath in for a few seconds before exhaling. Do the same at the end of your exhale. Remember: no straining. Find a comfortable rhythm for yourself.

Dynamic Balance

Your goal is to strike a balance between yin and yang traits, and between the yin and yang sides of the scale. You're aiming for a dynamic balance, though, not a fixed point, and not a precisely even split. For most people, the sweet spot is where either yin or yang is predominant—but only slightly.

> ***Don't be afraid to fall out of balance; embrace the feeling of returning to balance. That's the beginning of resilience.***

Just don't expect to hit your mark and then stay there. Everyone constantly moves in and out of balance in ways both large and small. You are just like a pilot flying from New York to Los Angeles: She doesn't take off and make a beeline from one airport to the next but constantly course-corrects across all 2,500 miles, moving higher or lower or north or south—and back again—depending on conditions. These deviations are not inefficiency, but rather the way to achieve optimal flying time and maximize safety.

Imbalance is inseparable from balance. You experience this in your own body when you stand on one foot. You don't stand stock-still—no one does—but make constant little adjustments that keep returning you to your center as you inevitably fall off of it. So don't be afraid to fall out of balance; instead, embrace the feeling of returning to balance. That's the beginning of physical and emotional resilience.

Rules of Yin and Yang

Taoist philosophy sets out several general principles describing the relationship of yin and yang, all of which will help you when you are trying to observe—and balance—them in yourself and, ultimately, in your relationship.

Yin and yang are relative. Yin and yang are opposites, but what is yin and what is yang is always relative. For example, relative to steam, water is yin (in this case, cool), but relative to ice, water is yang (warm). Generally, I am yang at work compared to how I am at home. But at work

I am yin when taking care of patients and more yang when I am dealing with administrative matters. When you are out of balance, you can boost what's low or curb what's excessive. Changing one always affects the other.

Yin and yang are interdependent. They cannot exist without each other. One is meaningless without the other. No one is all yin or all yang; your energy is made up of both, which is why the trick is to balance the two rather than pick one or the other.

Yin and yang are constantly shifting. Relative levels of yin and yang are continuously changing. They have no fixed value. Your goal isn't to get to one end of the spectrum or the other. It's to learn to see where you are—which may be different from yesterday, and may be different later today—and adjust so that you return toward center.

Yin and yang constantly transform into each other. Yang activates yin, and yin creates yang. Another way to think about it is that yin at its most extreme can become yang, and yang at its most extreme can become yin. You can see it in the yin/yang diagram: Just at the largest part of the black section is where a wisp of white comes in (and vice versa). If you push yourself at work too hard for too long (becoming more and more and more yang), one day you'll get sick (a very yin way to be, stuck in bed).

TRY THIS TONIGHT: The Loop *and* The Squeeze

You already know two of the most powerful exercises to nourish yin and boost yang: The Loop (page 61) and The Squeeze (page 85). So here's an excellent way to balance yin and yang: Combine the two!

Wait to practice this variation until you are quite comfortable with The Loop:

As you are inhaling, and energy is moving up your back, contract your PC muscle, as if to halt the flow of urine. Hold the contraction as you hold your breath at the end of your inhale, then relax it as you exhale and move energy back down your body.

This phenomenon is the root of the Chinese saying "80 percent is perfection": Anything sustained at its extreme transforms into its opposite, so it's best to dial it back just a bit if you want to keep it going.

Yin and yang can weaken as well as strengthen each other. Shifts between yin and yang are usually harmonious, but when one or both are too far out of balance they will eventually weaken or consume the other. Having too much of one can be just as unbalancing as having too little of the other. Too much of one will weaken the other. For example, someone who is very aggressive (yang) at work can weaken her yin to the point where she becomes too thin, and experiences dryness.

Emotional and Psychological Balance

Taking care of your emotional/psychological self is a crucial part of finding balance within yourself. It is just as important to a healthy sex life. Being emotionally secure and in a positive psychological state promotes healthy sexual desire, and good sex. Negative emotional states can block sexual feelings. Studies show that somewhere between 20 and 45 percent of American adults experience loss of libido due to psychological issues. If you are not in the mood, it may be because of your . . . mood.

Negative emotions deplete and unbalance your energy in general, and your sexual energy specifically. Positive emotions, on the other hand, nurture us, building up energy and keeping it flowing and balanced—prime conditions for wanting sex, and enjoying it.

Chinese medicine sees emotions themselves as a form of energy—and sex as one way to transform energy, including negative into positive. So not only will improving your mood improve your sex life, but improving your sex life will improve your mood. And then there's this: Lack of sex might be what's got you down in the first place.

I don't mean to imply that sex can prevent or erase any and all emotional or psychological problems. And you should never use sex to cover up a problem. Papering over something you really need to uproot is only going to create more, and worsening, problems. But sex—done right—will assist in the healing. In some, though not all cases, it *is* the healing.

It's pretty easy to get stuck in a loop of negative emotions and a nonexistent love life. But getting out of that loop can be pretty straightforward: Stop *not* having sex, and start having sex. If you can go ahead and just do it—with an attitude that is at least open-minded, even if you are not (yet) enthusiastic—you will find you can change the game. Some of the exercises in this book will help you do this—changing your mind-set, and just generally giving you a way to get started. This reflects the Chinese medicine philosophy that mind and body are one, and you influence both with physical acts, including sex.

When you do have sex, you will block some negative feelings with sexual feelings. You probably have already experienced how sex can take your mind off your troubles, simply by virtue of concentrating your thoughts somewhere else (somewhere nice!) for a while. Having sex releases endorphins, which make us feel good in all kinds of ways. Good sex lessens feelings of sadness, anxiety, anger, guilt, fear, and loneliness. And the effects last for up to a week!

But wait, there's more!

Good sex also creates feelings of pleasure, love, warmth, satisfaction, energy, strength, confidence, kindness, joy, gratitude, peace, harmony, and happiness.

And balance.

Warning Signs of Imbalance

Emotional or psychological imbalance shows up in all kinds of ways. Some are more serious, like clinical depression, and require more than just what's in this book. But there are a lot of more garden-variety behaviors that reveal imbalance, and even if they don't rise to the level of any diagnosis they can wreak havoc on your balance and your libido and, by extension, your relationship and your sex life.

The yin-yang scale in Chapter 3 hit the major themes, but I think you ought to have a sense of the wide variety of signals of imbalance, so you can be on the alert for them—and have a feel for what to do about it when you detect them.

Someone with yin that is low in relation to yang may:

- Have trouble adapting to change
- Seem insensitive
- Be uncomfortable receiving anything, even a compliment or gift
- Create conflict
- Be controlling, unyielding, or domineering
- Be overly aggressive, or even violent
- Not feel safe expressing herself
- Not be a good listener
- Insist on having things her own way
- Have trouble seeing someone else's point of view
- Play the role of martyr
- Lose herself in a relationship
- Give more than she has the personal resources to support, or neglect her own needs while taking care of others' needs
- Give what she wants to give, not what her partner wants or needs
- Be unable to give back to her partner
- Have trouble asking others to give, or difficulty asking for what she wants or needs
- Rely on her partner for nurturing and support, without being able to nurture and support herself
- Be unable to receive what she needs from a partner—including love—even when the partner is providing it (or trying to)

Someone with too little yang (or too much yin) may:

- Not assert herself or stand up for herself in relationships
- Fall back on passive-aggressiveness when she wants to get her way

- Have trouble setting boundaries in relationships
- Feel put upon
- Get stuck in a rut
- Withdraw or become secretive, creating distance in relationships
- Prefer being a "homebody" to engaging in outside world activities
- Seem unenthusiastic
- Neglect her appearance
- Be taken advantage of, dominated, or controlled
- Divert attention, energy, and effort to interests other than the relationship
- Focus on her own needs
- Put all attention on career or a hobby rather than on her partner
- Lose strength or leadership drive
- Rely on her partner for direction or leadership, without being able to guide herself
- Become less creative
- Be low on ambition
- Have trouble keeping up with the demands placed on her by others
- Become cold, withdrawn, or hard to reach
- Find it hard to define what she wants
- Find her relationship unfulfilling
- Feel easily misunderstood

Moving Back Toward Balance

At the extremes, imbalance is a very uncomfortable place to be, and whether or not people are consciously aware they are imbalanced, they'll be driven to try to rebalance. If they don't know how to center themselves in healthy ways, they sometimes try to do it in unhealthy ways, such as binge eating, compulsive shopping, drinking too much, or having an affair.

None of which can actually produce balance, of course, at least not any that lasts for any length of time. They will, in fact, only make things worse over time.

All the more reason to practice positive strategies for finding balance, so there's no need for it to come to that. Strategies like the ones in the To Do (It) List at the end of the chapter. You'll need a few preliminaries though:

Determine your dominant trait. Are you more often yin or more often yang?

Ask yourself if you are in balance or out of balance right now. In this moment. Then ask yourself if there are other times or places or situations in your life where you are out of balance.

Take time to identify when/where/how you are *in* balance. You can learn at least as much from that.

Keep in mind that you are the only person you can change or control. I'm sure we've all heard plenty of times that you can't change another person, but judging by the litany of complaints I hear from my patients about all the things their partners need to do differently, this is a message that hasn't *quite* sunk in yet. (File under Good to Know: When you do make changes to yourself, you will often trigger changes in your partner.)

Don't sweat the particulars. If figuring out the state of your yin or yang is stressing you out, try letting go of the details for a while. See if you can go with the flow through this process, at least at first. You probably know within yourself if you are out of balance—or anyway you will if you tune in—and that insight is really more important than being able to pinpoint whether that imbalance is yin or yang or just a basic lack of coordination, or what. Identify imbalance, strive for balance, and you will be doing the key thing you need to do for yourself. And as you become more familiar with the concepts of yin and yang, you will begin to be able to see it more clearly. You can then fine-tune your approach accordingly. It doesn't have to be perfect from the start to be effective.

TO DO (IT) LIST: Rebalancing Yourself

Having sex is one path to rebalancing your own yin and yang—one of the many reasons you may want to take a breath and just do it. There are, of course, other paths as well:

➜ **Take care of your general health.** Evaluate and make a plan to address any physical symptoms. Chapter 16, which deals with general health issues, can point you in the right direction. Work with a doctor and other health care professionals as necessary. Good health both signifies and supports balance—and an active libido.

➜ **Take care of your mental health.** A strong emotional state helps you keep yin and yang balanced—and goes a long way toward creating a healthy sex life. You need to evaluate and address any psychological or emotional signs of imbalance, just as surely as you do physical ones. Talk to a doctor or therapist if your feelings become overwhelming, or don't respond to self-help techniques.

➜ **Eat right.** A bad diet is another stress on your body, another thing to pull you off balance. A good one provides crucial resources the body needs for coping with whatever comes its way, allowing you to stay more centered.

➜ **Move.** Exercise is a famous stress-buster and energizer—and it helps develop balance, both literally as well as metaphorically. Exercise can also make you feel more at home in your body, building confidence about the way you look. And nothing is sexier than confidence.

➜ **Use both yin and yang.** Practice drawing on both yang (assertive) and yin (receptive) qualities to stay centered, without swinging over to aggressive or controlling or passive or needy. Look for opportunities to do this in your daily life. You can also use any of the exercises targeting yin or yang.

➜ **Build up your nondominant trait.** If you are generally more yang, practice tapping into your yin energy, and vice versa. If you tend to be fast in everything you do, put some effort into slowing down, at least sometimes. If you are all about calm, seek out some experiences that are all about stimulation. If you're more of an idea person, practice engaging with the practicalities of getting something done.

➜ **Practice mindfulness.** Be fully present in the present moment without judgment. Show up in the here and now, without dwelling on past pain or future fears. Adopt a "be here now" attitude. The Opening the Senses exercise—you know, the one with the chocolate (page 54 in Chapter 3)—is not only an excellent reason to stock good chocolate in your pantry and a great way to balance yin and yang, but also a classic way of practicing mindfulness.

➜ **Soothe yourself.** Learn ways of calming yourself down that don't rely on someone else. Use breathing exercises or meditations, like the ones in Chapters 2 and 6. Or try working out, or going for a walk, or listening to music, or doing yoga.

➜ **Be in nature.** For many people, connecting with the natural world is not just stress reducing, but it's also restorative. Connecting to the harmony in nature will nourish your inner harmony.

➜ **Do good.** Helping someone else, contributing something positive to this crazy world, has a wonderful side effect: It makes you feel good, too. The more you give, the more rebounds to you.

➜ **Reframe** the messages about your partner you have running through your head to make them about *you*. Since you're reframing anyway, go ahead and find a positive angle while you're at it. Are you thinking, "He always puts work ahead of me and the kids" or "He's never satisfied!"? Focus on these ideas instead: "I love spending time together so I'll plan more of it" or "I am making progress and will keep on moving."

➜ **Prioritize and delegate.** You can't do everything. You don't have to do everything. So don't!

➜ **Do something for *you.*** Get a massage. Sit with a cup of green tea in a café. Read for pleasure. Get a manicure. Meet up with a friend.

➜ **Be imperfect.** Accept that you are not, in fact, perfect, and allow your standards to "slip." In all likelihood, the world will keep spinning if you leave the office at five from time to time, or let your text messages pile up unanswered for the afternoon.

➜ **Sexercise.** All the sexercises will help you balance your own energy through tapping into your sexual energy. To name just one particularly useful one: The Loop (page 61) is good for absolutely everybody. See Appendix 2 for a guide to all the sexercises according to what they are especially good for, so you can choose what to try according to what you most need.

➜ **Try acupuncture.** It's all about balancing yin and yang, and getting qi moving again. Plus it eases muscle tension and causes the body to release stress-relieving endorphins.

➜ **Try herbs** according to whether you most need to move qi, nourish yin, or build yang (see the To Do (It) Lists at the end of Chapters 2, 3, and 4).

6

Putting Your Mind to It

Wanting Sex Starts with the Mind and the Breath

Sexual desire begins with being open to your own sexual energy. Sexual connection begins with being open to receiving someone else's sexual energy. Focusing on your breath is a way to anchor your attention in your body, so you can feel your energy. Meditation is a way of achieving the stillness necessary to receive energy from someone else.

Breathing—done consciously—can be a powerful way to cultivate and circulate, move and direct, your qi—and your sexual energy. Breathing can relieve stress and calm the mind—even lower blood pressure. Breathing circulates oxygen throughout the body, increasing your desire for—and receptivity to—sex. Equally important, focusing on your breath makes you aware of your body and what it is feeling.

Breathing can also be used along with, or as a form of, meditation. There are a huge variety of ways to meditate, and the best one is the one that works for you. You might want to test-drive a few before settling on your own practice.

For some people meditation is a spiritual practice. For some it is a religious practice, perhaps including prayer. But it need not be. Whether or not you approach meditation spiritually, it offers benefits similar to those of breathing: It reduces stress and calms the mind and body. It also improves focus. Many women have trouble reaching orgasm because they get distracted. Staying focused is a learned skill—and one of the best ways to start is by meditating.

Back to the Breath

You've been introduced to some excellent breathing exercises already in earlier chapters.

If you want to go back and refresh your memory, here's where you can review:

Take a Breath (page 25)

Belly Breath (page 96)

The breathing and meditation exercises in this chapter are meant to be either stand-alone activities, or a prelude to sex. It's your choice—just make sure you and your partner are on the same page anytime you are doing them together.

I recommend doing at least one every day. Even if it is literally for just a minute. You should begin feeling some results right away.

Progressive Relaxation

This is a very simple exercise. All you do is tighten and then relax your major muscle groups, one at a time, starting at your feet and working upward. Tense an area for a count of ten, holding it tightly. Then relax, enjoying the sensation of letting go. Make sure you keep breathing throughout (don't hold your breath as you tense your muscles):

1. Sit or lie down comfortably on your back and close your eyes.

2. Place your feet slightly apart, and, if you are lying down, your arms slightly away from your sides with your palms facing up.

3. Allow your breath to slow down. Put your entire attention on the breath as it moves in and out. Count to twenty, slowly.

4. Tense the muscles in the various areas of your body listed below, one at a time, in the order given. Once you've tensed, hold for a count of ten, then gently relax. Pause for another count of ten. Repeat, then move on to the next muscle group: Feet—Calves—Thighs—Stomach—Chest—Back—Hands (make fists)—Arms (bend at the elbow)—Neck—Head and Face.

The Three Locks

The Taoists conceived of this exercise mostly for men, but I don't see why they should have all the fun. It's an important exercise for everyone, and especially good for those who need to cultivate yin, because of the way it draws energy from the top of the body down into the pelvis.

The Three Locks enhances orgasm in several ways. It generates qi and distributes energy throughout the body. It increases the flow of blood and energy in and to the pelvis, which will intensify sensation. Used during sex (as in Variation 2) it distributes *sexual* energy, which helps make orgasm more of a whole body experience. The Three Locks also strengthens some muscles that are key to a satisfying sexual experience—similar to parts of The Squeeze exercise (page 121).

It's a good idea to practice the locks of this exercise before going on to combine them with the breathing and, eventually, sex. There are three locks you'll use: neck, abdominal, and anal, and they involve nothing more than contracting certain muscles in certain ways.

Sit comfortably, with your back and shoulders straight and well supported. Hold your head upright, looking straight ahead of you. Tighten your throat muscles by pulling your chin down toward the front of your neck, keeping your mouth closed, creating a sensation of closing your throat. You are simply lowering your head. Hold the position for a count of three, then slowly relax, raising your head.

You can do the abdominal lock in any position—and it's a good thing, too, since you're going to build up to doing it during sex. To create the lock, draw your abdomen in—moving your belly button back toward your spine—and up. Hold for a count of three, then release, as above.

For the anal lock, simply contract your muscles as you would if you were holding in a bowel movement. Hold briefly then squeeze more firmly still (you can feel the muscles higher up in your rectum contract), hold there a moment, then release.

Once you have familiarized yourself with these three movements, try engaging all three consecutively, without releasing the previous lock: Start with the neck lock, add the abdominal lock, then add the anal lock. This draws your energy down. Hold for a few moments, then release all three locks at the same time.

These locks are meant to work with your breath, so here's how you coordinate them: Begin by breathing out fully—slowly. Take a deep breath in, filling your belly. Now close the locks, working top to bottom, and hold as long as you comfortably can. Then exhale as you release.

Variation 1: At the point you have the Three Locks engaged, tense *all* your muscles. Let them go, along with the locks, as you exhale.

Variation 2: To deepen orgasm, begin to perform the Three Locks just as you feel orgasm approaching. If you find doing it distracting, however, it won't do much for your orgasm, so it's best to practice the Three Locks independent of any sexual activity for a while before you try this variation. And practice it during masturbation before you bring it into bed with a partner.

You Are Already Meditating

You've already learned powerful meditation exercises in previous chapters. To brush up on what you've read, see also:

Think About It (page 34)

Opening the Senses (page 54) This is wonderful on its own but is also an excellent prelude to any of the massage techniques or sexercises.

The Loop (page 61) This is one of the most important practices in the whole book, which is why it keeps coming up.

FOR THE GUYS: Why Meditating for Better Sex Is Not Crazy

If breathing and meditation seem a bit soft to you, and frankly not all that sexy, perhaps you'll like it better this way: These are exercises to intensify and extend orgasm. And they control the timing of orgasm, so you can last as long as you want to. *And* your partner will get similar orgasmic benefits, so if you practice together, you'll get some of the credit.

The ancient Taoists were *really* interested in male orgasm, and much of their texts are devoted to helping men perfect the way we do it. The Three Locks and The Loop are two of the key tools they use to that end.

Anytime you use the Three Locks just before orgasm, you will deepen the orgasm. But you can also use it to delay orgasm, even (or especially) if you are experiencing premature ejaculation. Either way, you should try this during masturbation a few times before doing it with a partner.

The Loop (pages 61 and 115), too, can help you delay orgasm, whether you're dealing with premature ejaculation or simply want to put it off a bit longer. During sexual activity of whatever sort, energy tends to build up in the pelvis around the genitals, and at some point it will overwhelm the ability to control ejaculation. Circulating that energy through the body lessens the focus on ejaculation until you decide it's time—and concentrates the energy where it'll provide the most intense experience.

Get Glowing

This Taoist meditation technique is meant to relieve stress and charge libido all at the same time.

Sit or lie in a comfortable position and close your eyes. Take about ten or twenty seconds to relax. Let your attention rest easily on your genitals. Then take a deep breath. Imagine the air moving through a soft tube from your nose to your vagina. Visualize the incoming breath as a beautiful stream of light. The light can be whatever color comes to mind, and the color can change as your feelings change. Let the warm glow of light remain in your genitals as you continue to inhale and exhale. The more attention you bring to the area, the more qi gathers and the more sensation is possible.

Sex Again in Real Life: Karen

When Karen first came to see me she told me she never felt like having sex, although on the occasions when her partner, Allen, would take the initiative, she would eventually warm up and enjoy their lovemaking. But having no desire worried her. She still found Allen attractive but said she never really felt sexual toward him. "We're like roommates," she said. "Compatible, supportive roommates."

I had started Karen on a program designed to give her more energy, build yang, and move qi. As a part of it, she began a daily meditative exercise in which she simply spent a few minutes visualizing having sex with Allen (Think About It, page 34). She quickly found herself feeling renewed enthusiasm for all kinds of things—not least of which was her partner. "If I don't set aside that time, I realize my mind just doesn't go there. It's like it just never occurs to me to have sex. But when I do focus on it, even just for a minute, it's at the top of my mind, and that can last all day."

Within six weeks, Karen found herself suggesting sex—a reversal Allen was as pleased with as she was.

Inner Smile

The ancient Taoists developed a meditation practice predicated upon the healing nature of a smile. It's one of my favorite meditations because it is so gentle, and it is an especially good one for beginner meditators for that same reason. I like to practice it outside, with the sun on my face, but really it's wonderful (and easy) to do anytime you find yourself with a few spare minutes. I find it grounds me for facing obstacles large or small with equanimity—and good humor. (Which also happen to be excellent ways to face libido issues.) Inner Smile helps induce a relaxed, happy, playful state of mind, which is ideal for good sex. In addition, it helps you feel warm toward yourself, and self-acceptance is an important part of a healthy sex drive. Smiling also evokes gratitude and positivity, which, when focused upon your partner as well as yourself, will increase your desire for and enjoyment of sex. Inner Smile is a great choice for anyone dealing with mood issues. Smiling, with or without meditation, will help rebalance yin and yang within you.

Here's how you do it: Sit comfortably with your spine as straight as possible. Close your eyes. Keep your neck and throat relaxed. Take a couple deep breaths, enough to make your abdomen really rise with the inhales. Use your exhales to help you let go of any thoughts not on the present moment—for now, set aside anything that's about the past, or the future. Rest your tongue on the roof of your mouth, near your teeth. Smile gently as if you have a delicious secret or a private joke. Not a big open grin, mind you—more Mona Lisa style. Continue with your slow, even breathing, and use it to help you direct your attention. Focus your attention on the space between your eyebrows—or, if you prefer, bring your energy there. Remember, where your mind goes, your qi will follow. Some people can feel energy from their smile expand backward toward the center of their heads. Move your attention/smiling energy gradually through your body, resting it in any area that needs healing—parts of your body you feel inhibited about, or that ache, or that otherwise need any kind of special care or attention, one by one. Spend a total of about five minutes shining this smiling energy onto each place. When you are ready to wrap it up, direct your smile to a point about two inches below your navel for a moment (in Chinese medicine this is the *dan tien,* the center of sexual energy). Hold there for a few moments, then release your tongue, and your smile.

Hard as it is to resist a smile, you may find some areas are particularly stubborn. Areas that seem to refuse the smiling energy, or remain otherwise tense and tight even when you are focusing positively on them, can point to where further attention would be useful. For people dealing with libido issues, the genitals are one such place—no surprise there—as are the breasts, so don't overlook them.

Sometimes these difficult areas are delivering a physical message, and sometimes there's a layer of emotional information in there, too. Problem areas can be a signal that you need to forgive someone, or let go of resentment, or work on staying in the present and not worrying so much about the future, or allow yourself to feel safe and secure, or find a way to relieve sadness, or release hatred you've been holding on to, or embrace compassion. One common scenario in people dealing with sexual problems is tightness in the ribs, which in Chinese medicine is seen as a sign of repressed anger. Smiling on these areas will help, but if that's not enough you should dig further to discover what's going on.

Modern science echoes the Taoist theories of the healing power of a smile.

Modern science echoes the Taoist theories of the healing power of a smile, by the way. We now know smiling lowers the stress hormones cortisol, adrenaline, and noradrenaline and produces hormones that stabilize blood pressure, relax muscles, improve respiration, increase your sense of well-being, and boost energy. That makes a good case for exposing yourself to anything and anyone that's likely to make you smile. But all the benefits hold if you are bringing the smile to your face on your own. Whether you prefer to see things in terms of Chinese or Western thought, five minutes a day devoted to smiling is good medicine.

Variation: Smile About Sex. You can focus this exercise however you like, but for our purposes it may be useful to center it around sex, and/or your relationship to your partner. The process is essentially the same as above, but while smiling think about your partner. Imagine him or her in your mind, and allow yourself to feel softness, compassion, and warmth. After a few minutes, gather the energy you generate that way and bring it with you while you send your smiling energy into your pelvic area.

Energy Meditation

The particular aim of this meditation, besides being relaxing and calming, is to help you feel deeply connected to the world around you. The ability to feel yourself truly a part of something larger than yourself is good practice, on a very basic level, for evoking that feeling with your partner. It is also a pathway to the even greater feeling of union with all of existence, which sex can generate.

Sit comfortably, close your eyes, and focus on your breath for a little while. Then begin to envision that everything around you is converting into energy, changing into small vibrating particles. Extend your vision to include everything in the universe similarly composed of energy. All that is solid, liquid, or gas is turning into an energy field. The universe is a huge mass of energy, energy that takes different forms and different states of matter. You are surrounded by an ocean of energy.

Now bring it back down to you, imagining your body is made up of those little vibrating bits of energy. See your whole body, every organ, changing into energy.

Start to see how your energy connects with the energy of the universe. Sit with this feeling as long as feels appropriate. Slowly open your eyes.

Advanced Loop

If I had to choose just one meditation for you to do to work on your libido, it would be The Loop. It's such a good one, I recommend you do it every day. This version is a bit more advanced than the basic model I hope you test-drove in Chapter 3 (page 61), for whenever you are ready or interested in stepping it up a bit.

Practicing The Loop will enhance sexual pleasure. It will cultivate more sexual energy, or help you tap into your sexual energy if you've been out of touch with it. The Loop combines breathing with visualization into a meditative exercise designed to balance yin and yang and circulate qi. It specifically helps move sexual energy from the pelvis through the rest of the body. Over the long term, practicing The Loop will lead to better orgasms—more intense, longer lasting, and a fuller, more whole-body experience. For some people, it will facilitate having multiple orgasms. Most people experience results after doing the exercise about five times, though some find it kicks in from the very first try. Either way, you will get better still with more practice.

One way to build on the basic version of The Loop is to do as the Taoists—who call their intense version of this exercise the "Microcosmic Orbit"—describe, and touch the tip of your tongue to the roof of your mouth, just behind your front teeth, as you imagine the oil reaching your head. This connects the two pathways you are moving energy through and makes it easier for the qi to flow as it should. In addition, Chinese medicine considers the pathway in front of your body yin, and the one in the back yang, so connecting them this way enables the balancing of yin and yang. The dual effects on qi and yin and yang are what make this process so central in the ancient Taoist texts.

Variation 1: Do The Loop in the sitting position, in the usual way, then add the following sequence at the end: Rest your hands between your navel and your pubic bone (on the *dan tien*, which is your sexual center in Chinese medicine). Focus on your sacrum—your low back where your spine reaches your pelvis. The idea is for your attention and energy to move through you from your hands to your back, bathing the sexual organs en route. After a few moments, move your hands to your sacrum and send energy back through to your lower abdomen (*dan tien*) for a little while.

Variation 2: Combine The Loop with The Squeeze, as described in Chapter 5 (page 98). You'll nourish yin and boost yang *and* move qi. Just wait to try it until you are comfortable with each exercise on its own. When you are ready, the key is to squeeze your PC muscle as you are inhaling, moving energy up your back—and relax as you exhale and move energy back down your body.

Variation 3: Do The Loop with your partner. Begin sitting or lying quietly together, with each partner doing his or her own Loop. Add in the PC squeeze if you wish (as above). When you are comfortable doing that together, you can move on to the full version of The Loop, party of two:

Get comfortable, face-to-face, and begin by synchronizing your breathing. When you are ready, go on to looping: As you are inhaling, imagine drawing energy from your partner into yourself and from there up your spine, just as before. Or stay with the warm oil image if that is better for you—warm oil pouring from your partner's bowl into yours. When it is time to exhale, imagine sending energy—or oil—into and through your partner, flowing down to refill their bowl. If you like, you can touch your foreheads together during this exercise—or during the time when energy is at your heads. Touching each other this way can give you a focal point for sending energy into your partner, as well as a concrete connection.

> ***Over the long term, practicing The Loop will lead to better orgasms—more intense, longer lasting, and a fuller, more whole-body experience.***

When you are ready to add in another component—and intensify the experience—add in the PC squeeze for both partners.

Another option is to use synchronized breathing, inhaling while your partner exhales, and exhaling as he or she inhales. You inhale and send energy/oil up your body just as before, while your partner is exhaling. Then your partner inhales and moves energy from their head back down to their bowl (versus exhaling on the way down, as in solo practice and earlier variations)—while you are exhaling and also imagining your collective energy moving through your partner. Your partner then exhales, and you inhale, while you both picture the energy transferring into your bowl and back up through the cycle. After a few rounds, reverse direction, so that both of you have a turn inhaling energy up before you end the exercise. You can do the PC squeeze as you inhale, as part of this exercise, but not when you are pulling energy down.

Variation 4: Do The Loop during sex, and be sure to include the PC squeeze. Doing The Loop together is a great way to kick things off. But you can also use it once you've been under way for a while—generating sexual energy together before pausing to focus on circulating it within and between you can give you quite an intense experience of The Loop.

You will be generating and experiencing a lot of sexual energy with this exercise, or the previous variation—especially if you are lying in bed together naked—so if you feel like skipping ahead to intercourse or whatever other activities come to mind before this exercise is "done"—I say go for it.

The Taoist texts consider this method of circulating energy through the body—especially the part where it eddies around in the head for a while—as the key to reaching higher states of consciousness. For those who are interested, this is indeed a pathway to experiencing sex as spiritual. Even if that's not your thing, The Loop does enhance the feeling of connection between two people and taps into the feeling of being part of something larger than yourselves.

7

Getting in Touch

Using Massage to Increase Your Desire

Sexual pleasure is dependent on energy moving in the body, and moving between two people. Massage moves energy—and massage with a partner exchanges it.

Beyond that, massage benefits both body and mind. It has all the benefits of touch in general—and then some. It is stress relief, relaxation, and even meditation and/or intimacy—depending on how you do it—all rolled into one. It improves circulation. It creates deeper connection to your own body—and to your partner, when it's a team effort. And massage can move qi and rebalance yin and yang.

I have drawn on the advice and vast experience of Nicole Kruck, LMT, massage therapist at our Center, for many of the exercises in this chapter. Most of the massage techniques here are designed to be done on your own—at least at first. In many cases, after you have explored solo, you may want to share an exercise with a partner. A professional massage is also an excellent option, if you can swing it. You may get insights and/or techniques that are beyond you and your partner. In an ideal world, you'd get a massage once a week. Not many of us can afford that at a spa, but you might just be able to work something out in trade with your partner, don't you think?

When you are massaging yourself, start slow and gentle, with light pressure, and use slow, full breaths. Allow time to relax into the experience and get used to your own touch. You'll be creating a relationship with your own body—a relationship that has, for a lot of us, become pretty distant. If anything ever feels uncomfortable, stop. Take a breath, shake out your hands to relax them, and try again. If it's still uncomfortable, let it go. Just rest your hands on the area for a few deep breaths, holding your awareness there to ease the body's response, and then move on to something else. Come back to that exercise, or that portion of the exercise, another day. It should work essentially the same way whether you are receiving a massage, or giving one.

Elements of Massage

You've already learned in earlier chapters a couple of techniques that are built on in this chapter, so you should take another look:

Buddha Belly (page 78)

The Squeeze (page 85)

My advice is to try all the techniques here at least once. What you most enjoy, or find most useful, you can put into regular rotation, or otherwise revisit from time to time when you want to change things up. Some of the massages described here are more special occasion events anyway. And some are meant for regular practice, like The Squeeze, which is important for everyone to do.

Buddha Belly

This exercise was introduced in Chapter 4 because it is good for generating energy, especially yang energy, and channeling it toward arousal. But it is good for just about anybody, regardless of how much yang you do or don't have.

The abdomen is a sensitive area for many people, and most people are uncomfortable focusing on it. We don't like to show it. We often don't touch it. The older we get, the less likely we are to welcome any attention to the area at all, even positive attention. But the abdomen remains a vital power center throughout our lives. There's much to be gained from reconnecting to it.

Yet modern lifestyles conspire to negatively affect healthy breathing and circulation in the abdomen and especially the pelvis—and that's not good for anyone's health or sex life. This massage can help counter the effects of poor posture that can come from hunching over computers or carrying larger and heavier bags and wearing restrictive clothing such as tight jeans, panty hose, and high heels. Of course better posture, less restrictive clothing, and stepping away from the screens once in a while are good ideas as well!

As mentioned earlier, in Chinese medicine the lower abdomen—the *dan tien*—is where sexual energy is generated and stored. Bringing nonjudgmental awareness back to the belly can help us tap back into our sexuality and renew our sense of sexual pleasure, as well as release old or unhelpful self-images and emotional pain, and support optimal health and strong relationships.

Do Buddha Belly once or twice a week to develop your desire, or anytime you feel the need to create sexual energy.

The Squeeze

If you were going to take only two things away from this book, I'd have this be one of them. (The Loop meditation would be the other.) So although you learned the basics in Chapter 4, page 85, here you'll learn the even more powerful full-length version.

Thousands of years ago the Taoists were avidly exercising their PC (pubococcygeus) muscles, just the way your ob/gyn might advise you to do nowadays to strengthen your pelvic floor and prevent or reverse stress incontinence. That's all well and good, but the Taoists put more emphasis on bringing blood and qi to the pelvic area to increase sexual pleasure. *Now* we're talking! The pelvic floor muscles are sometimes called "the love muscles" because they surround the clitoris and vagina (along with the urethra and anus).

Lack of tone in these muscles is one cause of painful intercourse. Even more compelling: Toning these muscles with a simple exercise increases sensitivity to touch and response to sexual stimulation, helping achieve—or prolong and intensify—orgasm. All while simultaneously increasing a male partner's pleasure during intercourse.

Having intercourse helps strengthen the muscles in the pelvis, especially the PC muscle, but not much else does, except very specifically targeted exercises like this one (which, by the way, does a much more efficient and effective job than "just" having sex does). This version, from the Taoists, layers in some massage to multiply the benefits of just the "squeeze" portion on its own.

If you were going to take only two things from this book, The Squeeze should be one of them.

A strong PC muscle bestows even more benefits than deeper orgasm—even more than dealing with stress incontinence! It also: stimulates production of estrogen and helps relieve PMS, menstrual irregularities, and symptoms of menopause; tightens the vagina and keeps it flexible (something male partners will enjoy); and supports the sexual organs.

The breast massage part of this exercise stimulates the nerves in the breast, particularly the ones around the nipples, which increases circulation, releases oxytocin, helps circulate lymph, and increases neural connections. It also strengthens the muscles and ligaments, helping keep the breasts looking full and buoyant.

All that from a few minutes a day spent this way:

Sit on the floor, or on the bed, in such a way that you can press the heel of your foot through your underwear against the opening of your vagina. If your body isn't put together in a way that allows you to do that, you can use a round object, like a tennis ball, instead of your foot. The idea is to provide a little gentle pressure and stimulation to the vaginal lips while you do this.

Rub the palms of your hands together vigorously until your hands feel hot. Place a hand over each breast so that you feel the heat from your hands on your skin. Rub your breasts in an outward circular motion thirty-six times.

While you are rubbing, tighten the muscles of your vagina and anus as if you were trying to stop the flow of urine. Hold it for a count of ten, then relax for a count of ten, then repeat. If at first you can't hold it that long, don't worry. Do what you can, and you will gradually get stronger and be able to hold it longer. Do a set of ten squeezes, three times a day. And that's all. Doing more or holding longer will overly fatigue the muscle, making it (temporarily) weaker, rather than stronger.

With practice, you will be able to do more and stronger squeezes.

Variation 1: Set aside the tennis ball, or your foot, for this one. Insert a finger into your vagina to help you feel when you are successfully contracting. Sometimes, especially when you are just starting out, it helps to have something you are squeezing against. You might also want to use this variation to experience the strength of your contractions so you can track the increase over time.

Variation 2: Do The Squeeze with a partner. Ask your partner to rub your breasts for you. Or have your partner use three or four fingers to apply gentle pressure to the vaginal lips (rather than your own heel or a tennis ball).

Variation 3: Do The Squeeze during intercourse. At this point we're referring to the loose interpretation of The Squeeze, no tennis balls necessary; breast rubbing in outward circles optional. Here's what you do: Contract as your partner withdraws, and relax as he thrusts. You'll be getting in good practice—and he'll thank you for it! While you've got your partner involved with this, ask him to give you feedback about any noticeable increases in the strength of your squeezes.

Variation 4: Ideally you'd do The Squeeze three times daily. Just in case you don't have three available time slots in your day to strip down and do the full Squeeze exercise, you can do the most essential component of it pretty much anytime, anywhere: squeeze, hold, and release while you're waiting in line, or driving, or watching TV. No one will know but you. Do try to perform the full Squeeze at least once a day, though.

♂ FOR THE GUYS: The Squeeze for Men

The Squeeze works a bit differently for guys but still offers very tempting benefits. The PC muscle is located at the base of the penis, and learning to control it strengthens erections and increases staying power. Research shows the effects are strong enough to combat ED. And it will also intensify and prolong orgasm, a very common theme in the ancient Taoist sexology texts.

Doing The Squeeze increases strength and circulation in the pelvis. It also has a protective effect on the prostate because the squeezing massages it a bit. Regular use of this exercise will stimulate hormone production and can increase semen production and sperm count. It's a great exercise not just for ED, but also PE or wet dreams—working with The Squeeze gives you more control over when ejaculation occurs. That's why it's a key part of "holdbacks" (see Chapter 14). But all guys will benefit from it, regardless of whether they are aiming for that far end of the Taoist sexology spectrum.

Do The Squeeze standing, sitting, or lying down. Get naked, and get comfortable. Rub the palms of your hands together vigorously until they feel hot. Gently cup your testicles with one hand, and place the other on the lower abdomen, about an inch below your navel. Move the hand on your abdomen in a circular direction, using gentle pressure. The Taoists insist on eighty-one repetitions, but I don't think you need to keep exact count. Estimate about one minute, and that should be fine. Either way, you should feel warmth—so if you don't, you probably stopped a bit too soon.

When you are done with your circles, the next step is to tighten the muscles around your anus and draw them upward—or, squeeze as if you are trying to stop the flow of urination—and hold for a count of ten. Relax your muscles for a count of ten, then repeat the contraction. Complete three sets of contraction and relaxation.

Variation: Do this with a partner. Your partner can do the cupping of the testicles.

Do the squeezes anytime you have a couple minutes. (Leaving out the testicle-cupping if you are out and about!)

Breast Massage

In our society, breasts are both overemphasized and overlooked. Despite a media fixation on size and shape, in everyday life breasts are hidden away, strapped into tight bras for most of the day. This hampers circulation and creates stagnation. That's on top of the negative vibes it is easy for us to pick up about our own breasts, when they fail to be large, or bouncy, or perky, or otherwise worthy of billboard advertising in Times Square. And do not get me started on the often hysterical response to breast-feeding in public! (Feeding hungry infants . . . the horror!)

Then, once a month, we *do* take out our breasts . . . and examine them for defects or danger. Or we think we should, but we often don't because we are somehow scared of them.

I'm suggesting switching to a new plan. Regular breast massage helps *prevent* disease, giving resiliency and suppleness to breast tissue and breaking up fibrocystic and scar tissue, and circulating healthy lymph throughout the body. Like any other part of the body, breasts require movement and circulation to keep them healthy.

Breast massage also reintroduces us to our own breasts, in an entirely positive milieu. It's a gentle way to be more intimate with our own bodies—and also with a partner, should we choose to share this process. Another great benefit of breast massage is the way it activates nerve receptors in the breasts that will create greater pleasure when stimulated. Finally, by massaging your breasts on a regular basis you will become very familiar with what they feel like in a state of health, as well as with their normal variations through your cycle (for those not in menopause). You will know, therefore, if there are any changes that need to be brought to the attention of a physician.

This exercise is not only good for the health of your breasts but is also an excellent way to stir sexual energy. This massage can be done directly on the skin or over a loose, thin shirt or sheet. You can use lotion or natural oils, such as olive, sweet almond, shea butter, coconut, or jojoba, preferably organic. Avoid mineral oil (which is a by-product of the petroleum industry, and difficult for your skin to absorb, so it tends to clog pores). If using oil, you may want to put down a towel under you to avoid stains.

Sit in a comfortable chair, or lie down. If you have larger breasts, you may want to tuck a pillow up under the sides for them to rest on. Rub your hands together vigorously, warming them and bringing in qi. Place your hands over your heart, taking several slow, deep breaths. Allow your qi to bring a calmness and warmth to your heart, then extend your awareness out to your breasts. Imagine a pure white light. Allow this light to fill the entire area of your upper body. If this imagery does not work for you, do not worry; just choose another color, another image, or forget it and simply continue with the breath.

Bring the palms of your hands to the sides of your ribs in an L-shaped position, with your thumbs pointed into your armpits and the other fingers pointing in toward the other hand, level with your nipples. Gently roll your hands over your breasts to meet in the middle of the chest. Return to the sides for your next stroke. Move your hands up your ribs a half inch each time, and repeat until you reach just under the clavicle bones, which run horizontally across the top of your chest. Repeat this whole procedure three times.

Bring one hand to the top of the head, simply allowing it to rest comfortably there. Bring the other hand over the breast to the opposite armpit (right hand on left breast). Starting with gentle pressure use the palm of the hand to spiral slowly around the outside of the breast, moving inward until just before the nipple. Stay off the nipple for now. Slowly spiral back out in the opposite direction around the breast until you reach your original starting place at the armpit. Repeat this whole procedure three times, then switch and do it on the other breast three more times.

Next repeat the same motions, but use two or three fingers and slightly increased pressure. (It should still be gentle.) Do three times on each side. Remember, none of these techniques should feel uncomfortable, ever; lighten up if they do.

Now using both hands, gently trace around your breasts in a figure eight pattern, using a sweeping motion. A sideways figure eight, that is—an infinity sign.

Next lean over with your breasts facing toward the ground. Gently cup one breast in each hand—or, for larger breasts, do one at a time, using both hands—and softly jiggle the breasts so they move in a gentle wave motion. Do this for at least one minute.

In the same bent-over position, gently hold and jiggle the nipples. If this does not feel good, skip this step, or repeat the whole-breast jiggle, above.

To finish up, return to an upright position and place your hands on your breasts again, feeling your heart and breath. Take a moment to acknowledge yourself for taking the time to love and nurture your body and yourself in this way.

The Mixing Bowl

This massage is aimed at improving circulation through the pelvis. Circulation—of blood, or of qi—is key to the health of the area and your whole body. And it is absolutely necessary for the development and spread of sexual feelings.

The "mixing bowl" that this exercise refers to is the "bowl" within your pelvis outlined by the hip bone on each side, the pubic bone, and the sacrum (the wider bone at the base of your spine, right where your fingers go in an "oh my aching back!" position). This bowl contains and conjoins the uterus, ovaries, bladder, intestines, arteries, veins, nerves, and lymph vessels within your pelvis. So it pays to make sure it is solidly constructed! Of course you are not actually constructing it. What you are building is a sense of its connectedness, of your pelvis as a whole, solid, strong structure, rather than a bunch of disjointed (or anonymous) parts.

Use a sweeping motion. Imagine you are painting a beautiful color all across your lower abdomen.

Before you begin, make sure your bladder is empty, so you'll be able to completely relax the pelvis. You can perform this massage either standing, or, if you are familiar with and comfortable in it, a yoga child's pose (sitting back on your knees, face bent down to the floor).

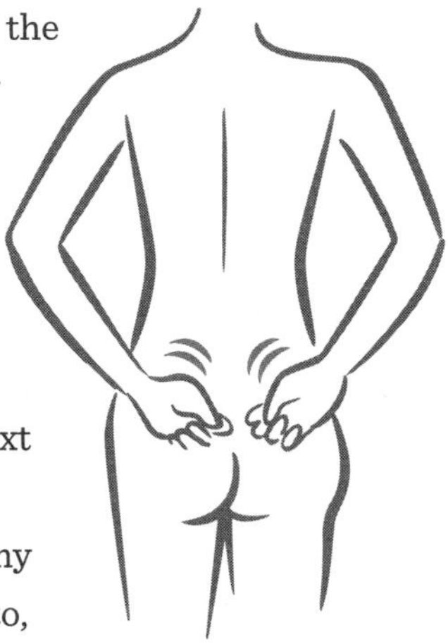

With your hands on your back, feel for the sacrum, between your hip bones. With your hands cupped or in loose fists, knuckles down, bounce them directly on the sacrum. Use the same force you would for clapping—and the same rhythmic motion, one to two seconds apart, allowing the impact of each bounce to ripple outward before the next one lands. Continue for one to two minutes.

This should feel good! If you experience any discomfort, use a lighter impact. If you need to, pause, breathe, and begin again more gently. If it still doesn't feel good, simply rest your warm hands there for a minute, and come back to this part of the exercise in another day or so.

For the rest of this massage, you can use oil or lotion on your skin if you like, or a thin sheet or shirt.

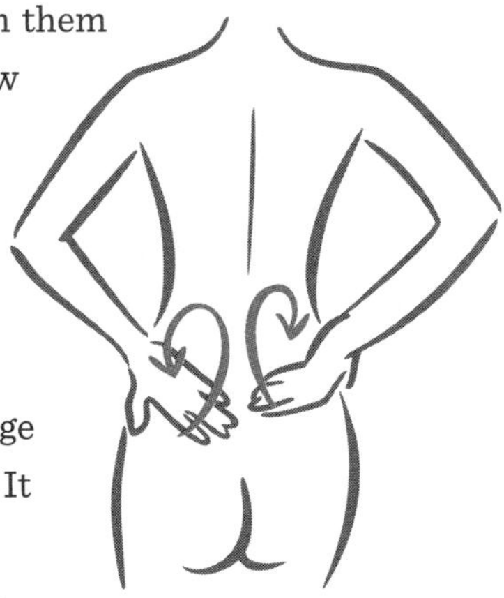

Rub your hands together briskly to warm them and draw qi there. Place your palms on your low back, and use them to draw spirals along either side of the spine from your lower back onto the sacrum. Massage up and down along the spine as far as you can comfortably reach. You do not need a lot of pressure. Don't forget your breathing. Massage your back this way for at least three minutes. It should feel warm and relaxing.

Now lie down on your back. Place a pillow under your knees or bend your knees and place your feet flat on the surface you are lying on. Rub your hands together again, then rest them palms down on your pelvis. Take some deep breaths and imagine the qi spreading from your hands into your pelvis—into the front of the bowl.

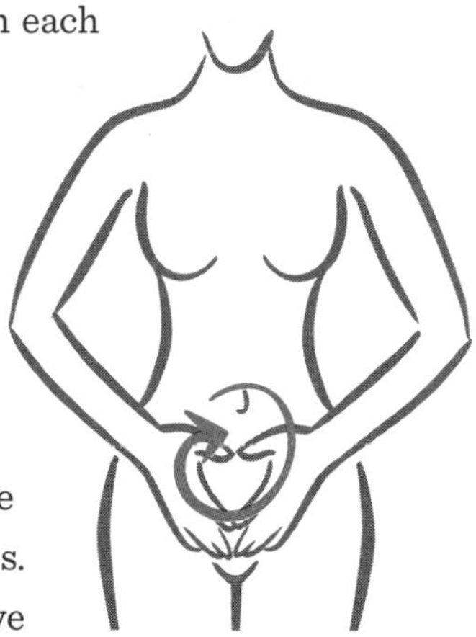

Breathe into your hands, feeling them rise with each inhalation.

Use your palms to make a big easy circle over your pelvis. Start at the navel line and use a sweeping motion. Imagine you are painting a beautiful color all across your lower abdomen, perhaps one color down to the pubic bone and another one back up to the navel. Cover the area completely from side to side, as well, and even over the side of the hips. Continue your breathing. Continue for about five minutes.

To finish, rest your hands back on your pelvis and check in with yourself. What does it feel like now? You may find it warm and cozy. You may feel a sense of connectedness in your pelvis, front to back and side to side. You may sense the whole "bowl," or feel as if all the contents of the bowl have been equally bathed with energy. The exact feeling evoked is not as important as taking a moment to notice whatever it is for you.

Exploring

This is a hunt for your erogenous zones: the areas of the body that are highly sensitive to touch, where even slight contact causes sexual arousal. These areas are different for each individual. The only way to find—or *remember*—yours is to explore the vast territory known as your skin. Knowing what areas arouse you—and sharing that with a partner—increases not only your pleasure, but also your participation, and your partner's. And probably your partner's pleasure as well: One way to feel great is to make someone else feel great.

This works best if you explore on your own first, then share your discoveries with your partner, as described in the variation following the main exercise.

Do this exercise naked but covered with a light sheet—and *without* lotion or oil. Lie down and get comfortable. Begin to breathe slowly and deeply, but easily, so you can keep it going through this exercise.

Use a light touch—just fingertips or the heel of your hand. Or perhaps a feather. Direct your movements toward your heart. You're aiming to touch every reachable inch of skin by the time this exercise is done.

Start at your head. Brush or stroke your scalp, and think about how that feels. Notice if you begin to feel sensations in other parts of your body. Is this area very sensitive to touch? Is touching it arousing? Relaxing? Do any pleasing images come to mind?

Move on to your forehead, lightly stroking or tapping around the face, again noticing any sensations and where they are and what they feel like. Continue over all the areas of your body you can comfortably reach, using these same techniques and reflections in each area. Be sure to check out all the most common erogenous zones: neck, breasts, inner thighs, buttocks, and lips. Don't miss the other common hot spots: wrists, fingers, feet, and toes, and inside the elbows, under the chin, around the ears, along the spine, and behind the knee.

Your purpose is to discover unknown (or recently neglected) erogenous zones. Not all of these spots will do it for everybody; the point is to find the ones that do it for you.

Your purpose here is to discover unknown (or recently neglected) erogenous zones, so you probably want to skip the genitals while doing your inventory. The more obvious sexual sensations could make it harder to discern the sexy signals from, say, your earlobe. Don't steer too far clear, however—you might be introduced to some near neighbors you'll be glad to know.

Not all of these spots will do it for everybody; the point is to find the ones that do it for *you*. So be sure to take note of the areas where you find particular pleasure, so you can go back and explore them more on your own—or with a partner.

To finish this exercise, lie quietly for a few moments, noticing your general state of well-being.

Variation 1: Vary your touch. How you touch an area can make a difference in whether it is pleasant or stimulating or ticklish or neutral. So once you've done your initial investigations, you should go back over the hot spots you've identified and experiment with different ways of touching them. Try light stroking, tapping, squeezing, mild massage, and deeper massage. Use lighter and firmer pressure. Use something light like a feather, or silk fabric. Blow on it. For those areas you can reach, try licking or sucking.

Variation 2: Explore with your partner. You'll want to share what you discover with your partner, and it's a good idea to do that sometime when you are not in the heat of the moment. (Doing so may end up creating that heated moment, but the only downside that I can think of is that you'll have to come back and do this exercise together again—and again—until you both manage to get through your whole list!)

Begin by embracing, bringing in all your senses. Take in your partner's fragrance, breath, and heartbeat, and the texture of your partner's body against yours. Keep drawing your attention into the moment.

When you are ready, lie down and get comfortable. Then guide your partner over your body the way you explored with your own hands earlier. Direct your partner to the areas you found most pleasing, showing your partner on *his or her* body where and how *you* want to be touched. As your partner complies, you should breathe deeply and notice your

That Tickles!

If a touch feels ticklish, don't automatically abandon it. The ticklishness is an indication of the kind of sensitivity we're talking about, so you want to see if you can get under that defensive maneuver. It might be worth it! So if it tickles, take a breath and see if it neutralizes. Ask for just a bit *more* pressure. Placing your hand on your body next to your partner's is another way to tame the tickles. If the ticklishness persists and a fit of giggles is not the mood you are after just now, move on to another body part. But this one may be an area to come back and explore more on your own, and then again with your partner another day.

sensations. If at any point you want to change anything: *Let your partner know.* And if your partner isn't comfortable with something you are requesting, ask for something else. This should be pleasurable for both of you. Your main job is to relax and enjoy, and allow yourself to receive their gift of touch.

Once you've covered all the territory, switch and let your partner tell you, and then show you on your body, where and how your partner would like to be touched. Each of you should be receiving touch for at least two to three minutes. But if you want to spend more time on certain areas, go for it. Just keep the time you spend giving and receiving approximately even.

Partner Massage

Partner massage is great as foreplay—besides feeling great, it opens up energy pathways through the body, leading to more satisfying sex.

But just because you might be naked and touching—or being touched—all over, doesn't mean you have to have sex. Partner massage is a very fine stand-alone activity. In fact, I suggest you aim to keep it not sexual, at least at first.

Partner massage is one good way to practice the kind of communicating about sex you need to do—*I like that; that's not a good spot; would you mind . . . ?*—in more neutral territory.

It is also a great way to mix things up, physically, with your partner, making it a great solution for the boredom that comes from being stuck in a rut. I've yet to meet the person bored by getting a massage! As an activity you do as a couple, focused on giving and receiving, it is a good choice in the face of almost any relationship issue you are working through.

Your first step here is to make sure you've got some clear space and time in which to luxuriate in this exercise. Then decide who's going first as giver, and who will be the first receiver. After you finish the exercise as described here: Switch roles. Some couples prefer to save "paybacks" for another day; sometimes it'll just depend on the time you have available.

Receiver, your part is as simple as they come: Get naked. Lie down. Cover up with a light sheet or soft blanket if you want to. Breathe deeply and relax, preparing yourself to receive your partner's touch and attention. And that's it for the "doing" for you, except for when you have to roll over partway through—and remember you must signal to your partner when you really dig what they are doing, want them to stop what they are doing, or have a suggestion for another area or method.

Giver, your prep is pretty simple, too: Put your focus on your partner, and on giving.

Now you're ready to begin: Massage gently, working from the head down (or the feet up) to be sure you get every body part. Use massage oil or lotion if your partner likes the feel of it. Work slowly, being sure to cover all the territory: legs, feet, hands, arms, face, head, chest, abdomen, back, buttocks. (*Almost* all the territory: Skip genitals and the breasts. Yes, your partner is naked in bed, but the goal here is not sexual arousal. If it happens, it happens, and I'm sure you'll know how to handle it if it does. My suggestion, though, is to finish the massage first.)

Experiment with different touches and motions to discover what you both like. Use different parts of your hands (fingertips, knuckles, fists, sides of the hand, heels of the hands, etc.) and use varying levels of pressure as well. Knead a little. "Karate chop" (gently) a bit. Rub broadly over larger areas. "Drum" on your partner (again, gently) with cupped hands. Squeeze. Pat. Sweep. Brush. Lean.

Dig in a bit over muscles, go easier over bone or really sensitive areas. (Although sometimes a sensitive area requires a firmer touch to avoid a ticklish sensation.) Various schools of thought on massage prescribe specific techniques, and if you want to investigate those, go for it. But for the purposes of relaxation, energy exchanging, and partner connection, you don't need any particular skill set or technique to make massage work for you. Some people, for example, will tell you to move your hands always outward, away from the heart, and if your goal is specifically therapeutic, to drain lymph or some such, that may indeed be the way to go. But here you're mainly after making your partner feel good, so your plan should be to use trial and error to find out what does that—and then do it!

Some areas are bound to be tenser than others, and you may want to concentrate an extra helping of attention there. Remember you want your partner to get—and stay—very relaxed, so push through the tension only when it furthers that end. If it's causing your partner to tense up more, you'll do better to choose a different emphasis. You can't go wrong with extra focus on what feels extra good!

You should spend at least thirty minutes on this massage. When it's over, you both may decide this has been an excellent bit of foreplay, and decide to move on to having sex. Or not. This exercise is useful and beneficial either way.

8

Sometimes It's All About You

Sex for One

To maximize sexual pleasure, it's important to understand how your body responds, and to what. Exploring is the only way to find out. And it's a good idea to explore by yourself, all focus on *you,* before there's a partner involved.

Masturbation can be a great way to connect to your own sexuality, hone your skills, and build your confidence. It helps you learn to control your sexual response. It will teach you about your own body, and how to satisfy it—and about how to teach your partner the same. It will help tune you in to your own energy flow. For a lot of women, masturbation is the best way to learn to have an orgasm—or, learn how to orgasm most easily or most intensely.

You get health benefits from masturbation, too. So if "it feels good" isn't enough for you, you can also go with "it's good for you." Masturbation can relieve stress, help you sleep, and relieve menstrual cramps. And it's much more fun than sending your liver yet another ibuprofen to metabolize!

Masturbation is also a great way to practice much of what you're learning in this book before trying it out with a partner. For people without a partner, or without physical access to their partner for whatever reason, it's a primary form of sexual expression. (And with a partner, mutual masturbation is one good way to keep changing things up.) Sometimes, you just need a quick release, and masturbation is the best route.

But masturbation can also be disconnecting and draining. Some people retreat into masturbation rather than having sex with their partners. The two sexual outlets can coexist, of course, but if the solo efforts begin to become a substitution for the twosome's activities, there's going to be a problem. I've also seen negative effects in patients with obsessions with Internet porn; it's striking how much energy is lost from masturbating to pictures of strangers. There's a clear lack of vitality. Chinese medicine explains the effect thus: Masturbating in this way cultivates yang, without any yin to tame it. It's not the use of porn per se—it's the lack of any counterbalancing energy coming in to replenish the sexual energy being expended. (See page 176 for more about the use and abuse of porn.) Any kind of masturbation, if overdone, will cause similar problems, as would any situation where you keep sending out energy but never get any back. Hello, imbalance!

All this is just to let you know you should use the awareness of your body and your energy that you are developing with this program to keep an eye on how you are using masturbation, so you can make it a healthy part of your life. Moderation is key.

For women, though, "moderation" can encompass quite a lot. According to Chinese medicine, women have a lot more sexual qi than men—and we lose less with each orgasm—so we get quite a lot of leeway in terms of how often we masturbate. For women, "moderation" is not so much about how much we are doing it and more about how we are using it—to connect with a partner and with our sexuality, rather than to avoid either, and to build rather than drain energy.

Dos and Don'ts

There's no how-to manual for masturbation. Pretty much if it feels good, do it. Beyond that, a few guidelines will set you up for an optimal experience:

- *Don't* rush. Allow yourself to go through all the stages of sexual arousal—and savor them on their own terms. Some women feel guilty, or just awkward, about masturbating, but those feelings are unjustified, so don't let them hurry you along just to get it over with.

- *Don't* focus on orgasm. Orgasm is not the be-all and end-all of masturbation, just as it shouldn't be in sex with a partner. Trying too hard to orgasm—alone or with a partner—is a sign you are rushing things. And Chinese medicine holds that when you try to force it, you are using muscles to push qi into your pelvis to compensate for low qi levels in your genitals—draining qi from other parts of your body in the process. We do it because it often works—but it also decreases the quality of the orgasm. Ironically, letting go of orgasm as your main goal makes it more likely you will orgasm—and orgasm more easily and more intensely.
- *Don't* overlook the less obvious erogenous zones. Sure, you know it feels good to stimulate your breasts and genitals, but don't forget about your earlobes, nape of neck, small of the back, bottom, back of the knees, inside of the thighs, and even your palms, navel, ears, feet, and toes. Find all your hot spots. Use them.
- *Do* involve your whole body—and all parts of your genitals. A lot of women tend to zero in on the clitoris to the exclusion of all else, and while that may be effective, you may be depriving yourself of a deeper experience.
- *Do* change things up from time to time, just as you do in sex with a partner. Don't rely on the same old, same old to bring you to orgasm. If you only ever go with what you know works, how will you discover what *else* works? Or, works even better? It's a little harder to surprise yourself than it is a partner, but you will still appreciate variety.
- *Do* take what you learn while masturbating and apply it when you have sex with a partner. Masturbation is a great way to test out new things or hone new skills. Of course you don't have to share everything. But you probably don't want to keep it all to yourself, either.

Sex Again in Real Life: Amanda

I'm pretty sure it was the first time in Amanda's life that a health professional had prescribed masturbation. Amanda had come to see me for help with resurrecting her sex drive, though she quickly explained that *she* really didn't care if she ever had sex again, but she was worried that her husband, Stuart, would have an affair if something didn't change in their bedroom. Amanda said she was busy with her year-old son—and *so* tired from looking after him—and felt quite fulfilled as a mother. It was almost as if she didn't need a sexual connection with her husband anymore, as if there wasn't room for one. All in all, Amanda was pretty shut down, at least as far as her sex life went. She had one specific complaint, too: She was still breast-feeding, her breasts were very tender, and she no longer enjoyed the way Stuart touched them.

I told Amanda herbs and acupuncture could help her fatigue—and the stagnation causing (among other things) her breast tenderness. But what I really wanted her to look at was her lack of interest in sex. Sexuality is a part of being human, so I doubted hers had actually vanished. More likely, it had been pushed aside. Amanda's role as a mom had become so consuming she didn't really see herself as a sexual person anymore. But I felt sure that was a reversible condition. I thought she was going to have to reconnect with that part of herself before she was going to be able to reconnect that way with her husband.

So I gave Amanda a pretty basic assignment—to masturbate at least every other day over the next week. She was hesitant. I explained some basic techniques—like those in this chapter—to help her get started. And I encouraged her to remember that sex is pleasurable, and to think about the importance of sex to her physical and mental health, her relationship, and to her*self.* Experiencing that pleasure again—creating it herself—would be the most powerful way to remind herself, and her body, of all that. Hence, the homework—which she eventually agreed to try.

By the time we next met, Amanda had managed to masturbate to orgasm—but only once. Still, she reported excitedly, that had been enough to start her feeling a bit more sexual already. She kept on with exploring her sexuality on her own for a couple more weeks until she felt ready to invite Stuart to the party. When she did, she was able to teach him quite a lot about what she'd learned about her body, and guide him to give her pleasure. Which he was quite eager to do! Amanda soon realized—a bit to her surprise—that she was matching his enthusiasm.

FOR THE GUYS: Masturbation

I think it's safe to assume we've got a handle on the masturbation thing, am I right? I've got science to back me up on that: Studies show 99 percent of men masturbate. We've got the "how-to" pretty much covered.

Men do tend to make a few mistakes, though. One is over-doing it. That depletes sexual energy and may leave you tired (especially in the late afternoon) and with weaker orgasms.

Or we misuse it, which means using it in a way that decreases connection or drains energy—like falling into a pattern of masturbating instead of having sex with your partner (not counting when you are apart or when your partner is not interested).

Another big error is rushing it, like someone is giving out a prize for how fast you can make yourself come. They don't—so take your time. Just getting off is not the same as cultivating your sexual energy, and the latter is what you should be aiming for. It has the bigger payoff anyway.

The other most common error is to only and always do the same old, same old.

So I want to make a pitch for some variety. Changing things up a bit is good for your libido, just as it is in sex with a partner. It also gives you a chance to discover all that works for you, and what works best. So experiment with varied and consistent pressure; varied and consistent rhythm; emphasis on the downstroke and the upstroke; using lube, and not. Try concentrating stimulation on the head of the penis, one hand on the head and the other on the shaft. Or, using one hand to press down on the base of the penis and the other to move up and down on the shaft. Stroke or tug the testicles, or stimulate the nipples or anus at the same time as you are working the penis. Touch yourself *not* on your genitals. Stimulate other erogenous zones. Try different positions. Use porn, or fantasy—or stay present with yourself in the moment. You might just learn a really good trick or two by branching out from time to time.

I am not exactly in line with the ancient Taoists in talking about best ways to masturbate: They advised men to ejaculate *only* inside a woman's body or risk losing precious sexual energy with each ejaculation. Instead, the sages were very excited about learning to orgasm *without* ejaculating. Ordinary mortals not committing to a serious spiritual quest for orgasm without ejaculation can still conserve their energy when they masturbate to orgasm, protecting both libido and future performance. One way to do this is to cover or hold your penis and testicles with both hands as you orgasm or for a moment or two afterward.

Another way is to do The Loop at orgasm or just after, circulating qi within you rather than releasing it. Focus on half a Loop: When using with masturbation, you want to move energy up without sending it back down to the genitals, where it could get lost or stagnate. You can also just stick with deep breathing, or simply focus your attention to the top of your head as a way of drawing qi upward. Another good strategy for just after ejaculation is to rub your hands together until they are warm and place them on your lower abdomen, letting their heat radiate into your pelvis.

Masturbation 101: Clitoral Massage

Having cautioned you about making your clitoris your exclusive focus, allow me to switch gears to tell you about *how to focus on your clitoris.* It *is* key to orgasm, so it pays to treat it right. You want to allow yourself time for plenty of warm-up, and plenty of side trips, but when you get down to business there are a lot of options you'll want to explore. Here are some of the things you might want to try to stimulate your clitoris during masturbation:

- Rub the clitoris directly with a finger, fingers, or your whole hand.
- Play with a variety of strokes: soft to hard, slow to fast, up and down, around and around . . .
- Massage the clitoris indirectly by rubbing the skin above and around it (the labia and/or clitoral hood).
- Press the clitoris against an object, such as a pillow.
- Try a vibrator, on or around the clitoris.
- Use water to stimulate the clitoris, such as from a handheld showerhead.

These are the basics, but there's still a lot of territory to explore before, during, and/or after clitoral stimulation. Experiment with:

- Rubbing the perineum (area between anus and vagina), periurethral area (around where you pee!), and/or the vulva
- Penetrating the vagina with a finger, fingers, dildo, or vibrator
- Stimulating other erogenous zones (nipples, inner thigh, buttocks, anus, breasts . . .)
- Different positions, like sitting, squatting, or standing

You'll also want to move further afield. Masturbating isn't only about your genitals, or even only about your body. Try masturbating:

- In different areas of your home
- In the bath or shower
- While reading erotica
- While fantasizing
- While watching yourself in the mirror
- While fully clothed

Not all of these things is for everybody. But you've got to test out everything to discover what does float your boat—you won't always be able to predict without hands-on experience.

Do The Squeeze

You should practice the most basic version of The Squeeze first, but once you have a little experience under your belt try The Squeeze during masturbation—especially the actual squeezing part. It's good for toning your muscles—and deepening your orgasm. And it's good practice for using it during sex with a partner.

The G-spot

The much-debated G-spot is located an inch and a half to two inches up the vagina on the "front" wall. That puts it directly behind the clitoris, just behind the pubic bone. It is most obvious once you are already aroused and lubricated, because it swells a little bit. Then you can find it by inserting your forefinger into the vagina, gently hooking it behind the pubic bone. If you go in up to about your second knuckle, that'll put you in the general area. Feel for a little mound of spongy tissue, slightly different in texture from the tissue around it, a little tougher or bumpier, about the size of a nickel or a quarter. The G-spot is exquisitely sensitive to touch, so it should announce itself pretty clearly when you land there (provided you are already warmed up).

It's worth hunting around a bit, if that's what it takes, because G-spot orgasms are very deep and intense. If you have not yet been introduced to your G-spot, you may want to find it on your own first. Then again, exploring with a partner would be fun, too.

Either way, here's a bit of advice: Pee before you get started. Part of what you may experience may make you feel as if you need to urinate, and if you are worried about wetting yourself you are certainly not going to be relaxed enough to orgasm. A little prevention goes a long way here. If you've emptied your bladder first, then if you do feel the urge to urinate you'll know you can safely follow this advice: Push through it. Don't hold back, and don't give up. The feeling will pass, and you won't in fact pee.

The sexercise here is to help you find and learn to "work" your G-spot. Begin by stimulating the G-spot with your forefinger, curving your finger to press a little on the vaginal wall, toward your belly. Start gently, and slowly increase the pressure. Some women like just a little pressure, and some like strong stimulation. Experiment to find out where you are on that spectrum. Vary speed as well as pressure. Slide your finger up and down inside the nook. Start above it, near the cervix, and slide down across it. Then repeat. Or, try rubbing in a circular motion around the nook, using gradually increasing pressure. You may want to try using two fingers.

The G-spot is exquisitely sensitive to touch, so it should announce itself pretty clearly when you land there.

When you are confident of the spot, you can teach your partner where it is and how to use it. It often takes some practice to get right, but you may find you enjoy simultaneous G-spot and clitoral stimulation.

The Chinese sex texts do not specify the G-spot (or the A-spot, see next section). But the positions recommended for intercourse as being the most satisfying for women are just the ones that stimulate the G-spot. They are: (1) the woman on her hands and knees, with her partner entering from behind her (see Tiger position, page 214). And (2) woman on her back with her legs raised and parted (see Monkey position, page 215).

The A-spot

The A-spot, also known (but not by many) as the anterior fornix, is an area of extra-sensitive tissue at the end of the vaginal tube, a little nook just in front of the cervix. It is by some accounts the female anatomical equivalent of the prostate. Whatever you call it, it can provide powerful orgasms when stimulated.

Your assignment is to find and stimulate it and see what happens. The A-spot is too high up to reach with your fingers, so the best way to access it is usually intercourse in the missionary position, with thrusts aimed high. You can also stimulate it with a dildo or vibrator, and this is probably the best way to begin figuring out how the A-spot works in your own body and discovering its power. Once you do this on your own, it is a lot easier to share it with a partner.

The A-spot is sort of a "you'll know it when you find it" kind of deal. During sex, you may want to adjust the position of your hips with a pillow until you feel as if your partner is thrusting against high up on the front wall of your vagina.

FOR THE GUYS: Prostate Massage

Chinese and Western medicine agree on the many benefits of stimulating the prostate, including strengthening erections, relieving inflammation, and helping prevent prostate cancer and the enlarged, hard, or painful prostate so common over age fifty. The Taoists add a few benefits to the list your urologist is unlikely to bring up: Stimulating the prostate strengthens and moves sexual qi, and helps balance yin and yang. And, for those on this particular quest, prostate massage is very helpful in developing the ability to experience nonejaculatory orgasms (see page 232 for more on "holding back"). Prostate massage also provides incredibly powerful orgasms.

I urge you to approach this with an open mind. This *is* an advanced approach, so don't pressure yourself if it's not the first thing you want to try from this book or this chapter. Maybe on one of your more adventurous days, you'll come back to it.

Now here's the part not everyone is on board with right away: The direct way to stimulate your prostate is to insert a finger into your anus and reach up to rub it gently. This is essentially how a doctor does your prostate exam, but I promise doing it as described below is considerably sexier.

You can do prostate massage yourself, and it should feel very good. And it's probably best to experience it first on your own before you involve a partner. But you should know you will experience even more pleasure when your partner does it for you. You can use prostate massage during intercourse or oral sex for particularly intense orgasms. (Anal sex, when you are the receiving partner, is a form of prostate massage all on its own.)

Here's how you massage your prostate:

Insert a finger into your anus and reach back and up, curling it toward your navel, until you feel the prostate. Use a bit of lubricant to make insertion easier (look for lube with all-natural ingredients). If you are not accustomed to anal play, insert your finger gradually, pausing frequently to take deep breaths and relax. It's normal for the anus to contract as something comes in, but it will relax as you get used to the sensation. Don't force it. You may find that stroking your belly, buttocks, or genitals creates just enough pleasurable distraction to allow you to relax into the experience.

Proceed gently until you feel the prostate's smooth, round surface. Apply gentle pressure—perhaps nothing more than resting your finger against it at first. When you are ready, progress to more of a massage: Vibrate your finger a bit, or slide it back and forth. Keep taking those deep breaths, and enjoy the sensation. This should never hurt, so if it does, ease up.

Sex Toys

Toys were familiar territory for the ancient Chinese sexologists. In fact, they invented them! Dildos, for example: Ivory carved into the image of a husband's penis, with his portrait carved at the end, were given to wives when their men went off to war. The Chinese used penis rings to help maintain erections—some with little bumps to arouse the clitoris—thousands of years ago. Also little balls were inserted into the vagina to stimulate the G-spot . . . the list of this type of paraphernalia goes on. And much of it was dreamed up as a way to improve masturbation for women, so they could stimulate all parts of their vagina and vulva even when they

The Loop Remix

Once you've practiced The Loop (see pages 61 and 115) enough times to be quite comfortable with it, you can try it while masturbating. There are many benefits to the combination, but one of them is that you create an experience that is more energetic than just orgasm alone.

You might want to begin with a few minutes of The Loop before moving on to masturbation. Or, try masturbating for a while first, then taking the sexual energy you've generated and circulating that in the usual Loop way.

Whatever your approach, go ahead and throw in The Squeeze, too, when you're ready for that.

The Loop is also a great idea after you've had an orgasm—you can circulate the qi you've built up within your body, rather than lose it. Focus your energy upward, toward the top of your head. While you are at it, rub your hands together until they warm a bit then lay them on your lower abdomen (*dan tien*) to replenish the energy of that area.

were working alone. The sages dispensing advice on using various items this way were not exactly a Girl Power group. Their thinking was that in these ways, women would strengthen their muscles and develop their sexual skills—which would be pretty awesome for their male partners. Actually, I can't really argue with them there. It's just that it is also pretty awesome for the women themselves.

Sex toys are often just the ticket for mixing things up to relieve boredom. The most common ones are probably vibrators and dildos, and both come in a variety of forms. I don't have a lot of advice on what sex toy you should get—you just have to play around with them to see what you like—but you should start with something pretty basic. Later, if you want to branch out, or add bells and whistles, go right ahead. Remember, it doesn't have to be sold on some website as a sex toy to be fun in bed. I bet if you try you can find a few different ways to make a simple silky scarf sexy.

In any case, the trick, once again, is to use toys in a connected way—or else they will put you on an express lane to less sex, less sex with your partner, or less satisfying sex. Or all three.

When you are having sex without a partner, but with some kind of toy, the questions to ask yourself are: Do you use a toy to connect to your body and your sexuality? Or are you using it to avoid feeling or exploring aspects of yourself?

Whether sex toys are connecting or dis-connecting depends mostly on where your mind is; and where your mind goes, your qi—your energy—will follow. When using toys with your partner, if your focus is on your experience with your partner, it's all good. But people who use toys as a way to avoid connecting, or instead of having sex with their partners, will run into trouble along that path.

One of my patients, Renya, and her partner had a successful experience with their toy of choice after a friend raved about vibrating cock rings. Renya suggested her husband wear one of these little gadgets during intercourse—and thereafter they were both big fans. The ring helped him maintain his erection longer, and at the same time stimulated Renya in a way that dramatically changed her "I rarely orgasm" experience of sex. Sex became much more enjoyable for both of them—and much more frequent, too.

Renya's experiment paid off in part because this toy is worn during intercourse (that is, it didn't interfere with intercourse), in part because it benefited both of them, and in large part because they used it together. Renya and her husband used it to create, rather than disrupt or avoid, connection.

9

Do It Yourself

Putting It All Together

The plan presented in this chapter is designed to get you comfortable with a core set of exercises for moving qi and balancing yin and yang within yourself. So following it should: (1) get you unstuck and well balanced, and (2) get you all the practice you need to master these techniques to the point where you'll be able to draw on them whenever and wherever you want them, no crib notes needed.

Because let's face it: It's one thing to read about or even learn all these ways to recharge your libido—and another thing altogether to actually fit them into your life. But for them to work as intended, you do of course actually have to do them. And pretty regularly, at least over a short period of time, until you have successfully powered up again and many of them have become sort of second nature. There's an official Sex in Six program coming up, for you and your partner to work on together, but that's only going to work as well as you prepare for it. So this is where you practice doing your own handstands, so you'll be ready to perform with another person when the time comes.

Because the plan in this chapter is streamlined to a handful of exercises, it hits many highlights—and all the truly crucial skills—but doesn't cover every strategy in the book. Still, my hope is that you will try most if not all of the strategies more informally on your own. Probably you've been doing a little of that on your own already, as you've worked through the chapters up to this point. And I encourage you to keep that up, so you can discover the full range of what is most useful for you. With a little practice, you will figure out which things help, which you like, and which you'll want to keep coming back to when you need them—and which you'll want to keep coming back to even when you don't need them. Some things you will learn so well that you will no longer need to "practice" them because you will just use them naturally. For example, many of my patients use The Loop so often and so well that eventually they simply "know" how to circulate their energy and do it almost automatically during sex, or whenever the need arises. They no longer have to intentionally set out to accomplish a Loop, or find a time to coordinate doing it with their partners. Though if things get chaotic, they may well sit down for a few minutes to focus on The Loop as a means of getting through whatever it is.

How to Do It Yourself

There is no specific time frame for completing this part of the Sex Again program. But you should plan to do all the phases, to do them in the order given, and to **devote a minimum of about a week to each.** And you should be prepared to **spend a little time essentially every day** on it. (Most days' assignments can be completed in twenty minutes or less—many days, you'll only need five minutes.) Working the program this way, you'll be immersed enough in the techniques you are learning to really make them *yours*—and to feel the results for yourself.

That said, if you skip a day, or two or three, no worries. Just pick up where you left off and keep going. As long as you don't let it happen all the time, it can't impair your results—though stressing about doing it "right" definitely can.

If your partner is so inclined, he can do this part of the program, too—but he doesn't need to for you to reap benefits from it. He definitely doesn't need to be doing it at the same time as you—though if there are exercises you want to practice together, that is certainly fine.

You can also work this part of the Sex Again plan at the same time as you undertake the Sex in Six program that's coming up (in Chapter 15). Of course that requires more of a time commitment. And for some people, it would be biting off more than they can chew. But if you are up for it, you'll see results that much faster.

PHASE 1

Think About It (page 34)
Take a Breath (page 25)

Take a few minutes each day to do each of these exercises.

PHASE 2

The Loop (page 61)
The Squeeze (page 85)
The Loop AND The Squeeze (page 98)

Continue with daily doses of Think About It and Take a Breath.

Add to them by practicing The Loop and the full Squeeze, once a day—and the most basic element of the latter (the actual squeezing) three times a day. If pressed for time, you can alternate days doing The Loop on one and the full Squeeze on the next. But get in at least those PC squeezes every day.

PHASE 3

Qi Moving exercise and/or
Yin Nourishing exercise and/or
Yang Boosting exercise

Add a fifth exercise daily. That means you'll be continuing with Take a Breath, Think About It, and The Loop and The Squeeze—and adding one more of your own choosing, according to what you most need to work on—your yin, your yang, or your qi. If you have more than one problem area, odds are one of them is going to be stuck qi, and you can prioritize that over yin/yang balance when it comes to choosing an exercise. Or, if you are up for the challenge, you can pick more than one exercise and alternate which one you do each day. A full list of exercises appears in Appendix 2, but here are the choices when you are working solo:

To Move Qi

Three Locks (page 109)
Mixing Bowl (page 127)
Breast Massage (page 125)
G-spot (page 142)
A-spot (page 143)
Tease and Release (page 198)

To Nourish Yin

Three Locks (page 109)
Inner Smile (page 112)
Progressive Relaxation (page 108)
Breast Massage (page 125)
G-spot (page 142)
A-spot (page 143)
Tease and Release (page 198)

To Boost Yang

Belly Breath (page 96)
Three Locks (page 109)
Energy Meditation (page 114)
Mixing Bowl (page 127)
Tease and Release (page 198)
To the Edge and Back (page 228)

PHASE 4

Buddha Belly (page 78)
Opening the Senses (page 54)

Replace the exercise you chose last week with Buddha Belly and Opening the Senses. Continue with Take a Breath, Think About It, and The Loop and The Squeeze daily. But alternate days doing Buddha Belly and

Opening the Senses. This supports balance by giving you yang boosting one day and yin nourishing the next.

PHASE 5

Progressive Relaxation (page 108)
Exploring (page 129)

Take a break from your practice of Buddha Belly and Opening the Senses, and add in Progressive Relaxation and Exploring instead. Continue daily with Take a Breath, Think About It, The Loop, and The Squeeze. Do Progressive Relaxation and Exploring at least once each.

PHASE 6

Masturbate . . . (Chapter 8)
. . . With The Squeeze (page 142)
. . . With The Loop (page 146)
. . . To the Edge and Back (page 228)

Retire Progressive Relaxation and Exploring for now, but continue daily with Take a Breath and Think About It. You're going to keep going with The Loop and The Squeeze, too, but with a twist: Use them while masturbating. That will intensify your experience, and also get you ready to use those techniques during sex with a partner. When you are ready for another challenge, add To the Edge and Back, as well. You can do all three during one session of masturbating, but if that's overwhelming, practice one at a time before combining. And if you are not used to masturbating in general, you might want to begin with some of the suggestions in Chapter 8 before layering in other techniques. This is the phase most likely to require more than one week, depending on how much masturbation you are able and wanting to fit in—and how much you'll need. To the Edge and Back is pretty easy to "get," so you may not need more than one trial run to feel comfortable with it (and understand its power!). And you may be so good at The Loop and The Squeeze by now that you find it's a simple thing to bring them into a sexual context. But you should extend this final phase until you find all these variations easy to do—and easy to remember how to do—as you are reaching orgasm. You have to have as many orgasms as it takes to achieve that. It's just the price you'll have to pay.

FOR THE GUYS: Improve Yin or Yang—for Men Only

Almost all the exercises move qi, nourish yin, or boost qi in the same ways for men and women. One men-only exception is Prostate Massage. It is good for yin deficiency or yang deficiency. (Another exception: Breast Massage doesn't do much for a man.)

part **three**

Balance and Connect

10

Yin, Yang, and You Two

Finding Balance with Another Person

Finding or creating dynamic balance between two people is a beautiful thing—the basis for a deep, powerful, and long lasting connection, and the foundation of a strong libido and active sex life over time. It's the setup for good sex—really good sex. That is to say, sex that not only expresses that balance and connection but also reinforces it. Sex that makes you want more of it.

Just as each person in a relationship has his or her own yin/yang balance, so does the relationship. And just as an individual's ideal balance is usually struck with just slightly more of one than the other, two people will achieve optimal balance when one partner is slightly more yin and the other slightly more yang. You already know from playground experiments on the seesaw that if you want to balance you better have one person on one side and one person on the other. If both people are on one side, then you're going nowhere but down.

At the risk of stretching the image too far: If one person is out to an extreme and the other is closer to the center, you are also not going to be able to balance. And then there's this: Someone on the very end of the teeter-totter requires more weight to balance than someone closer to the center of the board.

In the same way, it is good to have one person be more yang—but just by a little, while the other is just a little more yin. And the more centered you are in yourself, the easier you will be to balance.

Strong relationships need both yin and yang. Yang energy creates passion, pulling a pair together in the first place. But it is yin energy that creates intimacy, for connection over time. Yang energy allows for offering what a partner needs; yin energy allows for accepting what a partner offers. Yang energy takes the lead; yin energy rounds up the resources to execute the mission. It operates this way both in the relationship in general, and in the sexual part of the relationship specifically. No relationship—and no sex life—can thrive with only yin or only yang.

Balance Each Other

Finding your own balance will serve you well in all aspects of your life—not least of which is preparing you to connect strongly and deeply with another person, and find balance with that person, come what may. Being in balance, and knowing how to find your way back to balance, allows you to deal with whatever comes your way. It can even prevent, avoid, or eliminate problems from cropping up in the first place. But no couple can skirt all problems, so having the balance and the ability to weather them when they do arise is crucial.

This is one of the brilliant things about being in a relationship: You don't have to do everything all on your own.

It starts with individual stability. That's what makes it possible to strike a balance with another person. When you are centered in yourself, you can forge close emotional and energetic bonds without losing sight of yourself. You can stay true to your own ideas and values, even as you engage with someone else's. You can agree without losing yourself, and disagree without feeling alienated. You can empathize with and support a partner who is having a tough time without getting drawn into the whirlwind yourself. You open yourself to nurturing and support from a partner without spilling over into neediness. You can share your whole self.

And you can help your lover do the same. This is the distinctive sign of a healthy relationship. And the foundation for a healthy sex life. Ideally, a relationship is the coming together of two people who are balanced within themselves, and who thereby can strike a balance with each other. And then, when one or both people fall out of balance, or the relationship between them does, one can reel the other back in. No one strikes one perfect balance and stays there forever. We are constantly moving a little too far one way or another (and sometimes a lot too far!) and adjusting back toward balance. Being in a relationship means you have another person who can rebalance with you. It's like the circus performers I mentioned earlier: If the flier up top bobbles a bit, the person forming the base will shift to restore stability.

Recently I had a run of a few months where I was managing serious conflicts at work every day, so I was maxing out on the yang end of the spectrum. During that time, my husband picked up a lot of slack at home, especially when it came to cooking dinner, which drew up more yin in him. At a time when I probably didn't have enough yin in myself, my partner could shore me up and keep me from going off the deep end.

This is one of the brilliant things about being in a relationship: You don't *have* to do everything all on your own. Your partner can do some of the balancing for you. And when you strike a balance with your partner, balance in other spheres of life will follow.

You may not be there at the moment, but in any relationship worth keeping you can get there. You can get there sexually with the Sex in Six program—and the effects will carry over into other areas of your life.

Having two people to balance is also one of the really tricky things about relationships, however. For as often as one person balances the other, there are equal risks of an imbalance in one person amplifying imbalances in the other, or in the relationship.

When there's imbalance in a relationship, there are bound to be relationship problems. (And where there are problems, there's bound to be imbalance.) Relationship issues are often at the heart of libido issues, whether it's a strained relationship, a general lack of intimacy (not just sexual intimacy), or simply boredom with having sex with the same

TRY THIS TONIGHT: Synchronize Your Breathing

This exercise emphasizes connection, so if and when your relationship takes a wrong turn, it is a great way to come back together. It's particularly useful when you are in conflict, as a way to put focus on how you work together. It is a very literal way to get in sync with each other—or experience how in sync you are. It is a good way to focus your concentration on each other, tuning in to your partner's body while also regulating what's going on in your own—a solid foundation for connected sex. It is aimed at creating and reinforcing intimacy, setting the stage for sexual intimacy. So this is a great way to begin a sexual encounter. But it is also an excellent exercise all on its own. As explained in the ancient Taoist texts this practice harmonizes your qi. The exchange of energy during sex begins here, with the breath. This is how you begin to create a sense of union. Once you master the more chaste version, try branching out with some of the variations.

Sit facing each other and look directly into each other's eyes. Rest your hands on your knees, palms up. Take gentle, deep breaths in through your nose and out through your mouth, inhaling and exhaling in time with your partner. You will not start out even with each other, but you will get there as you focus on the rhythm of your partner's breathing. Begin to gradually shorten or lengthen your breaths until you match your partner's timing. Find a pace that is comfortable for both of you. If one of you shifts away from that pace eventually, the other should adjust accordingly. Breathe together this way for about five minutes. (You may want to start with a shorter session and build up the time gradually.)

You can also do this exercise with your eyes closed. This makes you tune into each other in a different way, without visuals to rely on. You may need to place a hand on each other's chests to feel the breathing, or make a soft sigh as you exhale so you can hear each other. If at first you feel uncomfortable having extended eye contact with your partner, then this is a good way to ease into this exercise. You can also begin with your eyes closed, and open them partway through to gaze at each other.

Variation 1: Do this exercise lying in bed, facing each other. Eyes open or closed. Clothed—or not. Touching—or not. You should be comfortable.

Variation 2: Do this exercise lying down "spoon" style, one of you curved around the other from behind. This is another good way to adjust if the eye contact is too intense at first. But "spooning" also gets you in touch in a very direct way: You'll be able to feel each other breathing quite easily, even feel each other's heartbeats. You should breathe in unison this way for about three minutes—estimate, or just go long enough to experience easy, natural breathing for a while—then switch positions and synchronize again for a few more.

Variation 3: Hold your breath for a few seconds after each inhale and exhale, keeping in unison by taking your lead from each other. This requires a bit more concentration to pull off, so wait to do this one until you are experienced with the earlier variations.

Variation 4: This twist is known as Close the Circuit. Position, timing, and eye contact are all the same as above, but now you are going to exhale as your partner inhales, and inhale as your partner exhales. In Chinese medicine the breath carries energy, so this is a way to physically experience the exchange between you. The circuit you'll be creating, connecting the two of you, is a way to harmonize your qi—and balance yin and yang between you.

partner over long periods of time. Restoring balance is often the key to healing the relationship, both sexually and in general.

Lack of libido may indicate not just imbalance but also that energy is not moving between partners as it should on the occasions when they *do* have sex. It may also be a symptom of energy not flowing properly within one partner's body (or both). And just as with imbalance, the problem probably exists not only in everyday life but also in the bedroom.

Good sex encourages partners to be vulnerable and open with each other, which in turn encourages tenderness and compassion in all areas of their life together. And if that sexual relationship has gone on for years, then there has been quite a lot of energy invested in it. The more energy that goes into that bond, the more profound it is.

TRY THIS TONIGHT: The Squeeze and The Loop—for Two

To balance yin and yang as a couple, try the Squeeze/Loop combination (see page 98)—with your partner. Start by doing it sitting quietly together, as a meditative (but not yet sexual) practice—just until you get the coordination down. Then do the combo together lying down. And then naked. Then you're ready to use it as part of your sex life—as a great way to kick things off, or to generate energy during sex.

The Yin and Yang of Sex

Any sexual experience—like any relationship—needs both yin and yang to succeed. Intercourse is a physical embodiment of the relationship of yin and yang, yang entering yin, transforming once again into yang. Not much is more yang than an erection bound for insertion or more yin than a receptive (lubricated) vagina. That's from a heterosexual framework, of course. But good sex, gay or straight, has both participants shifting from giving to receiving and back again over and over. Sex combines and exchanges yin and yang as partners give and receive.

When you do it right. Both people need to access both their yang (giving) and yin (receiving). If either or both partners are out to an extreme of yin or yang, or if both partners are too closely matched in their levels of yin and yang, the sex isn't going to work that well, either physically or emotionally. When it *is* well balanced, sex is both more enjoyable and more meaningful. Not to mention more satisfying and longer lasting.

For those on the yang side, sex is a way into the emotional connection with another person. For those on the yin side, an emotional connection is the route to sexual arousal.

At a very basic level, it takes an interplay of yin and yang just to get things rolling. It is yang energy that initiates sex. But without yin energy to receive and respond to an overture, no one's getting any. Other distinct characteristics of yin and yang as they apply to sex demonstrate why you need both energies within a couple—and both within yourself—for a satisfying sexual experience.

For example, yang energy tends to move up, and yin energy down. As it applies to sex, this means people who are more yang (in a heterosexual relationship, typically that's the man) tend to be turned on by direct stimulation of the genitals—with response flowing up from there to heart and mind—while people who are more yin (most often the woman) generally need to have their head and heart sparked first, with response moving down from there to the genitals. This is true not only of an individual sexual exchange, but also of the function sexual acts have in the relationship. For those who are on the yang side of the balance, sex is a way into the emotional connection with another person. For those on the yin side, an emotional connection is the route to sexual arousal.

Yin is slow and yang is fast. People with more yang tend to get aroused quickly, while people with more yin turn on more slowly. Someone more yang will also burn through a burst of sexual energy faster, while for someone with more yin it will last longer.

To nourish a strong sexual connection, both partners need to play to their lover's dominant aspect. That may require tapping into your non-dominant trait at least a bit, until you find that exquisite balance between you and another. Just be careful not to move too far too fast in another direction; you need to allow time for your partner to join you on the journey. If your partner is normally the initiator and then one day you decide to come on like gangbusters, for example, you might both enjoy the changeup very much, but you can expect it to take a little while for your partner to get with the program.

Sex as a Yin/Yang Tune-up

Having sex is an important way to balance yin and yang—both within yourself and between you and your partner. In part, that's because having sex is a great way to get qi moving, and free-flowing qi is an important precondition for balanced yin and yang.

But having sex also has a direct effect on yin/yang balance, both in the moment and over time. Sex can help yin transform into yang, and yang transform into yin, re-creating balance. When a couple isn't getting this periodic yin/yang "tune-up," it is easier for any imbalance to grow to the point where it would cause problems. On the flip side, when two people restore their yin and yang, within and between themselves, their libidos are usually restored, too.

Sex also *unites* yin and yang. It's the exchange of energy between partners, and the coming together of yin and yang, that creates a powerful experience of two becoming one, where the whole is greater than the sum of the parts. In the early phase of a relationship, sex is a big part of what forms the bond between two people. As time passes, we no longer need sex to *create* the bond between us, but we do need it to keep that bond strong. We make a mistake when we let that slip away. Sex literally, physically, joins two people—and their energies—together; it nourishes the relationship in a way nothing else can.

There is a potential downside to this exchange of energy: Not all energy shared this way is going to be positive. Even in the best relationship, you are vulnerable to sharing any negative energy your partner

TRY THIS TONIGHT: Morning and Evening Meditation

My patients love this exercise, which is meant to promote connection separate and apart from intercourse. It also puts focus on closeness, harmony within oneself, relaxation, intimacy, and a feeling of oneness with another person. It moves qi, and nourishes yin. It's a quiet moment in your day—a form of meditation. In the morning it enlivens and in the evening it relaxes.

Here's how you do it:

Begin with a bit of foreplay warm-up to get to the point where there's enough lubrication to allow for penetration. Use lube as needed. Embrace in the missionary position (The Dragon, see page 214). The man should penetrate and use just enough movement to maintain an erection, but not enough to ejaculate. Actually, it doesn't even matter if you maintain an erection—once you are in, the both of you can just hold still. Just experience being there.

And that's all there is to it. Continue for as long as you both like—just a few minutes is fine—sharing and enjoying the stillness between you. Sometimes a couple will turn this practice into sex, and that is perfectly fine, as long as that is what both of you have in mind, but it is designed to end without intercourse. The one thing you don't want to do is set out to do this exercise, but then skip the slow, still part in a rush to get to intercourse. If you want the full benefit, I advise a bit of patience.

may have. And we all have some, at least sometimes. And whatever the level of energy, negative or positive, we are never more vulnerable to it—or open to it—than when we have sex. When the energy is negative, an infusion of it in this way can touch off or intensify negative aspects in you. Or, you may have to expend your positive energy fending off the incoming negativity, when surely you had more appealing plans for how to spend it.

People with a strong internal balance, though, may be able to absorb that energy without taking on its toxicity. They might even be able to take that negative energy into their bodies and transform it into positive, which can then flow back to their partners. Sex is one of the best ways of doing that. Add that to the list of reasons you want to maintain a healthy libido!

Sex Again in Real Life: Jess and Mike

Jess was yang deficient and always tired, and sex was the last thing on her mind. When she did have sex she seldom climaxed and so found the whole experience rather unsatisfying. She did have sex every now and then but confessed she felt like she was just doing it to keep her husband, Mike, happy.

Just the thought of having sex made Jess feel overwhelmed. But she said she missed physical closeness and worried that her relationship with Mike was suffering. I suggested the Morning and Evening Meditation. Jess liked the sound of the low-key intimacy and, assuming Mike was game to give it a go, committed to trying it at least once the next week. The next time she was in the office she couldn't wait to tell me how great it had been. Somehow the fact that it was a meditation rather than sex had made her feel much freer, she explained, like she didn't have to try so hard. And she definitely felt the connection between the two of them: After a few minutes, in fact, they felt so close and warm toward each other that they seemed to just flow naturally into having sex. Jess said it didn't take long for her to feel her body really responding when Mike began moving inside her. She proudly reported that with the pressure off, she was able to orgasm—without really thinking about it.

FOR THE GUYS: You Want Me to Do *What* But Not Have Sex??

It seems to be more obvious to women than to men why anybody would want to do Morning and Evening Meditation. It is a very yin activity, which means it may be a bit out of the comfort zone for some men. Those are the men for whom it will be especially

beneficial! So I'm going to clue you in the same way I do my patients, because I've heard from them over and over again how quickly they change their mind about this exercise once they try it.

First of all: This is a meditation, and thinking of it like that (rather than as "not having sex") is the first key to understanding it.

You may have to be patient with this process. If it doesn't seem very rewarding at first, give it a little time. This is about creating and strengthening connection, and that doesn't always happen instantly for everybody. For a lot of men, however, just one experience of Morning and Evening Meditation makes its appeal clear. If you don't happen to be one of them, remember: There will be time for other things later. And putting in the effort now, even if this wouldn't be your first choice on the menu, builds a strong, energetic connection and a stronger relationship and, therefore, better sex. And then there's this: Delaying pleasure builds anticipation and therefore creates greater pleasure in the end.

Opposites Attract Versus Like Attracts Like

If you want to witness the complementary nature of yin and yang, spend some time in an "opposites attract" relationship. Two people can be (or appear to be) opposite in all kinds of ways, but often the underlying opposition is in fact between yin and yang. This usually works out to a yin-dominant woman and a yang-dominant man, but it could just as well be the other way around. And it works exactly the same way in same-sex relationships as it does in opposite-sex pairings.

In the most successful relationships both partners are comfortable in both yin and yang roles. How else are they going to be able to balance each other across all the many different situations their life together will entail? Opposites-attract relationships (in the yin-yang sense) work when partners respect each other's strengths, and can draw on them to bolster their own weak spots.

There are danger spots in an opposites-attract scenario though. If either or both partners are at an extreme of yin or yang, the balancing act between them will be precarious at best. There are also going to be problems if one partner is frustrated looking for her partner to be more like her all the time, or if one partner is dependent on the other's strength without ever being able to tap into her own resources for it.

Opposites-attract relationships work when partners respect each other's strengths, and can draw on them to bolster their own weak spots.

This is why in some cases it is the two-peas-in-a-pod relationships that are the successful ones. Couples where both are predominantly yin, or both predominantly yang, tend to have a lot in common right from the get-go, and that's good for bonding. These partnerships can run into trouble over time, however, unless both people can also tap into differences between them to balance out each other's weaknesses as well as bolstering each other's strengths. Both partners need a strong ability to access their non-dominant trait—more so than in an opposites-attract relationship. Without that, they won't be able to support each other when the going gets rough.

Sex Again in Real Life: Laura and Adrian

Laura and Adrian made his-and-hers appointments at the clinic to deal with a range of health issues: PMS, painful periods, and migraines for her, and fatigue and neck and shoulder pain for him. They both had a litany of complaints about their marriage, too. No coincidence there!

Laura complained that Adrian had no get-up-and-go, and Adrian said Laura tended to nag. Laura felt Adrian's passivity backed her into a corner—like she always *had* to be the one initiating any kind of action or else "nothing would ever move forward in our lives." Adrian, for his part, felt disempowered by Laura—and reacted by retreating further into himself.

No surprise, this dynamic extended into their sex lives. They rarely had sex and were both happy to list the reasons: *Adrian doesn't try hard enough to give me an orgasm. He never starts anything anyway. It's always about sex when* Laura *wants to have sex. She is so hard to please, most of the time I prefer just to masturbate.*

To me the pattern was clear: As Laura was becoming increasingly yang (outward-looking, aggressive, initiating), Adrian was becoming more and more yin (inward, passive, receptive). With both of them at extremes, Adrian and Laura *had* struck a balance between them—but it was a rickety one, at best, because it was built between two unbalanced individuals. I explained to them that their current balancing act was the opposite of what it should be: They were finding balance by pushing further away from each other, rather than gathering each other toward the center.

To find a healthier balance between them, Laura and Adrian both had to begin by focusing on themselves. (That's true in any relationship, but for the two of them, this was also a way to nudge them toward taking responsibility for their own issues. They both reflexively pinned blame on their partner for whatever was going on in themselves, as well as in their relationship.) But I told them to notice how changes in themselves helped support their partner's changes.

I recommended herbs to both of them, to get qi moving, support yin/yang balance, and address their specific health issues. And we spoke about other ways they could each work on their internal balance. Laura decided to look for ways she could be more receptive in her day-to-day life—and not just at home. Adrian planned, in part, to practice being assertive—again, in all areas of his life.

As the weeks went on and both Laura and Adrian began to come back into balance physically and emotionally, their symptoms started to dissipate—and they could start to help each other balance in positive ways. Laura was having fewer headaches, and Adrian's muscle spasms eased. Adrian planned a few activities and projects for the two of them, and Laura had gone along gamely—*and* overlooked some chores left undone.

As their health and relationship improved, so did their sex life. Adrian initiated sex with Laura for the first time in *years*—as his yang built up, this was easier to do. And Laura, with her new focus on being receptive, gladly responded. Laura explained that she tried looking on the experience as an exchange of energy between them, instead of trying to get

Adrian to do things her way, and she discovered that by letting go in this way she had an orgasm almost without trying: "I always thought I had to work hard to come—or get Adrian to work hard. So I was pretty surprised it happened so easily when I *stopped* trying." With their yin and yang internally balanced, Laura and Adrian were able to shift the dynamic of the balance between them to a place that supported them both, rather than leaving both of them feeling precarious.

As their sex life picked up and became more satisfying, the last of their symptoms resolved. Not only had moving stagnation to create yin/yang balance made them more sexual, but being more sexual had moved more stagnation, improved balance, and made them healthier.

Signs of Imbalance

Relationships, just like people, display telltale signs of imbalance. When one partner is way too yin or way too yang, his or her imbalance will create imbalance in the relationship, and the imbalance in the relationship tends to create imbalance in the other partner, as that partner burns through energy, trying too hard to correct for the other person's extreme. Alternately when one partner gets out of whack, the other shuts down in response to the pressure to compensate. So while I've framed the "symptoms" below as the result of one person's imbalance, it's really about the pattern created by the subsequent chain reactions.

You're not going to see *all* of these in any one relationship (let us hope!), but several are likely to cluster together.

When one partner has too little yin (aka too much yang), sex tends to be:

- Disconnected
- Mismatched in how fast (or slow) partners become aroused
- Rushed
- Mismatched in how much each partner wants it
- Unsatisfying, or not emotionally supportive

And the relationship and/or the couple may:

- Lack intimacy
- Have a lot of conflict
- Be dominated by one partner
- Seem unsupportive
- Be full of anxiety, resentment, insensitivity, frustration, irritability, and/or neediness
- Be inflexible or uncompromising
- Be disorganized
- Lack good listening
- Not be emotionally expressive
- Have one partner neglecting their own needs, losing themselves in the relationship, giving more than they have to give, and the other partner feeling unmet
- Feature one partner using the other (or one partner *feeling* used)
- Lack empathy
- Struggle with commitment
- Experience aggression or even violence
- Be inflexible

When one partner has too little yang (aka too much yin), sex tends to:

- Slack off for lack of someone to initiate it
- Slack off for lack of interest
- Slack off due to tiredness
- Be slow to get going
- Be overly dependent

And the relationship and/or the couple may:

- Seem boring or unexciting
- Be rather rudderless
- Just run out of steam
- Find it hard to make changes
- Find it hard to adapt to change
- Be unsupportive
- Not be emotionally expressive
- Fall prey to brooding, gloom, hopelessness, passive-aggressiveness, worry, overthinking, withdrawal, secretiveness, distance, coldness, or feelings of rejection.
- Lack creativity
- Lack motivation or ambition
- Lack leadership, or only ever be led by one of the partners
- Be dominated by one partner
- Have trouble where one partner focuses too much on their own needs and the other feels taken advantage of
- Get overwhelmed
- Shut down
- Be too tired to deal
- Have trouble setting boundaries
- Be homebodies, or have a mismatch in how close to home the partners like to stay
- Neglect their appearances
- Divert effort away from the relationship and into something else, like a career or hobby

Is Your Relationship Stuck?

Qi stagnation can occur between people, too, as well as within individuals. And—this should come as no surprise—stuck qi between partners will undermine their yin/yang balance. Here's what that usually looks like:

- Poor communication
- Lack of connection
- Erratic behavior, alternating between being needy and nurturing
- Periods of just shutting down
- Dramatic arguments
- Suppressed emotion
- Periodic outbursts of emotion

FOR THE GUYS: Bringing Out Your Best

Balance is not just about picking up your partner's slack. It's not just about shoring up weaknesses. Sometimes partners inspire each other to be their best selves. Sometimes you simply find you are a better person in the presence of your partner. This is a powerful bond. Who doesn't want to be with a person who brings out your best? Who makes you feel like (and act like) the person you really want to be? Or who gives you the desire to actually be that person?

This feeling is one manifestation of yin/yang balance between two people. Being with someone with a complementary energy to your own may pull you a bit out of your natural comfort zone—but that doesn't mean it doesn't feel good. In fact, it may be a bit of a revelation—you know what you know about yourself, and then, bam!, with someone else in your life you may see a new side of yourself, and experience yourself as more dynamic than you realized you were. And all that might have remained undiscovered if the two of you hadn't crossed paths.

This is true for any two people in a relationship, but I think it sometimes hits men harder—especially men who are very yang and who, with a partner, find a way to tune into their yin. Getting a respite from the all-yang, all-the-time channel can be quite a relief. That moment when you look at another person and realize *this person makes me want to be better*—well, there's not much that beats that for emotional bonding. *And* for deepening a sexual connection.

That's right. If your sex life is in the doldrums, getting it back on track is not a matter of crazy underwear or an expensive vacation or anything else external to you two. Nothing wrong with a trip to Victoria's Secret, or Turks and Caicos, if you can pull it off, but what's *really* hot is using your bond with your partner to share and exchange your energy, shore each other up, and inspire each other to new heights—in and out of bed.

The Yin and Yang of Conflict

One of the great benefits of balancing the yin and yang of your relationship is the way that sets you up to handle conflict. All relationships face conflict. And it can be quite the passion-killer, in both the short and long term. But it doesn't have to be. Couples who learn how to deal with conflict actually increase their bond through handling it constructively and compassionately.

Conflict is inherent and inevitable in yin and yang. (Then again, so is coming together.) But it also triggers strong emotions. It may help to know that conflict is just another way energy moves between two people—and as energy in motion, it can be transformed. Conflict is one way to clear a space for something new to emerge. It may not always feel like it, but conflict is an opportunity for growth, within yourself and within your relationship.

Most people have a go-to response to conflict. People who are prone to yin deficiency tend to get agitated, while people who are prone to yang deficiency tend to withdraw. People who are prone to stagnant qi either bottle everything up—or vent rather explosively.

When partners are centered, within themselves and between the two of them, they can be calm in conflict, comfortable with their emotions (and their partner's), and respectful of the other person's position. They are able to prioritize finding a resolution over "being right." They are able to compromise. And when the conflict is over, they are able to move on, forgiving and forgetting. You might not feel very sexy right in the middle of a fight, but getting through it together might just put you in the mood. You know, makeup sex.

Sex Is Not Boring. But You May Be Doing Boring Things.

Now is a good time to remind you that yin and yang are in *dynamic* balance. It is ever changing; it'll be different today than it was yesterday, and different again tomorrow—unlike sex with a long-term partner, probably. For a lot of my patients, boredom is one of the big reasons they think they are not interested in sex. Many think of it as being bored with their partners, but what they describe is actually boredom with their sexual routine. This is the boredom of couples who have slid into going through the motions in their sexual relationship without focusing on their emotional—and energetic—connection. Likely, there's stuck qi involved—a very literal stagnation. I also notice this in patients who are yin deficient or otherwise yang dominant (or in relationships that are): Yang is structured and relatively rigid. If your sex life is, too, that can be a sign of yin deficiency—and a shortcut to boredom city.

Fortunately, this issue isn't really about the relationship, or the person you are in the relationship with, but about doing the same thing over and over again, with nothing new. This suggests a straightforward solution: *Change it up.*

You'll be glad to hear that yang is also responsible for making change. So even if thus far it has led you to being stuck in a rut, you can also use it to dig back out, by tapping into your natural energy in a slightly different way. You can use it to come up with something to freshen things up. Because let's face it: Even the most effective "technique" gets stale with overexposure over time.

Please don't think I'm suggesting stunt-sex or anything like that; there are plenty of ways for us mere mortals to spice things up without having to pretend we are porn stars or gymnasts. If you're up for something out there, by all means, go for it—whipped cream, blindfolds, whatever. But pretty much any change to the routine might be all you need. Have sex in the morning if you always have it at night. Try being on top if your partner always is. Kiss a part of your partner's body you usually overlook. Early on in your relationship, you likely tried lots of different things as you got to know each other's bodies. You can't get back the big "new and different" feeling of a new partner, but doing the things new partners do will go a long way to keeping things interesting.

I do want to add that sex is *not* a good way to escape from boredom in the relationship itself (apart from your sex life). Avoiding a problem is never a good idea in the long run; it is better to face it so you have a chance to resolve it. Anyway, sex that is an attempt to avoid boredom is bound to be unconnected sex that leaves you drained of energy rather than energized.

FOR THE GUYS: Porn

One surprising—and surprisingly common—source of loss of libido in men is use of pornography. And not just loss of libido: The latest research reveals heavy use of porn, and especially Internet porn, can cause ED—even (*especially*) in men young enough to be presumably *decades* away from that experience.

Pornography is not a problem in and of itself. How it is used often *is* a problem, however. When porn is used to create more connection, then it's fine in a relationship—even beneficial. More often than not, however, porn distracts from energetic connection.

The thing about looking at porn is: You don't get anything back from it. Yet sexual energy pours out of a person using porn. And most often there's no one there to receive that energy and shift it back to you. Using porn together—still depending on how, exactly, you use it—may be able to spark a couple's flame, and that's all to the good. But if they don't then transition to being with each other, rather than relating to a screen or unreal images, sex can't build their connection. In fact, both partners will *lose* sexual energy in the deal. That's no big deal every now and again, but if it becomes a regular routine, you're headed for trouble.

Using pornography on your own could help strike a balance in a relationship—if one partner desires more frequent sex than the other, or partners aren't available to each other over some period of time—or help you channel your sexual energy if you are not in a relationship. But it is a very fine line between that and the use of pornography in such a way that it creates separation between two people rather than connection.

Also, pornography has to shoulder much of the blame for the outsize expectations of sex our society has come to hold. Mainstream pornography is a purveyor exclusively of sex between young, chiseled people in every scenario except the ones played out in homes across this country every day. Not a lot of sales, I suppose, for videos like *Let's Have Sex If We Can Ever Get the Kids to Sleep* or *Household Chores as Foreplay* or *Let's Try a New Position. This One Hurts My Back.* It's easy to become desensitized to real human sexuality by the cartoon version presented in porn. I've heard guys describe heavy use of porn leading to their inability to be turned on by their actual partners—compounded by an aversion to efforts their partners make that strike them as porn inspired. It is a real challenge to overlap real life and porn just enough—but not too much.

So ask yourself: What are you looking to get out of using pornography? Are you getting what you really want? Is it a good way to get it? If your goal is just getting off, porn might well do the trick—if that is all you want. But patients often tell me they are watching porn to connect with their partners, or to stave off boredom. And they recognize that, however satisfying it is in the short term, porn is very repetitive—and therefore not a great antidote to boredom.

If you suspect you are using porn in a way that's interfering with your sex life, try this: Lay off the porn for two weeks and notice what effect that has on your libido and sexual satisfaction. In the meantime, do something connecting (lots of choices in upcoming chapters), *especially* if you feel any kind of void while on your porn fast.

Deciphering "Lack of Attraction"

Some people bored with their sexual experiences wrongly construe the feeling as lack of attraction to their partners. But lack of attraction is actually a somewhat different problem, with a somewhat different solution. You're not going to solve it by trying out a nifty new trick in bed. (And if you do, then it wasn't lack of attraction: It was boredom.)

"Lack of attraction" is also not always what it seems, however. Sometimes the underlying issue is really one of anger or resentment—and, in those cases, stuck qi. It might also be more about lack of *motivation* (and a yang deficiency) or lack of receptivity (and low yin). In all these cases it's not so much that the attraction is gone; it's more like something is hiding or blocking it. Most of the time, then, getting qi moving again, working back toward balance, and focusing on your compassionate and tender feelings for your partner will allow you to dig out and reconnect to the underlying attraction.

Consider this process a treasure hunt. None of us can claim the same visual charms we had when we were younger/thinner/less wrinkled. We have to move beyond fixating on this surface level so we can reach the deeper, more powerful stuff. In a mature relationship the sexual bond—and the attraction—are based on intimacy, caring, security, affection, shared experience, and mutual support . . . with a dash of "you look great!" in the mix. So if just one of those things drops out—if there are, say, several extra pounds of "looking great" to go around—there's still a lot of glue to keep the whole thing together.

Still, there may be items that bear discussing with your partner. Think about whatever way your partner has "let himself go" that's pulling on your attention, and what it says about him. Is he fine with it, or oblivious to it? Is he depressed, lacking in motivation, or dissatisfied with his life? Check in with yourself, too. Are you legitimately worried about your partner's health? Are you reflecting thoughts about your own body? Is this about your own self-esteem? Do you need your partner to look a certain way in order to feel good about yourself? Then talk to your partner. Be direct and nonjudgmental: "I love you and I want to be attracted to you, but your lack of care for your appearance is affecting our relationship and I want us to address that."

Sex and a Surge of Emotion

Sex can sometimes trigger a surge of emotion. (Actually, any intimate touch can.) This happens more often when the sex is good, when there's a connected, intimate space for strong emotions to flow safely.

The feelings released might be about your partner, or your relationship, or sex in general, or they may have nothing obvious to do with what is going on at the moment. The outburst might be related to feelings from the past, or it might be a response to current events in your life. Sometimes it's just an explosion of raw emotion, with no particular focus at all. It might not really surprise you, if you know you are in turmoil. But it can also come seemingly out of the blue. When you think about it, though, it's not all that surprising that an experience that can be intense, vulnerable, and emotional all on its own can stir up feelings of similar depth.

If you experience a surge of emotion like this, pause for a few slow deep breaths and allow the feelings to float by, as if they were clouds. If there's an area or technique that seems to have been a trigger for these emotions, you can leave it alone for now. (But don't preclude coming back to it some other time.) There's no benefit to "pushing through" something that doesn't feel good, whether physically or emotionally. Honor your body's responses by being gentle with yourself.

If you like, you can chat with a therapist about why, how, and when exactly these things come up. Chinese medicine explains it as sexual energy moving stuck qi, freeing up buried emotions. Either way, talking about it with *someone* is probably the best response. I nominate your partner as the listener of first resort. The key thing is to go ahead and have the feelings you are having. Experience them. Express them.

If you are the partner of someone who's had this kind of intensely emotional response to sex, here's what you do: Listen. Empathize, encourage, reassure. Pay attention. Show you care. As far as these emotions go: better out than in. Besides, it's pretty clear no one around here is getting any sex until this blows over! And that's just the way it should be—strong feelings like this need to be processed before you proceed. And once they are, picking up where you left off is probably just the ticket.

Doing something physical together that *isn't* sexual can often be helpful. Go to the gym together, attend a yoga class, learn how to kayak, spend time gardening, take a walk together every day. You may find you both feel better—and sexier—just by taking positive action and engaging in something new or challenging or invigorating or relaxing, *together,* even if no one's physical appearance really changes. You might get a similar charge by cooking healthful meals together, or by doing something else that nurtures you physically.

Dealing with Outside Attraction

The other way attraction causes problems between two people, of course, is when one of them is attracted to someone else. *Acting* on attraction to a new person when you are committed to someone else is a big screaming sign of imbalance within your primary relationship. (And probably within you.) But simply feeling an attraction isn't. Or, it doesn't have to be. Committing to one person does not mean you will only ever be attracted to one person. What it does mean is that you need to know what to do about it—what you want to do about it—when it happens. That's an important part of a healthy relationship.

The stakes are very high. Your whole relationship is on the line. And if you think it can be "only" about sex, you should know that when sex is "cheating," it is always draining rather than revitalizing. You squander your own energy when you scatter it widely. That steals from your primary relationship, of course: You have less energy to give it, as well as less for yourself. Sex with the new person won't be all it could be either, for the same reason: Some of your energy is withheld from it.

Seeking more than one partner at a time is often an attempt to cover up fear of true, deep intimacy with one person—real connection. Or even fear of really getting to know yourself. But guess what: Acting on the outside attraction won't fix imbalance or fear. It'll only create more problems—and/or push existing ones to extremes.

So you have to ask yourself: What needs am I trying to meet by looking outside my relationship? Be honest with yourself if there's something you are trying to avoid. Does the outside attraction represent freedom from routine and responsibility, for example? That's a really common one, but the people making the association often can't see it very clearly. It's worth looking closely. The next phase is to think of ways you could meet those needs on your own, and/or with your partner—and make a plan for making them happen.

If you've already acted on an outside attraction—or, if you have been cheated on—the essential questions are the same: Is this relationship destroyed, or is it bigger than this occurrence? Can we move on? Do I want to? What am I after? What can I do to fix the hurt? Am I playing the fool? Cheating is breaking a contract, and just as in business, when that happens, either the show is over—or you renegotiate.

"Renegotiating" may require help from a therapist or from another third party. Therapy may be the way to learn to process feelings of betrayal—and to decide if you want to forgive. One way or another you'll need not only to express your pain—but also to hear your partner's, even if he is the one who cheated. You'll need to know what he was thinking and trying to achieve by cheating. If the relationship is to heal, you'll need to make a plan for reestablishing the connection between you and your partner—and learning to trust it again. Cheating interrupts your energetic connection in a serious way, and both of you will have real work to do to build it back. It can be done, but not easily, not haphazardly, and not alone.

FOR THE GUYS: It's Never Just One Thing

For men, there's a lot of overlap between and among boredom, lack of attraction, and outside attraction or even cheating.

Typically, we're more strongly inclined toward wanderlust. Not that only we do it, and not that all of us do it. But, as a general guideline, men tend to have more yang energy, and yang energy moves outward. It's a mistake to try to ignore this. It's also a mistake to dwell on it. The thing to do is to acknowledge and address it. You might feel the urge, but you need to consciously decide what to do about it.

Boredom is often at the root of cheating and lack of attraction, for that matter. What I'm saying is: If you are feeling bored in your sexual relationship, you'll want to do something about it. Something *with your partner.* Be proactive. Come up with new things to do together. Set out to surprise your partner. (Not with anything really big—really big deserves advance discussion.) Recognize your strong suits, but don't rest on your laurels.

If you address any boredom you may be feeling, what you thought was lack of attraction might dissipate. You might also take a new look at your partner—using the "old" eyes you used to have for her or him when you first met. If you are committed to every other thing about this person and relationship, and keep your focus on the depth of your love, upon reflection "lack of attraction" might not even register as a problem. You have to consider the big picture and assign physical attraction its proper weight.

Don't get me wrong: Physical attraction is no small thing. It probably played a big part in bringing you two together in the first place, and it can certainly add a charge to your relationship in and out of the bedroom. But physical attraction doesn't *only* come from outward appearance. And some wrinkles or a bad hair day can't squash it in any relationship worth its salt.

Still, we are bombarded all day long with sexual imagery that probably doesn't much resemble our real-life partners. It's easy to get your idea about what is attractive pretty skewed, so don't beat yourself up about it. Then consider: Do you really want to get hung up about her belly flab when you're not exactly sporting six-pack abs yourself? Even more important, do you really want to get hung up about her belly flab when, given a few minutes, you can reel off so many great things about her?

Feeling you might cheat, or might like to cheat, does not mean you will cheat. But it does mean you should take action. If you feel like cheating, quick, before you open your mouth, or your zipper, consider: Why? You owe it to yourself and to your partner to figure out what's going on and how you can unravel it before you go too far. Take inventory of the costs *before* you do anything. That's your responsibility to your relationship. Why are you doing it (thinking about doing it)? What are you after? Is it worth it?

For most of my patients the answers have to do in large part with imbalance leading to a lack of deep connection to their partner. Or, with being out of balance themselves and turning to external experience to try to make themselves feel whole, or escape pain, or validate themselves.

Qi stagnation underlies most cases of cheating (or contemplated cheating)—energy is not flowing between partners well enough to sustain a strong connection. Typically anger and resentment, dammed up along with qi, are used to justify cheating. This weighs doubly on men who already tend toward stagnation/stress/frustration themselves. Men who tend to yang deficiency usually respond to thoughts of cheating by just sucking it up. Those who tend to excess yang are more likely to express those feelings some way.

What I hear most often from men struggling with the idea of cheating is that even with a lot of choices out there, and a lot of temptation, mostly they want to stick with the partner they have. The partner that has nurtured them. The partner they have already come so far with. Even if that's not what you think, cheating is never going to be the Right Path. But you can't go wrong working on nurturing your connection with your partner, improving communication, dealing with any boredom or lack of attraction, and focusing on what is really important. That will most likely put any thoughts of cheating from your mind, or keep them from lodging there in the first place. That is something you will never regret.

Wherever you are in the array of feelings of boredom, lack of attraction, outside attraction or cheating, here's how to put or keep the focus on nurturing your relationship:

Look to yourself first. Be honest with yourself about your end of the bargain, whatever it may be. You can't change your partner, but you can change you. (When you do, there's a good chance your partner will shift in response.)

Identify imbalance. Assess the yin and yang of your relationship, and any places it may be out of whack.

"Own" your judgments. Take responsibility for your views and expectations of a situation and reframe them, as necessary, to be about you. If you are thinking "My husband is a slob," shift to "I don't like an untidy bedroom." One way to maintain balance is to make sure you aren't stacking all the weight on one side.

Focus on what you love about your partner. List three things that you find attractive about your partner, and allow your attention to settle on those things. Practice having soft, nonjudgmental, and compassionate feelings about your partner's "flaws"—as you would want him to feel about yours. Resolve what you can, and let the rest go.

Communicate. Talk to your partner about what you need—and what he needs—and discuss ways you can create that together. Look for the balance between meeting someone else's needs and getting the love you want.

Trust your relationship to shift and change as necessary. The whole point of forming an energetic bond between two people is being able to rely on it this way.

Be a sounding board for your partner, in both senses of the word. Be there to receive his or her thoughts and emotions and help test and understand them. But also be the reflector who helps send the best of your partner out into the world in its most potent form. Both roles require a combination of yin and yang. When your partner does the same for you, you've found your balance.

Be choosy about what energy you allow yourself to absorb from your partner. As long as it is positive energy, go for it. But be cautious about any negative energy, unless you are in a place where you will be able to neutralize it, or even transform it into something positive. Doing so requires excellent balance and provides excellent support, but you should only take it on if you know you can handle it.

Put in the work. Issues won't resolve themselves. In any relationship there is work to do, and you have to show up for it if you want to resolve problems. You are part of creating the solution.

Meet in the middle. Somewhere between whatever territory you've staked out and whatever ground your partner is holding, there is a sweet spot that will be acceptable to both of you. Meet there. In Taoism this is called the Middle Way, and this kind of balance is central to Chinese philosophy.

Give yourselves credit when you are able to resolve conflict in a relationship: You now know your relationship can survive challenges and disagreements. Resolving conflict together builds trust.

Blow off steam when things get intense. Get some physical activity. Talk it out together. Spill to a friend, or a journal. Take a break to get some space, and perhaps some fresh air. Any or all of these things will help move qi so you can move toward balance.

Ask yourself if this is a conflict, or a calamity. "Catastrophizing" the event in your thoughts makes the conflict worse and harder to resolve, and makes the effects last longer. Don't overreact to your partner. Don't let whatever it is build inside you. Recognize the severity of the issue at hand. Deal with it, so a small thing won't grow into a big thing. If it is small, don't make it big. But do give big things the attention they deserve.

TO DO (IT) LIST: Connect and Balance with Your Partner

There are some quick tips and tricks you can use to help you balance and exchange energy with your partner in the moment—and when you build up enough of those moments you can construct something long lasting. Having sex is one of those ways, which should be no surprise to you by now. Have sex and you'll move qi and rebalance yin and yang between you, highlighting your connection. An experience of intimacy is especially powerful when circumstances are conspiring to pull you two apart, so there's no better time for sex than when the going is tough. (Caveat: Sex cannot take the place of working on what you need to work on. Also, it's not a good idea to have sex when you, your partner, or both are in extremely emotional states.) If you are still not ready to *just do it,* the suggestions below will help get you ready—or compound the benefits you accrue when you are ready to do it.

➜ **Make an effort** when it comes to your sex life. You don't have to go to the lengths you did when you didn't know this person was going to be in your bed each night. Not having to is one of the prime pleasures and privileges of a long-term relationship! But do try to please both of you with what you bring to bed—in your head or on your body.

➜ **Change things up** in your sexual routine. Anything, really. If you didn't do it the last few times you had sex, do it. If you always do it when you have sex, drop it out this time and see where that takes you. Perhaps try out a new position from Chapter 13.

➜ **Surprise your partner.** Many of my patients worry they will feel silly or self-conscious staging a sexual surprise of whatever kind, but their partners usually respond enthusiastically.

➜ **Practice any of the breathing, meditation, or massage exercises** you learned to do yourself—this time, with your partner (see Chapters 6 and 7). All will help you balance and exchange energy. Synchronize Your

Breathing (page 160) is an especially good choice for connection and balance.

➜ **Kiss.** When people feel bored in their sexual relationship, this is usually one of the first things to go. Or, could it be that we feel bored because we stopped kissing? In any case, Chapter 11 has plenty of suggestions to get you restarted.

➜ **Have a "quickie."** Often what feels like lack of attraction is actually a kind of sexual shutdown. A quickie can be a low-pressure way to get things started again. And assuming it is a change of pace for you, a quickie can combat boredom as well. Try it someplace other than the bedroom, if that's where you usually have sex. (See In Defense of "Quickies," page 199.)

➜ **Try Morning and Evening Meditation** (page 165) as a way of emphasizing connection. It is especially wonderful after there's been conflict.

11

Bringing Kissing Back, and a Lot More

The Lost Art of Foreplay

Whatever you do, do not skip this chapter. You'd be better off reading only this chapter and skipping the rest of the book! If you did that, I'd say you'd still stand a decent chance of restarting your libido with just what's here. (Though, of course, you will be better—and even happier—doing the stuff in this chapter when you understand the insights and strategies from elsewhere in this book!) You can't really overestimate the importance of foreplay—or the number of couples who have slid into sexual doldrums for lack of it. The same is pretty much true of kissing—kissing as its own activity, and kissing as a part of foreplay.

Kissing

Kissing is one of the first ways we connect sexually. It sets off intense physical and emotional reactions in the body. It decreases levels of the stress hormone cortisol. And it increases oxytocin, the bonding hormone. That's how, chemically speaking, kissing induces relaxation and builds connection.

Kissing creates closeness, both literally and emotionally. It's just about the most intimate thing you can do. The lips and tongue are exquisitely sensitive. Your lips, for example, have a thinner layer of skin than anywhere else on your body—and under that skin, more sensory neurons than almost anywhere else. Kissing is a sensual and sexual trigger: Kissing warms us up for sex.

Kissing is sexually arousing because it excites primarily yin energy, which moves downward from the mouth to the genitals. Kissing, especially tongue kissing, produces not only pleasure, but also a sense of attachment. What Western medicine ascribes to oxytocin, Chinese medicine attributes to the mouth and tongue being connected to the heart.

The ancient Taoists touted kissing as a way for two people to connect energetically, and a way to exchange qi. Kissing stimulates yang along with yin, harmonizing yin and yang by facilitating sharing between two people. The only way to do all this any better is through intercourse.

Yet while most intimate relationships begin with kissing, and lots of it, it is common for kissing to fall out of the repertoire over the long haul. I don't think it is any coincidence that relationships become less passionate when kissing falls by the wayside. The relationship loses vibrancy and fullness. The state of your "kissing life" is a pretty good representative of the state of your sex life.

I don't think it is any coincidence that relationships become less passionate when kissing falls by the wayside. That's why we're bringing kissing back.

That's why we're bringing kissing back. There's a list of tips below to help you step up your game, and a few exercises after that to give you some ways to practice. But you don't really need directions from me to get started on this, do you? Next time you are near your partner—maybe right now?—go ahead and plant one on him.

My recommendation is for a certain amount of kissing for kissing's sake. In other words, kissing that is not part of foreplay. That covers romantic kisses, affectionate kisses, comforting kisses, and all the rest. But it does also include deep, passionate kisses. In fact, a few minutes spent kissing is one of the things I recommend to patients who are having trouble having sex for one reason or another—especially people who feel too tired or too busy for sex.

Even if you don't fall into that category, kissing just to kiss can be a very enjoyable pastime. Remember "making out"? For many, many people their most passionate memories are about kissing, not sex. Those memories often come from a time before they were having sex, or before they were having sex with that partner. Even long after that particular bridge has been crossed, however, trying to recapture some of that feeling is an excellent goal. It's good for a couple to sometimes enjoy passionate kissing that *doesn't* lead to sex—even if you get to feeling like you really wish it would. Especially when you do, in fact: It's a little shot of that longing that probably used to be part of your relationship but may not be anymore. It generates heat! Kissing apart from sex, when it stirs up sexual feelings, also gives you a little more appreciation for the sex when you do finally go there.

My other recommendation is to make sure you do use kissing as part of not only foreplay but also any sexual activity. Long-term couples tend to drop kissing out of their sex life the same way they lose track of it in their everyday life together. Put it back on the menu!

Whether kissing is the appetizer or the main course, here are some ways to optimize the experience:

- **Use your hands.** Create a physical connection in addition to the one your lips are making. Where exactly you place your hands on your partner's body is not important—do what feels natural, what feels good. Try the shoulders, back of the neck, lower back, or face. This is not a complete list, and in any case should vary from time to time. And if those hands should roam a little while the lips are in action . . . well, happy trails!
- **Make eye contact.** Imagine you have to communicate what you are feeling with your eyes alone. Looking into each other's eyes may be

more of a prelude to a kiss than something you do the whole time you are in a lip-lock. Chinese medicine understands the high erotic potential of kissing this way: The eyes are related to the energetic pathway that surrounds the genitals. Western thought says the eyes are the windows to the soul. In either case, this is a connection you don't want to miss.

- **Have a heart-to-heart.** Here's a thing you probably haven't thought much about: Which way do you tilt your head when you kiss your partner? If you both tilt to your own left side, and lean into your embrace a little, your hearts will be touching. This is more than nice symbolism or sappy sentiment. This is a subtle but clear way to experience the deep connection between you, especially when you bring awareness to both your heartbeats. Which, by the way, will be elevated by kissing—if you are doing it right! (Studies show that most people tilt right, however, so you may have a bit of a habit to undo here.)
- **Relax your mouth and tongue.** You want to *use* the relevant muscles, but not tense them. You will enhance their sensitivity this way. And isn't relaxed what you'd want to encounter in your partner? In Chinese medicine, tension creates stagnation, and as we've discussed, stagnation will limit your sex drive—beginning with your enjoyment of kissing.
- **Vary pressure, speed, and technique.** One thing you *don't* want kissing to be is boring. Luckily all it takes to avoid that is a little variety. Pay attention to how your partner responds, and you'll know which things you should emphasize in any given moment.
- **Know what you're doing with your tongue.** Gently slide your tongue into your partner's mouth—then move it a little deeper. Besides lighting up all the many nerve endings inside the mouth, the idea is to stimulate the salivary glands, which are located under the tongue next to the back teeth. Saliva contains testosterone, and testosterone provides a jolt to the libido, so swapping spit is actually

key to activating your sex drive. Exchanging saliva may not be the sexiest way to think about kissing, but the ancient Taoists were way into it—without even knowing about the testosterone thing. We can leave the words *spit* or *saliva* out of it, but we do want a nice juicy kiss. The wetter the better—and it is deft use of the tongue that makes it happen.

FOR THE GUYS: Kiss Her

I know a lot of men are less interested in kissing than their female partners are. But it's a mistake to skip it, and I'll tell you why: If you want to have sex with a woman, the first thing you need is for her to want to have sex with you. Passionate kissing is an almost surefire way to turn her on. Western medicine might explain it as the presence of testosterone in the saliva you're sharing during a kiss—and testosterone boosts female libido. Or you can think about it this way: Kissing primarily stirs yin energy. And yin energy moves downward. When you kiss, that energy moves from the mouth on an express lane right toward the genitals. So kissing is sexually arousing for any yin-dominant person—which includes the majority of women.

Guys tend to be more yang and therefore more goal oriented and less enthusiastic about what seem like preliminaries. But take the time: Kissing triggers the release of the bonding hormone oxytocin—even more in men than in women. And by invigorating yin and calming yang, kissing makes both partners more open to each other. That's the connection thing—and that makes for good sex.

You'll probably find your enthusiasm for kissing increases once you are under way. Men don't usually "need" kissing to become aroused, like many women do, but they enjoy it when they are already turned on. Chinese medicine ascribes that to the fact that kissing also stimulates yang, and yang energy makes us feel like kissing.

Kissing isn't only an "on" switch for sex. You can use kissing in all kinds of other ways—and bring good things to your relationship with each of them, like intimacy, a sense of connection, and a balancing of yin and yang. But if kisses, from small and sweet to deep and passionate, do get you sex—everyone wins.

So work on restoring kissing to your relationship. It doesn't always have to be sexual, but the more you do it, the more naturally the sexual kissing will flow. Make kissing a part of every day, with everything from "Have a nice day" kisses to "Let's get naked" kisses. Lots of them.

DAILY KISSES

Kiss before you part in the morning. Kiss when you are back together at the end of the day. Kiss before going to bed. And those are just the minimum daily requirements! At least once a day make one a *real* kiss. Like you mean it. And lasting longer than, you know, it takes to *sneeze*. You don't have to spend all day on it, but luxuriate in what you're sharing for a few moments. Everyone, no matter how busy, has time for that.

UNEXPECTED KISSES

Kiss your partner when and where they least expect it. While you are cleaning up the dishes, or in the middle of a movie, or while waiting for the light to change. On the neck, or inside the elbow. A little element of surprise keeps things interesting. It also makes the point that you are often thinking about your partner. The accumulation of these little sparks between you helps keep the embers burning so that when the time comes, it doesn't take much to fan them into flames.

CHOCOLATE KISSES

Chocolate and kissing stimulate the mind and body in very similar ways—with chocolate actually producing the more intense and longer-lasting response. Both kissing and chocolate induce brain states that are alert yet relaxed—and decrease anxiety. Both rev up your heartbeat—in a good way. Chocolate has some unfair advantages, like the mental stimulants caffeine and theobromine and the serotonin-assisting tryptophan. Chocolate also provides a "natural high" thanks to the release of the dopamine that its sugar and fat content triggers in the brain.

But the chocolate feature I want you to take advantage of right now is the conveniently sexy way it melts at body temperature. Try taking a bite of chocolate and, with it melting in your mouth, kiss. Enjoy the silky smoothness, as well as the extra sensory stimulation. Or try passing a piece of chocolate back and forth with your partner while you kiss. Can't think of anything better to do with a Kiss!

KISSING LIKE YOU WANT TO BE KISSED

Take turns kissing each other the way you like to be kissed. Experiment with soft, gentle kisses, and deeper, more aggressive kisses, and so on. Learn what you like—and teach your partner!

I WANT TO KISS YOU ALL OVER

You can't go wrong with lip-to-lip kissing, but be sure to venture further afield as well. Ear nibbling and neck nuzzling are particularly popular outings. Remember all those erogenous zones you mapped out with the Exploring massage? Odds are they are even more responsive to attention from the lips and tongue. Set aside time to test this hypothesis together.

Foreplay

Foreplay gets qi to rise, which increases sexual energy and so precipitates desire. It's also the most common area that a couple's sex life seems to lack. If you could only address one thing, it is the single thing most likely to solve your whole problem. In other words, if you work on nothing else together, work on this.

A lot of people rush through foreplay, or essentially do without it, and this leads directly to specific sex problems, such as uncomfortable or even painful intercourse. It also means that couples miss out on a lot of the benefits of sex. Without good foreplay, sex is never going to be as pleasurable or satisfying as it could (should) be. Lack of foreplay is also a pretty reliable sign that there are some communication issues for the couple. And both those things make low libido more likely—poor sexual experiences do not exactly inspire one to want a lot more of the same.

Good foreplay makes sex a deeper and richer experience. It adds variety to the sexual experience. It builds intimacy, sensitivity, and openness. Good foreplay helps ensure orgasms for both partners—and more-intense orgasms at that—and reduces "pressure to perform" and the resulting performance anxiety. Foreplay helps bring mind and emotion into an equation that might otherwise be all about the physical body. Of course the other great benefit of foreplay is that it does prepare the physical body for intercourse; women's bodies, especially, are likely to really *need* foreplay to become fully aroused.

The ancient Taoists touted foreplay because it generates qi and harmonizes yin and yang, both within each partner and between two people. Foreplay calms yang (which is quick to arouse and so may be creating the feeling of wanting to plunge straight into intercourse) and nourishes yin (which is harder and slower to arouse). Yin takes longer to move to the pelvic area than does yang. Yin is what makes it possible for each partner to receive the energy that is exchanged during sex; without yin the sex won't be connected. In other words, the sex won't be *good.* Intercourse that begins too soon will have low levels of yin circulating; yin-dominant people are less likely to end up satisfied under these circumstances, and their partners will not get the maximum benefit of sex either, because the yin-dominant people will have less yin to give.

The key is to involve the whole body in foreplay, and to use all your senses.

It all works better when everyone just sloooooows down. Yin needs time to come into full effect. And yang won't go anywhere. Trust me, it'll wait.

In Chinese medicine, energy pathways, or meridians, run all over the body, so the key to moving sexual energy everywhere it needs to go is to involve the whole body in foreplay. This is also the recommended way

What You Already Know About Foreplay

Kissing is often the first way we connect with our partners. While kissing does not always lead to sex, sex very often begins with kissing. Kissing during sex, and foreplay, completes an energetic circuit between two people. To make the most of it during foreplay, you may want to brush up on your technique, along the lines described earlier in this chapter.

Many of the massage exercises, when done with a partner, can be used as foreplay, or as part of foreplay. In particular, you might want to try:

Exploring (page 129). **Partner Massage** (page 132)

to unstick stuck qi, which will make it easier to enjoy sex and easier for women to reach orgasm. Best to go ahead and invest in the kissing and stroking all over to help the qi flow. Pay special attention to the breasts because not one, not two, but *three* energy pathways run through them—in both men and women. That's good for both the receiver of the extra attention, and the giver; they are an easy place to stimulate the energy, and an easy place to drink it in.

Chinese medicine also dictates using all your senses as you go about getting your partner's qi in gear. Good foreplay uses eyes, ears, nose, tongue, and lips as well as hands. Awakening all your senses awakens all your body.

You've already heard the two most important rules of engagement: Foreplay should be a whole-body/five-senses affair. Here's what else to keep in mind:

- The Golden Rule of Foreplay: Do unto your partner as they would have done unto them. *Not,* in other words, what you'd like done to *you.*
- Allow plenty of time to spend on foreplay. Don't wait until the last minute to have sex, when you're already tired.
- Aim for variety; try to maintain a sense of surprise.

- Do what works—but branch out into techniques related to what you know works. That way you will add to your repertoire.
- Communicate! Good foreplay, like good sex, depends on it.
- Delay penetration as long as possible.
- Enjoy foreplay on its own terms. It may be an appetizer (though it doesn't have to be), but you should still savor it.

The directions to these exercises are fairly specific, so I do want to mention that if you have the urge to freestyle, go right ahead. Following the maps laid out here concentrates your efforts on your partner's energy pathways, which is an extra boon for both of you. But even more important is what your partner is feeling, and signaling to you, and what you are inspired to do. If it's lighting your partner up, you are obviously hitting the right places! So don't get hung up on exactly what to put where and when and how. On the other hand, if you are not brimming with ideas on just what to do to begin your sexual encounter, you can't go wrong following these to a T.

Sex Again in Real Life: Allie

Allie came into my office complaining that she had trouble achieving orgasm—and her attempts to do so were getting less and less frequent. After I listened to the details of her tale of woe, it seemed to me that Allie had stuck qi. As she described it, she was pretty disconnected from her partner, Joel, and her frustration with that was causing more stagnation, which made it harder still to get moving sexually.

My main suggestion was that she and Joel spend longer on foreplay. I advised Allie to talk to Joel about not moving on to intercourse until they were both sure she was fully aroused. Allie assured me that she and Joel hadn't been leaving out the foreplay—but also admitted it pretty much had all been genitally based. I encouraged her to discuss taking more time together before anyone's genitals were involved at all.

She asked for suggestions that might inspire Joel to branch out a bit to ensure that her whole body got stimulated and her sexual energy fully activated. I described Tease and Release (see below)—which layers some additional techniques on top of the genital stimulation they were already using—and she set out to recruit Joel's participation.

Allie was delighted with the results, happily reporting back about how easily she had an orgasm the very first time she and Joel tried it. She was even more excited about how much she enjoyed the entire sexual experience, and told me she was feeling her sexual desire again in a way she really hadn't lately. Even better, Joel was also enthusiastic about her enjoyment: "I've got the feeling we *both* can't wait to do it again!"

TEASE AND RELEASE

This is a good way to warm up the whole body and, as Chinese medicine would have it, get all the energy pathways of the body flowing.

First, imagine three levels of erogenous zones in the body. The primary zones: lips, breasts, nipples, genitals, and labia. Secondary zones: earlobes, nape of neck, small of the back, bottom, back of the knees, and the inside of the thighs. And the tertiary: palms, navel, edge of pinkie finger, nostril, anus, ear opening, soles of the feet, and big toe. If you haven't already done it, now's the time to get cracking with the Exploring exercise (page 129). With that under your belt you'll know which out of all these are best for you—and your partner—and you'll be able to focus, then, on the most pleasing areas.

You're going to begin with stimulating the secondary zones, then move to the primary, and finally to the tertiary. This makes sure foreplay begins somewhere other than the genitals—as the Taoists insisted upon. Once again, those old Taoists knew what they were doing! This gradually activates all the erogenous zones for a full-body experience. It provides a gradual buildup by teasing sexual energy without getting explicitly sexual at first, then releases it through direct sexual contact, then teases it again. Or, as the Taoists thought of it, this approach arouses sexual energy slowly (yin) and then releases a little (yang), and then arouses more.

As you approach each area, begin with a touch or kiss, then breathe or blow on it, then lick. Light strokes are best on the inside of the thighs.

In Defense of "Quickies"

Sometimes sex without foreplay, or a minimum of foreplay, is just the ticket. I know, I know, this comes in the middle of a whole chapter devoted to encouraging heaping helpings of foreplay. But "quickies" can be a way of connecting that takes the pressure off. That's why I sometimes suggest them to my patients who think they don't have the time or energy for sex. A quickie from time to time is one way to add variety and perhaps an element of surprise to your sex life, especially in long-term relationships. It can be a different kind of excitement.

Of course you need both people to be on board for it—one partner ready and one just going along without any enthusiasm for the project is definitely *not* what I'm recommending. Your best bet may be to suggest a quickie sometime when the mood strikes you—maybe you're already turned on, so getting lubricated isn't an issue. Or try planning to surprise your partner with the offer of a quickie. Plotting it out may mean it lacks a certain spontaneity for *you*, but it may also get your juices flowing.

The problem arises when quickies are all you ever do. If that's the case, then you're not so much having a fun or spontaneous or particularly randy quickie—you're just having bad sex.

Try circular strokes on the palms and navel. Don't get caught up in the particulars of techniques here, though; the point is to provide a mixed bag of stimulation, and to work out what you like best.

Take turns being "giver" and "receiver" in this exercise, and complete the whole thing one way before switching roles. If one partner is yin dominant, that partner may need or want to receive more foreplay, and that's OK. The time and attention devoted to each person needn't be equal—though it can be when that's how you both like it.

FOR THE GUYS: Why Men (Should) Care About Foreplay

I sense some eye rolling going on about all this foreplay stuff. We're men, and we have a deep, primal, genetic ability to go for straight-ahead *sex* that has very little to do with kissing, eye contact, or "connection" other than the most basic physical kind. It definitely doesn't include fifteen minutes of warm-ups!

I hear you. And I'll remind you that you also have a natural drive to bludgeon enemies into something unrecognizable, but you hardly ever decide to act on it. You know there's a better way.

So it's not that sex can never be quick-and-dirty (see In Defense of "Quickies"). In fact, sometimes it probably should be. Less connected sex can be very fun. It's just that that's not the only way. Or, shouldn't be. There's a balance to be struck between meaningful and meaningless sex. They are not mutually exclusive. But you should never mistake one for the other.

The difference usually begins with foreplay. There's a stereotype that men "fake" foreplay the way women fake orgasm. Let me just say I'm not a fan of either approach. Good foreplay is almost inseparable from good (connected) sex. And foreplay can and should be enjoyable in and of itself—for *you,* not just for your partner.

You're not going to get into it yourself, however, if your whole attitude is "gotta get her lubricated *some*how." You're right that if you want to have sex with a woman, you'd best bring at least a little foreplay to the table. But you're missing out if you do it grudgingly—and if you think it's something for women only. Make no mistake, though: If you stop faking it with the foreplay, she won't *need* to fake it with the orgasm.

Aside from that, you should know that foreplay can strengthen erections and increase endurance. That's thanks to the way foreplay stirs up yin energy to support the yang energy of arousal—yang which may be quick to leap to attention but then have a hard time sticking around if it doesn't get yin support. The balancing of yin and yang is one of the great benefits of foreplay. Investing that time up front is very yin, versus the all-out yang of heading straight to orgasm as quickly as possible. In the balance is where connection happens.

You should also know that when women are considering who is good in bed, *this is what they are thinking about.* They don't care nearly as much about size, or endurance, or whatever fancy thrusting technique you think you're impressing her with. Not that women don't appreciate all those things. It's just that foreplay is, quite simply, what turns a woman on.

Foreplay can help bring you into the moment and create that sense of connection—both when you are playing and when you are being played. And it should feel really, really good. (If it's not up to snuff in that area, it's up to you to teach your partner what *would* feel really, really good—and if necessary, do more research yourself to find out.) Sometimes women orgasm during foreplay, and that's all to the good. But men should try *not* to.

All that said, foreplay is about giving and receiving, and sometimes the receiving is more popular with women than it is with men. So while sex should just about always contain plenty of time for foreplay for a woman, your "turn" doesn't need to take as long (except when you want it to).

By now I hope I've sold you on the importance of foreplay. If you need or want some ideas on how to proceed from here, you might want to check out the guidelines and exercises in this chapter. Then feel free to improvise from there!

That's basically what Gus did. He came in for treatment, complaining of painful ribs. As I was taking his history, he did rather sheepishly bring up that he wasn't as "enthusiastic" about sex as he used to be. "My wife Julee wanted me to mention it," he said. "I don't think she's as into it as she used to be, either." I asked if either of them had any specific complaints about their sex life, and he said not really, his wife just said she usually felt rushed. A few more questions revealed that Gus and Julee didn't spend much time on foreplay, and she didn't always orgasm. And that, even setting aside sex, he didn't feel all that connected in his relationship these days.

My diagnosis was stuck qi and yin deficiency, which was causing both disconnection in his relationship and a hurried approach to sex. And, I thought, his rib pain as well. Gus admitted to drinking a bit too much alcohol on occasion, which, although probably an attempt to relieve symptoms of stagnation, was surely contributing to his yin deficiency. I not only recommended herbs and acupuncture—and moderation with the alcohol—but also suggested that he try just slowing down a bit—in life and in sex—to improve his health and support his relationship. Specifically, I "prescribed" fifteen minutes of foreplay every time he and his wife made love. He looked at me like I was nuts and blurted out, "What would we do for all that time?"

I encouraged him to ask Julee what she enjoyed, at which point I think he surprised himself with the realization that he'd never done that—or at least, not in a really long time. I also explained some of the strategies described in this chapter, which he agreed to try.

At his appointment six weeks later, Gus was eager to tell me about the changes in his sex life. (I had to ask him about his rib pain—which, he told me like it was an afterthought, had resolved.) All that foreplay felt a little strange at first, he said, but he quickly became a fan when he saw the results it got. His wife was having orgasms every time now, for one thing. And for another: They'd been having sex a lot more often ever since they tried this new plan. Julee was a lot more interested, and his enthusiasm grew right along with hers. He told me that at first the foreplay seemed like a bit of a chore, but now he actually looked forward to it.

But that wasn't what surprised him most about the whole experiment. "Everything seems better between us," he said, "not just the sex."

Spending time on foreplay was helping to emphasize the connection between Gus and Julee during sex, and that was carrying over into their life outside the bedroom. The sex—having increased in quantity and quality—was helping move Gus's stagnation, both physically and emotionally. And that, in turn, was ensuring happier and more fulfilling sex—and a happier, more fulfilling relationship.

HEAD TO TOE

This exercise is divided into two phases. The first covers the top half of the body and stimulates important energy pathways there. The second half covers the lower body and targets another set of pathways there. So really you're going to work head to groin, then feet to groin. This should be a leisurely process, taking up to twenty minutes altogether. For some women, this process will bring them to orgasm—though another, deeper orgasm may follow during intercourse afterward.

Embrace your partner, and with a free hand rub and press the vaginal opening and clitoris or, on a man, the perineum (area between anus and base of penis) with small circular motions. Meanwhile you're going to kiss, lick, and breathe on various body parts, working your way down one side of the body from head to genitals: eye, cheek, ear, mouth, neck, shoulder, and so on. At the chest, gently kiss the nipple and lick in a circular motion. Continue down over abdomen to the genitals—then take it from the top down the other side of the body.

For phase two, begin at one foot and move gradually back up to the genitals, kissing, licking, and breathing-on as you go. The Taoists describe specific points to stimulate (similar to acupuncture points), but it is not necessary to know them to make this exercise work. If you work the territory basically as described here, you will be hitting those points! Meanwhile, remember, one hand is still manipulating the genitals, as above.

In this exercise, too, partners take turns giving and receiving.

12

The Tip of Your Tongue

A Big Thumbs-up for Going Down

The Taoist sexologists were great proponents of oral sex as a powerful way to create energetic connection that was almost equal to intercourse. It often bests intercourse at increasing intimacy and trust. It's also a particularly effective way to balance yin and yang; performing and receiving oral sex tends to bring out whichever energy you are low in. Oral sex also helps pull sexual energy and desire—once it is aroused—down through the body to focus it in the genitals.

At a more basic level, oral sex is a great way to mix things up a bit. Having sex through activities other than intercourse is a key way to keep variety in your sex life, which is a key way to keep your libido humming along. Oral sex, specifically, provides an opportunity to revel in receiving, without the concurrent obligation to give. (The "69" position excepted.)

You can make oral sex your main course, or you can incorporate it in your foreplay. Either way, it's a simple enough thing to do: Stimulate your partner's genitals with your mouth. Bonus points for caressing other body parts while you are at it. If you are new to the sport, or in need of a refresher course or simply some new ideas to try out, you'll find some tips below. If either of you is uncomfortable at all with oral sex, begin by trying it for short periods of time, without the intention of reaching orgasm, and gradually lengthen the sessions over time.

Fellatio

Fellatio is Latin for *oral sex performed on a man,* from the word meaning "to suck." Yes, this is one of those rare activities where your highest aim should be to really suck at it. Here's how:

- Get comfortable. Try kneeling over him while he lies on his back, kneeling on a pillow between his knees while he sits on a chair, or kneeling in front of him while he's standing up.
- Men tend to respond to visual images, so keep in mind what he is looking at. Clear the sightlines so he has a good view of the action. Or maybe put on bright lipstick to emphasize the scene, if that excites him.
- Have some water or warm tea at hand so you can keep your mouth moist.
- Build tension by starting slowly, perhaps kissing the inner thighs and abdomen to begin with.
- When you're both ready (maybe a little while *after* he is!) take his penis in your mouth. Move up and down along it, varying pressure, speed, suction, and any other part of the technique you can change up. Lick it like a lollipop. Lick it like an ice-cream cone. Try humming at different pitches to create pleasing vibrations. Experiment.
- Use your hand to stroke his perineum, cup his testicles, or rub the shaft of the penis while your mouth focuses on the head. Try twisting your hand gently around the shaft as your mouth continues in an up-and-down motion. Or apply pressure with your hand. (Your hands are also useful in stopping his thrusting so it won't go uncomfortably far.)
- Get feedback—verbal and non-. If you like (or he does), ask him to guide your motions, or cue you verbally.

- Find a rhythm. Once you're in a good groove, stay consistent as he approaches orgasm. You can use your hands to give your mouth a little break from time to time, but right at the end is not a good time to switch techniques!

FOR THE GUYS: Reasons to Get a Blow Job (As If You Need Them)

I'm sure I don't have to sell you on the awesomeness of the blow job. What you might not realize is that getting one can improve your sexual performance. For a lot of guys, it's a welcome change of pace to have their partners be in the driver's seat for once. And it's a great way to relieve the pressure to perform.

The blow job was actually the way Kieran overcame ED. (Sometimes you just gotta do what you gotta do!) He'd been having trouble getting and keeping an erection during sex with his partner, and the more it happened, the more he got worked up about it—and the more it happened. Kieran's style was to rush into things, and sex was no different than anything else in his life. He felt a lot of pressure to perform. This fast and anxiety-producing approach was very yang, without enough counterbalancing yin to make it stable.

My advice, then, was for Kieran to nourish his yin. What better way than to do something that's completely receptive: Receive oral sex—and *only* receive. This was an ED "treatment" Kieran felt he could really get into! I'm sure his yin made great strides as a result. But Kieran also felt relief at not feeling he had to perform. He soon found that he could sustain an erection better during oral sex than during intercourse, and this went a long way to restoring his confidence, further relieving his performance anxiety. It wasn't long until the effect carried over into other, more mutual sexual activities with his partner.

Now if you want oral sex, here's your end of the bargain: Do your partner a favor (and make yourself an appealing target!)

by maintaining basic standards in the hygiene department. If you get any complaints that your semen tastes bitter, salty, or otherwise unpleasant, try cutting out alcohol for a week—it can make a dramatic change. (An "off" smell or taste that persists could be a sign of infection, so in that case, you should see your doctor.)

Also—and this is key—return the favor.

Cunnilingus

A surprising number of women are reticent about receiving oral sex. Let me just say: That is a big mistake. For one thing, most women who receive oral sex regularly—and well—love it. Why miss out? And oral sex is usually a more reliable way than intercourse for women to reach orgasm—and probably the best way for a nonorgasmic woman to learn to orgasm.

You do have to be able to relax into the experience, and if that is not second nature to you, it is well worth the effort to acquire the skill. Nourishing your yin is often helpful in improving your ability to receive anything at all—and that includes oral sex. Remaining non-goal oriented during sex, including oral sex, helps. So does anything that keeps you in the moment, or intent on the pleasurable sensations—focusing on your breathing, or letting go of extraneous thoughts as they cross your mind. Doing The Loop will help you feel the energy moving through your body as well as facilitating a "be here now" attitude.

Experiment with using oral sex as part of foreplay—or as the main course. Either way, it should not be the very *first* thing on the agenda—be sure to include some kind of warm-up first—kissing or massage, for example.

There are a few logistical things you should keep in mind about receiving oral sex, too. You can improve your partner's experience—and probably yours, too, since you won't be worrying about this—by practicing good basic hygiene. And, more surprisingly, by watching what you eat (and drink). Cut back on alcohol and caffeine, drink lots of water, and prioritize fruits and vegetables, and you'll ensure that the tastes and odors your partner experiences during oral sex are nothing more than the powerfully attractive pheromonal ones nature conveniently has in place to encourage sexual activity. Despite what you may think and what advertisers sell you, douching does not "keep you fresh." Douching kills off protective bacteria and will leave you susceptible to infection—as well as the unpleasant smell that comes with it.

Speaking of which: It is a good idea to be familiar with the scent of your own secretions. The best way is probably just to know what your hand smells like after masturbation. If you do notice an off odor that isn't going away, it could be a sign of infection, and you should see your doctor. For the same reason, if you notice an off odor in your partner, find a way to break it to him gently. He can find out if there is a problem—and you can look forward to a more pleasant next encounter!

Sex Again in Real Life: Chloe

Chloe had a problem some women *wish* they had: a husband who liked to go down on her. The charm was lost on Chloe, however. She said she never liked being the center of attention, and that during sex she was more comfortable giving than receiving. This made oral sex something of a point of contention between her and her husband, Daryl. She was fine with performing it. (This part, Daryl did not mind at all.) But when it came time to switch roles, she just felt unsettled and awkward lying there while her husband focused on giving her pleasure. Her attempts to avoid this situation had somehow morphed into avoiding sex altogether, which had been going on for long enough that Chloe had gotten sort of used to it—to the point where she said she thought she just wasn't interested in sex anymore.

Now, Chloe had not walked in the door of my office asking for help with oral sex. She'd come with a list of physical complaints that led me to diagnose yin deficiency—symptoms like her tendency to flush dramatically and her barely there menstrual flow. Chloe's yin deficiency manifested emotionally, too, I noted, as she described feeling restless and anxious. She also pled guilty to being resistant to change, reluctant to try new things, and, at times, rather inflexible—all of which can be traced back to yin deficiency. I explained that yin is what makes us receptive, and that yin deficiency can make us uneasy with receiving.

Chloe quickly connected the dots to her sex life, and her issue with oral sex in particular. I pointed out that enjoying oral sex would be a great way for her to nourish her yin—and a great way to revive her libido and her sex life. Nice work if you can get it! For Chloe, though, the trick would be to truly allow herself to receive.

At first Chloe begged off, saying she worried that Daryl didn't really like performing cunnilingus. But she eventually agreed to ask him and, if he really didn't mind, give it another go. (Spoiler alert!: Daryl reassured her that it was fun for him, too, explaining that, among other things, he drew pleasure from bringing her pleasure.) I suggested that Chloe ask Daryl to start with just a few minutes of oral sex, without her even thinking about if she would have an orgasm. That seemed more manageable to Chloe, so she gave it a whirl, and while Daryl was on board with this plan, Chloe herself still found it hard to focus during the deed. My advice was to try bringing her mind right back to the present moment each time she realized it had wandered—without any internal commentary about the fact of the wandering. Chloe decided to try focusing on her breath as a way of connecting herself back to her body, and the moment.

The next time I saw Chloe, two weeks after her last visit, she could hardly wait to report that she'd finally been able to just go with the experience—and even have an orgasm that way. To her surprise, she'd found she was now eager to keep trying! As time went on, Chloe noticed she felt more flexible, and more open in general, to new experiences or new ways of doing things. And she felt a greater sense of closeness and intimacy between her and Daryl.

FOR THE GUYS: Her Turn

I was thinking of calling this section "Performing Oral Sex: What's in It for You?" but decided that sounded a bit too self-centered. That doesn't mean there are not some very good answers to the question! The first is: She will feel great—and you'll get the credit. It's a sure-fire way to turn her on, and that's going to work out well for you. It also shows her that you care about her experience and her orgasm—which will definitely boost your rep. Receiving oral sex builds yin for her, just as it does for you, and a side benefit is more energy for her to share with you. Oral sex is an important way of balancing things up, too—when you are reciprocating, of course, but also as a way of exchanging yin and yang energy in general.

The "best practices" for going down on a woman are below, so I'm just going to add one overall tip about approach for men looking to be at the top of their game in this area: DON'T dive right in. Start slow. Explore. Play around. Try not to be goal oriented, or in a hurry. A lot of men feel a need to zero in on the target and get the job *done,* but let me assure you that simply isn't what most women have in mind. As always, if in doubt, ask her. As a matter of fact, ask even if you are not in doubt! Let her guide you and tell you what feels best.

Cunnilingus is Latin for *oral sex performed on a woman,* literally formed from the words meaning "vulva" and "lick." So the instructions are pretty much right there in the name. But here are a few more specific suggestions:

- **Get comfortable.** Find the position that will give her the most stimulation—and you no neck strain.
- **Remember the foreplay.** It's better to begin after she's relaxed and aroused. Here's a clue you're good to go: Her legs are free of tension and naturally separated, with the knees a bit bent.
- **Build anticipation.** Start slowly, kissing the inner thighs and abdomen, say. Even once you are at the vulva, take your time before turning your attention to the clitoris. Gently touch, kiss, and lick around the labia and entrance to the vagina first. Use your fingers to open the labia.
- **Stimulate the clitoris with your tongue.** For some women the tip is far too sensitive for direct contact, and you'll do better to stimulate the shaft, or to use indirect stimulation. Check in with her: Find out what she likes.

- **While your mouth is busy,** give your hands something to do. Some suggestions: stroke the perineum, massage the vagina, find the G-spot.
- **Vary the speed and pressure you are using,** as well as the area you are working on. You should also make use of the full range of tools: tip of the tongue, flat of the tongue, the whole mouth, and so on. Try forming the letters of the alphabet with your tongue, or making figure eights, or creating suction. When in doubt, slow is better than fast and soft is better than hard. Speed up or increase pressure only if she signals you to. Which brings us to:
- **Communicate.** Ask for her feedback—and keep an eye (and ear) out for the nonverbal feedback you'll be getting throughout.
- **Whatever she really likes, keep doing it.**
- **Be patient.** Sometimes it takes a while for a woman to climax this way.
- **Stop.** Once a woman has had a clitoral orgasm (or in some cases two), her clitoris tends to get hypersensitive, similar to the way the penis behaves after ejaculation. That's your signal to move on to other activities, like more foreplay, or intercourse.

13

Take a Position

The Top Ten Sexual Positions—and What to Do Once You're in Them

The most significant thing about having sex is the way it unites two people. The most significant thing about *how* you have sex may be the position in which you have it. The position you choose affects the flow of energy, within you and especially between you.

The Taoist sexology texts go on and on and *on* about sexual positions, and which ones are good for which organ systems and which ones activate which meridians, and which ones will lower your blood pressure or relieve your back pain or what have you. I am happy to report that unless you have a burning desire for the details—for which you will have to consult books other than this one—we can boil down all this great variety into three basic positions that will allow you to enliven your sex life, accommodate your own specific body and preferences (and your partner's), and, yes, reap the energetic, healing, and even spiritual benefits the ancient texts refer to.

The three basic positions are: one partner on top of the other, one partner behind the other, and side by side. Everything else—including the Top Ten list that follows—is a variation on these. The Taoists conceived of these in the context of a heterosexual couple having intercourse, but in essence they apply to same-sex couples as well, though a few commonsense adjustments may be called for here and there.

Having a variety of positions at your command adds fun and adventure to your sex life, and increases the pleasure, and benefits, of having sex. Different positions may feel different emotionally. For example, how much of your bodies are touching, and how open you need to be, and whether or not you can look each other in the eye, or whether you need to maintain or relinquish control can change the way a position affects you. Some positions require more energy to put into action than others, and some require more energy from one partner than the other. Some positions are better than others for some body types, or some combinations of bodies, or some physical issues. Some positions emphasize shallower or deeper thrusting; some are more conducive to female orgasm; some are better or worse for ED. Different positions are better for certain movements, angles, depths of penetration. Different positions create different sets of sensations. As always, add lube as necessary or desired.

There's no one Right Position. There's not even a Best Position for any given sexual encounter—and there's nothing wrong with changing positions in the middle of the action.

For example, intercourse with a man on top of a woman allows for stimulation of the clitoris with the man's pubic bone, and stimulation of the A-spot with deep thrusting (especially if she brings her legs up or puts a pillow under her bottom). A woman will have more control over the depth and speed of thrusting if she is on top, and more ability to stimulate sensitive areas. For some women this is the only position they can orgasm in. And for men, this position provides a chance to sit back and relax a little. A man entering a woman from the rear allows for deep thrusting and G-spot stimulation with the penis. Side by side (spooning) allows for sensuous, slow lovemaking with whole body contact.

All that said, there's no one Right Position. There's not even a Best Position for any given sexual encounter—and there's nothing wrong with changing positions in the middle of the action. The list below is not comprehensive, just suggestions, or starting points. What's important is for you to explore, experiment, and discover *what* works for you *when,* and *how.* The Top Ten is here to provide inspiration. Pick according to your preferences. Adapt to meet your own (and your partner's) needs and wants. Expand your repertoire. Make variety an important component of your sex life. Not that you have to do every single thing in this section, this chapter, or this book, and you certainly don't have to master them all, but I would recommend you try most of them. How else will you work out your favorites? Do whatever you have to do to not get stuck in a rut. At the same time, be sure not to forget about old favorites and proven winners.

The Top Ten

The Taoists gave animal names to the various positions, and while their reasons may not always be obvious to us today (just what did they know about actual dragon sex, anyway?), I rather like the playful note they add.

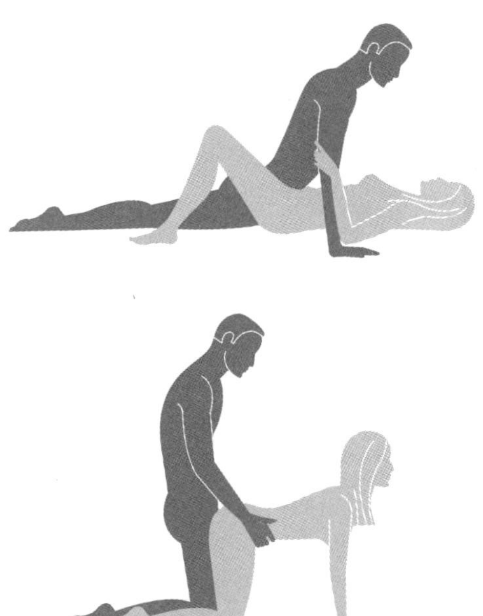

1 Dragon

Already familiar to you as the missionary position, this is where the woman lies on her back with her legs spread apart, and the man lies on top of her.

2 Tiger

Familiar as "doggy-style," this position has the woman on her hands and knees with the man entering from behind.

3 Monkey

In this position, the woman lies on her back with her legs raised and resting over the man's shoulders as he kneels in front of her to penetrate. Most of the movement should be done by the woman.

4 Cicada

Here the woman lies on her stomach, and the man lies on top of her to enter. This position allows only shallow penetration and tends to build anticipation. Arrange pillows as necessary to get comfortable; you may want to use them to raise the woman's bottom a little.

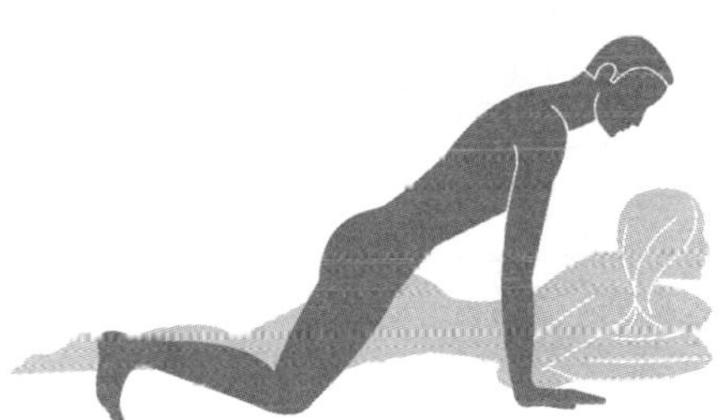

5 Turtle

The woman lies on her back with her legs raised and bent back, knees toward her breasts. The man is on his knees, penetrating from the front, with the woman doing most of the moving once he's in. The man can use the woman's legs to rub her breasts. This position requires more flexibility and coordination than some of the others, so it won't be for everyone. Try it if you like; if it's uncomfortable . . . stop! If it doesn't appeal, skip it and choose something else.

6 **Phoenix**

The woman lies on her back with her legs raised, and the man, on his knees, holds her legs in front of him as he penetrates from the front.

7 **Rabbit**

The man lies on his back, with the woman on her hands and knees over him, facing his feet. The woman does most of the moving.

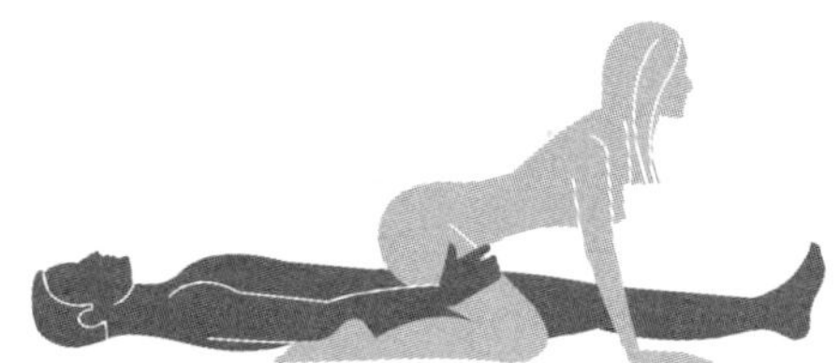

8 **Fish**

The man lies on his back and the woman lies on top of him, face-to-face. She does most of the moving. **Sideways Fish** is the man and the woman lying on their sides, facing each other. She raises one leg onto his side, and he supports the leg with his hand as they rock back and forth together.

9 Crane

The man sits on a chair, and the woman sits on his lap, facing him. She does most of the moving, but he helps move her hips and buttocks with his hands. You can also do this with the man sitting on the floor or bed.

10 Mandarin Ducks Joined

The man and the woman lie on their sides, the man behind the woman. She bends both legs and raises the upper one. He supports her raised leg with his upper leg, and enters from the rear.

Like and Unlike

Positions that match partner's body parts like against like (hand to hand, belly to belly . . .) are more relaxing and harmonizing, according to Taoist philosophy, while those that pair "unlike" (mouth to genitals, back to belly) are more stimulating and exciting. So you can choose (or shift) positions according to what your aims are. Keep in mind, however, that good sex most often involves a mixture of the two approaches. Perhaps that's one of the reasons for the popularity of the missionary/Dragon position: It simultaneously hits both aspects, with penis-in-vagina contact being unlike, and stimulating; and the matching up of other body parts being like, and more harmonizing.

OK, We're in Position. Now What?

With choosing a position, the variations have only just begun. Whatever position you're in, you want to continue to mix it up by way of speed, angle, depth, and style of penetration. Combined, of course, with a wide array of stroking, kissing, rubbing, blowing, licking, etc.

Many women leave control of the thrusting up to their male partners. How's that been working out for you? Allow me to suggest some strategies for doing your part to introduce variety to the proceedings.

The most obvious one is: Get on top. Now you're in the driver's seat. You control the angle of entry, the depth of penetration, and the speed. You set the rhythm—or the syncopation. Most often the woman-on-top kneels, but if you really want to play with angle of entry, try squatting instead, crouching over your partner with your feet flat on your bed, lowering yourself onto his penis. Kneeling or squatting, experiment with different actions, see what you like. Whatever techniques you develop up there, you can use in other positions. Here are some other things to consider, whatever the position:

- Shift the angle of your pelvis. Rock forward or back, or twist slightly to one side or the other.
- Vary the angle of your legs. Bent or straight? In the air or planted on the bed? (Some movements will affect the angle of your pelvis.)
- Use tension in your vaginal muscles, increasing and decreasing it, and using it at various points in the thrusting—when it is deep, or shallow, or on entry, or with withdrawal. Now's the time to show off your Squeeze-derived skills!
- Use your hands to change the depth of penetration—pull your partner into you, or, to keep it shallower, press against your partner's hips or groin, or place your fists between your pelvises.
- Stay still. When your partner takes the hint, together you can use pauses to build anticipation—or just to rest. Or to focus for a moment on the sensations you are experiencing.

FOR THE GUYS: Thrust

If you are like a lot of guys, you have basically a fast-and-deep autopilot setting in almost any position. That's a lot of intense stimulation (for you, anyway) and probably the fastest path to orgasm. But this is not a race, and you will both get more out of it—and therefore also get more—if you slow down (at least sometimes) and develop a bag of tricks to mix things up. You're basically playing with three things: speed, angle, and depth.

Speed is fairly self-explanatory. Your best strategy is to change it up from time to time, so your approach is not totally predictable. Start slow and pick up speed as you go along, perhaps. Even within the same in-and-out you might vary it: quick entry and slow withdrawal, for instance—or vice versa. You should also consider "pause" a speed. When in doubt, take it slow and steady. Most men err on the side of going too fast, especially at the beginning. Don't worry, if and when she wants you to pick up the pace, she'll let you know!

Angle is probably the most overlooked aspect of thrust, but also the most important for a woman's pleasure. If you're only and ever headed straight ahead, you are minimizing your chances of stimulating the interior of the vagina; different angles allow you to stimulate different areas—not to mention different parts of your penis. Angle upward and you can get the G-spot. Angle downward and you may be able to provide clitoral stimulation. Don't neglect side-to-side, though, for yet another set of sensations. Try swivelling your hips while thrusting, for a combination of angles. Or "stir" your penis around, using your hand rather than your hips to get the motion just right. These may not be the sensations moving either of you directly to orgasm, but by adding to the total variety of sensations you are intensifying the whole experience.

Depth is a favorite topic of the Taoist sexology texts, and different sages have different spins on the perfect ratio between shallow and deep thrusts, and the patterns in which they should be deployed. There are specific benefits at each depth. Shallow thrusts give the most stimulation to the most sensitive parts of the penis and vagina—the head and the vulva, respectively. They build excitement, especially in the woman. Deep thrusts stimulate the base of the penis, and the deeper inside portion of the vagina (which is more sensitive to pressure, whereas the outer portion is more sensitive to touch). Deep works best when the woman is already very aroused.

Does Size Matter?

This is where you are expecting me to say *no, the size of the penis doesn't matter* very reassuringly. But the truth is: It does matter. Whether too big or too small (and remembering that these are relative terms), the size of the penis can interfere with optimal pleasure for both partners.

I can still be very reassuring, however: Whatever the size, the issues that arise are entirely solvable.

If your partner's penis is "too big":

- Use positions that keep penetration shallower, and positions that give you control.
- Use plenty of lubricant. (Read labels to pick one with healthy ingredients—no petrolatum, no fragrance, no parabens; look for water-based rather than oil-based.)
- Take your time, and make sure you are fully relaxed and aroused before you begin intercourse.

If your partner's penis is "too small":

- Put a lot of emphasis on foreplay.
- Choose positions that optimize clitoral stimulation.
- Use The Squeeze—the actual squeeze portion—during intercourse.

With these tricks up your sleeve, it won't matter that size matters.

Angle, Depth, and Speed

As you and your partner experiment together with the three basic variables of thrust—angle, depth, and speed—here are a few techniques to throw in the mix:

- *The Thigh Master.* For this technique, the woman provides resistance to entry by keeping legs closed, initially, with tension in her thighs. The man slowly parts her legs as he enters, but the woman keeps tension, not letting go altogether, maintaining steady pressure. Don't try this until the woman is well lubricated.
- *Keep on Rocking.* This is a way to stimulate the clitoris during intercourse—without using your hands. In the missionary position, the man enters as far as he can while leaving his pubic bone resting on his partner's mons (the slightly raised pad of flesh just above the vaginal opening). Then both partners rock together, staying connected in this way.
- *Open Wide.* In this technique, either partner places their hands on either side of the vulva and gently pulls the labia apart as the man enters. The woman will need to keep her legs wide open, or raised, for this to work.

As always, communication is key to getting the most out of any or all of these variations. Find out what you like, find out what your partner likes, figure out how to maximize both. As with anything new, practice makes perfect. Don't expect this to be effortless right away; give yourselves permission to take some time to develop your technique. Some things you may need to build up to gradually.

Nine and Nine

The Taoist sexology texts contain a variety of instructions for using deep and shallow thrusts in alternating patterns, but I think one version is plenty to give you the general idea—and all the benefits. This particular gloss on the subject I learned from Dr. Stephen T. Chang's book, *The Tao of Sexology.* You can use this technique with many of the positions mentioned in this chapter (or whatever other ones you dream up), as long as it is one where deep thrusts are possible, and where the man has a sufficient amount of control over how deeply he penetrates. You can also combine Nine and Nine with The Squeeze (the during-intercourse version, see page 123); a woman can increase both her own and her male partner's pleasure by contracting during the deep strokes. Alternately, contract during the withdrawals, increasing friction and stimulation in that phase instead.

Chinese medicine considers shallow strokes yang and deep strokes yin, making this a particularly good way to balance yin and yang energy.

To begin, the man will insert only the head of his penis into the woman's vagina—nine times. Then the entire penis once. That completes one set of ten strokes. Next decrease the number of shallow strokes by one, and increase the number of deep strokes by one, and continue doing so for a total of nine sets. The full pattern looks like this:

nine shallow and one deep
eight shallow and two deep
seven shallow and three deep
six shallow and four deep
five shallow and five deep
four shallow and six deep
three shallow and seven deep
two shallow and eight deep
one shallow and nine deep

This alternates a feeling of being tantalized with a feeling of being satisfied, which is a highly pleasing combination for most women—and a good path to orgasm.

The pacing is up to the two of you, but in general slower is better. A lot of couples prefer slower entries and quicker departures.

Beginning with more shallow and moving on to deeper thrusts maximizes pleasure, especially for the woman. This alternates a feeling of being tantalized with a feeling of being satisfied, which is a highly pleasing combination for most women—and a good path to orgasm, even for women who haven't been able to orgasm during intercourse previously. Doing the Nine and Nine can speed up the path to orgasm for women, and/or heighten the orgasm experienced.

While the varying of strokes creates a sense of anticipation that intensifies the experience for most women, for men it tends to spread out the intensity, helping extend intercourse by delaying his orgasm. That's because the stimulation varies between targeting the head of the penis and the shaft. Stimulation of the entire penis increases desire to ejaculate; stimulation of the head of the penis alone decreases desire to ejaculate.

That said, one time through this whole exercise totals ninety strokes, and no matter how you spread out the area of stimulation, this can be a lot for many men. If you finish a set of nine without having an orgasm, feel free to do the whole thing over again. But if it's tricky getting all the way through, just do shorter sets, at least to begin with. Do sets of five, or four, say. Whatever works for you.

However many sets you are doing, try not to approach this too mechanically, or be too rigid about keeping count. If you do sevens twice in a row, or skip from eights to sixes, I promise, nothing bad will happen. And should you get halfway into this and both be overcome by an urge to abandon the pattern for all-out thrusting . . . go right ahead. You can always count sets another day.

Real Sex in Real Life: Sharona

Sharona had trouble achieving orgasm—until she and her husband, Javi, tried out Nine and Nine. The variation kept them engaged, together. Done slowly, this exercise built anticipation for Sharona, which made her clench her PC muscles, and kept her focus on her pelvic area, all of which increased her pleasure and hastened orgasm. It also moved Javi's focus just enough to delay his orgasm. So Sharona and Javi were on a more even pace toward orgasm, which helped free Sharona to aim for her own.

In Chinese medicine terms, this exercise moves more energy (qi) in and to the pelvic area, helping to unstick what is stagnant. Sharona took an herbal formula (Xiao Yao Wan, or Relaxed Wanderer) too, also designed to move qi, and smooth hormonal transitions (including arousal and orgasm). But as far as Sharona was concerned, it was Nine and Nine that kept her coming back for more.

Now you officially have no excuses left for lack of variety in your sex life. You don't *always* have to be doing something new, but there's also no reason to *always* do the same old, same old. As you audition these various approaches for a recurring role in your life, you should notice more than just spiced-up sex. You should notice increased *desire* for sex.

14

Peak Experience

Come When You Want To

I don't think the Taoists ever met a cycle they didn't like and so naturally saw sex, too, as a cycle. Of which orgasm, as the release of sexual tension, is the completion.

Orgasm feels great, obviously. It has some less obvious benefits as well: It relieves stress and tension, reduces pain, improves sleep, induces relaxation, pumps blood and qi through the pelvic region, rebalances hormones, and releases a flood of hormones that bond humans together, spur feelings of security and trust—and make you feel like cuddling. Which is to say, this is not a thing you want to miss out on. Or rush. It *is* a thing you want to optimize. Having orgasms—really good orgasms—is the main motivation of anyone's sex drive. You can boost your libido by improving your experience of orgasm. You can do this by just having them, if you haven't been. Or by having them more easily, more reliably, or more often. Or by prolonging or intensifying the ones you do have.

When the ancient Taoist texts talk about orgasm, they more often and most famously direct their instruction toward men. And when they do, they spend most of their time on the subject of *not* having orgasms—or so it can seem. (Really, they separate orgasm from ejaculation, and advise having the former without the latter.) They are very much in favor of the female orgasm, however, even if they don't give it near as much press, so I think we can all agree those sages are indeed very wise. Taking another page from their playbook, however, this chapter has even more info for men than for women—because the information for men is more complicated. Everybody benefits from orgasm, but not everybody gets there the same way.

Female Orgasm

An orgasm can be gentle or intense, fun or serious, forceful or mellow—as varied as women and their moods. It can be a solo or partnered activity. An orgasm can happen before, during, after—or instead of—intercourse. And any of those kinds of orgasms can be completely satisfying. But without orgasm, or without a "full" satisfying orgasm, sex can be frustrating, isolating, or otherwise unhappy, and leave you feeling let down, angry, sad, restless, or alienated. A sexual relationship that *sometimes* includes sex without orgasm for one partner is fine; where you run into trouble is when orgasm is desired but consistently lacking. A complete orgasm, one that is fully satisfying, brings pleasure to the whole body—and is noticeably energizing.

Where your mind goes, your qi follows. The trick is to have an intention for orgasm and focus on the sensations that will take you there.

The ancient Taoists identified nine stages of female orgasm. Here's the kicker: The one most of us are familiar with/aiming for is merely a stage four! So for those adventuresome enough, there are five more levels to be explored, taking you through multiple orgasms and spiritual peaks. I'd recommend setting your sights on having regular (meaning consistent, as well as "stage four") orgasms before you spend any energy searching for levels five through nine. Once you've got that squared away, you can decide if you are satisfied where you are (as many of us will be), or you want to continue your quest.

The Taoist sexologists also advocated for a woman having an orgasm before intercourse, believing more and better orgasms could then follow during intercourse. Even without that possibility, the preintercourse orgasm was preferred, because having gotten the orgasm out of the way, a woman would be able both to more completely lose herself in the spiritual experience of intercourse and to more fully connect with her partner during it. My advice, however, is not to worry much about whether it's before, during, or after—except to the degree that this is another way to incorporate variety into your sex life.

As for how to have those orgasms: Chinese medicine promotes the idea that where your mind goes, your qi follows. This one I'm totally on board with. To put it another way: Place your attention where you want your energy to go. This is a very helpful concept when it comes to achieving orgasm. A pro-orgasm mind-set is half the battle. The trick is to have an intention for orgasm, and a focus on sensations that will build to orgasm, without becoming fixated or obsessed to the exclusion of all the other wonderful things that are likely going on while you are having sex. Your mind can open a pathway for your energy to follow, and pouring your energy toward orgasm is a great way to have a great one. Where your mind is *not* helpful in having an orgasm is when it is either sending you negative messages (*I'll never orgasm* or *He doesn't know what he's doing* or *This is taking forever, he's going to give up*) or off on some other business altogether, planning tomorrow's to-do list or coming up with snappy comebacks you *should* have made, or what have you. Should you find one of these types of thoughts crossing your mind during sex, you have to do what you'd do during meditation—let it go. No judgment—that'll only get you further off track—just release it, and bring your mind back to where you want it to be: attending to your orgasm. It may help to focus on your breath, or the sensations in your body. It's a good situation in which to employ The Loop. Doing The Loop on its own (not during sex) is a good idea, too—it gives you practice with the kind of physical and mental focus that will help you achieve orgasm. The same goes for meditation in general.

TRY THIS TONIGHT: To the Edge and Back

This is an easy exercise to help you have an orgasm. If you reliably have orgasms, this exercise is good for building them up, taking you to higher heights.

It's a good idea to practice this on your own first, before trying it with a partner.

All you do is bring yourself right to the edge of orgasm, using whatever method you are in the mood for—then back off. Coast for a few moments, until you feel you are back to more like halfway there, then go back to the brink . . . and back off again. Come close to coming about three times before you finally let yourself go over.

Some suggestions for pulling back:

- Pause. Just stop what you're doing for a minute.
- Change the stimulation. Adjust to something else that feels good but isn't moving you toward the edge.
- Take a deep breath. At orgasm you automatically go into short, shallow breaths. If you breathe short and shallow, you will hasten rather than forestall orgasm. If you start breathing short and shallow on automatic pilot, you are on the edge and now is a good time to put on the brakes. Right now. And taking big, slow, deep breaths for a few moments will create a little space between you and the edge.
- Do The Loop to move energy away from your pelvis.
- Relax the muscles in your pelvis—sort of an anti-Squeeze. The best way to learn to do this is to do a Squeeze contraction, and then release it and pay attention to how it feels to relax.

In fact, to the same degree relaxing those muscles delays orgasm, tightening them prolongs and enhances it. So when you are ready to come, do The Squeeze and the effects of going to the edge and back will be even more intense. You should also try tilting your pelvis slightly so your back arches a little.

FOR THE GUYS: Why You Want Her to Come

Make no mistake: You want your partner to orgasm. Frequent and fully satisfying orgasms will boost her libido, and you are going to benefit from that nearly as much as she is.

But there's something else in it for you, too: When a woman orgasms, that's a big release of yin energy . . . and it's headed right at you. The better her orgasm, the more energy you get. This is one of the key ways sex functions to balance yin and yang—in you, as well as in your partner, and in the relationship. Just one more reason to add to the list of why you should care about your partner's orgasm almost as much as your own.

Exercises specifically for improving orgasm follow, but I'm starting with a few basic tips and tricks you can use to make reaching orgasm easier:

- **Keep your socks on.** You are 30 percent more likely to experience orgasm if your feet are warm. Dutch scientists at the University of Groningen have done the study to prove it, but Chinese medicine has known all along that cold feet mean poor circulation—and poor circulation makes it harder to orgasm. If slipper socks aren't your idea of sexy lingerie, there is a more romantic option: Start things off with a foot massage.
- **Try Zestra Arousal Oil,** a natural product containing herbs and vitamins to help warm and bring blood to the genitals. Many of my patients have had very good results with it.
- **Start with a warm-up exercise.** Once you are ready for penetration, try the Around-the-Clock: Lie flat on your back and have your partner penetrate as deeply as possible—then stay still. Rotate your pelvis clockwise several times—for as long as you like, then switch to counterclockwise for a while. And so on. This is a great way to rev up slowly, with emphasis on highlighting genital sensation.

- **Do Nine and Nine** (see page 221) once you are warmed up. It's a good way to help keep your mind focused on your genital sensations. It also helps you learn to let go and enjoy the ride.
- **Do The Squeeze.** Tensing those muscles increases blood flow to the area and heightens arousal. If your partner is in the area, he will thank you, too.
- **Focus.** Having an orgasm requires you to be present in your own body and focused on the sensations you are experiencing and the connection you are creating. If you find that extraneous thoughts are intruding on your experience, you've already taken the first step to resolving the problem: noticing you are getting distracted. Next, imagine any extraneous thought encased in a bubble—and let it float away. The Loop is always good. So is just feeling your breath and your body.
- **Synchronize your breathing.** Matching your inhalations and exhalations will keep you and your partner in the same rhythm, and help bring you to the same level of arousal. If one of you is ahead of the other, matching your breath can bring you together again.

FOR THE GUYS: To the Edge and Back

This exercise is essentially the same in practice for men as it is for women—approach orgasm, back off, re-approach—but the point of the whole thing is inverted: For men, the idea is not to encourage orgasm, but to put it off a bit. For everybody the payoff is the same: intensified orgasms.

The trick to this is to really tune in to the sensations in your body, so you know for sure when you are at the last moment before ejaculation. What does it feel like when ejaculation is inevitable? What does it feel like just *before* that?

It's a good idea to practice this on your own first. But you can also do it with a partner, during intercourse (or not), once you have a little experience under your belt.

All you do is bring yourself right to the edge of ejaculation, using whatever method you are in the mood for—then back off. When you are just learning, try stopping a little bit further back from the edge, and gradually build up to stopping right at the edge. Most of the advice for women on cooling off a bit holds for you, too (see above). With some tweaks (see following). One big difference:

- In men, doing The Squeeze contractions helps forestall orgasm.

And one key addition:

- Pressing The Point (see page 233) will pull you back from the edge.

As for the tweaks:

- Pause when you need to pause. In or out, or partway, doesn't matter. Should you lose your erection, don't worry: If you got one in the first place, you can be confident it will come back when you resume stimulation.
- You don't *have* to just stop. You can change the stimulation you're getting to something that won't move you so quickly to ejaculation. Move more slowly or more shallowly. Or change angles, or make circular motions rather than in-and-out thrusting.
- Pay attention to your breathing. Remember to breath deep to slow yourself down. And that if you are already breathing short and shallow, you will be swimming against the current to stop ejaculation now and may have to really work on big, deep breaths for a few moments.
- When relaxing the muscles in your pelvis, it is the ones around the penis you most want to target.

You can use any or all of these, alone or in combination.

When you feel you are back to approximately halfway to orgasm, you can get back to business . . . until it is time to back off again. Back off two or three times before letting yourself go over the edge. (And not more times than that, because you could desensitize yourself a bit if you go on too long.)

FOR THE GUYS: The Squeeze, The Loop, the Three Locks, and The Point

Male orgasm is at the very center of Taoist sexual philosophy. Specifically, the aim is to orgasm without ejaculating. These "holdbacks" are as famous as Taoist sexology gets. So let me emphasize right up front about this approach: I'm not a big fan.

At least, not for most of us. I don't question the positive effects attributed to suppressing ejaculation to retain qi. It's just that to really master the technique takes serious dedication to a spiritual and philosophical quest that is, I think, beyond what most of us are going to do in real life. And *semi* doing it is not only not going to help, but it may actually cause harm—starting with creating stagnation and running the risk of "blue balls." It's likely to be frustrating enough to put you right off sex. And I wouldn't want to see all of the accessible, useful things the Taoist texts have to offer tarred with the same brush.

Still, there's a lot to gain from some of the techniques used to prevent ejaculation. The techniques can help you better control ejaculation, preventing premature ejaculation or extending intercourse as long as you like. They can strengthen your erections. They can build intimacy between partners, increase pleasure for both partners, and make orgasm a full-body experience. For all these reasons and more, practicing these techniques will improve your sex drive right along with your sex life.

You already know about three of the most powerful techniques used in holdbacks: The Squeeze (see page 124), The Loop (see page 61), and the Three Locks (see page 109). The fourth is The Point (see next page). In essence, devotees of holdbacks do The Squeeze and the Three Locks at the moment just before ejaculation, and then The Loop, to draw energy away from the pelvis and upward and recycle it (rather than let it go out with the semen). At least that's what they do after years of serious practice. This is believed to strengthen, energize, and heal the body, and achieve for the practitioner a heightened spiritual state. And, not for nothing, extend orgasm—until they last up to five minutes each!—and make a man multiorgasmic. With this kind of holdback, a man experiences orgasm, but doesn't ejaculate—and retains his erection, so he can go back for more of the same.

With the use of The Point, precise pressure can stop ejaculation without stopping orgasm, but the erection will be gone after orgasm, meaning the multiple-orgasm thing is pretty much out. That's why the Taoists consider use of The Point to be for beginners: Advanced practitioners of holdbacks eventually learn to reverse ejaculation with just The Squeeze contractions, thereby maintaining their erections.

For most men, living out here in the real world, we're not talking about using these techniques to stop ejaculation altogether. What we are talking about is using these techniques to basically delay or control ejaculation—so it happens when you (and your partner) want it to—and to lengthen and intensify orgasm. My advice is to experiment with using The Squeeze, The Loop, and The Point as ejaculation approaches, to find what works for you and what you, and your partner, enjoy or find useful. This is one of those times you will probably want to practice solo before trying it out with a partner.

The Point, as I'm calling it, is an acupuncture point located halfway between the anus and the scrotum (the perineum); you'll feel a slight hollow. Press firmly on it *just* before you are going to ejaculate—if you want to prevent (at least temporarily) ejaculation while experiencing (or building toward) a powerful orgasm. You might want to start out using three fingers, to increase the chances you'll get the right point, until you get more intimately familiar with the territory. Take several slow, deep breaths as you press.

This works by inhibiting the contractions that move semen through the urethra for ejaculation, slowing the rate at which the prostate empties, so it extends orgasm, as well as intensifying it. Or, as the Taoists would have it: It interrupts energy flow to the penis, sends qi up the body, and helps balance yin and yang.

It's best to learn to work The Point on your own at first, but when you are ready, go ahead and press it during intercourse. Then show your partner how to press it for you. You might also want to arrange a signal for *when* you want her to press it. Most men find it feels even better to have someone else press this point than it does when they do it themselves.

Also for when you are practiced up a bit: You may want to use Squeeze contractions while the point is pressed. Your prostate will thank you, and I think you will find it to be quite an enjoyable (and effective) bit of multitasking.

Owning your ability to orgasm when you want to is the final component of a satisfying sex life—and a strong foundation for an active libido. Women might view this ability from a different standpoint than men, but the effect on our experience of sex, and our desire for sex, is the same: It's all upside.

FOR THE GUYS: Steven Gets The Point

Steven came to see me when he (and his wife, Kath) became sufficiently frustrated by his premature ejaculation. His interview revealed him to be a classic case of stuck qi, overworked and stressed, and trying to drink his way out of it. When I pointed out that his nightly drinks were only making the PE worse, he agreed to cut it out—and to try acupuncture and herbs to treat stress and stagnation instead. I also suggested several exercises from the ancient Taoist texts (the ones we're calling The Squeeze, The Loop, and The Point). Steve protested because he'd heard a bit about Taoist sexology and was dead set against giving up ejaculation. But I explained that the Taoist "holdback" techniques could be used to hold back ejaculation *temporarily* (rather than retaining semen indefinitely), which is pretty much the definition of PE therapy.

Steven started out doing The Squeeze daily for a week, strengthening his PC muscles to the point where they could help control ejaculation. For the next week, he added in a daily Loop (solo version), which I explained he could deploy to reabsorb the energy behind ejaculation, to save it for when he needed it. Finally, he found and practiced pressing The Point. During the time he was learning and practicing these techniques on his own, I suggested he focus carefully on his own sensations during sex with Kath, so he could clearly identify the point just *before* he would ejaculate.

From there he moved on to doing The Squeeze during sex, and then The Squeeze with a Loop, and finally, The Point—first pressing it himself, and ultimately teaching Kath to press it.

As he became better tuned in to the signals from his own body, and the stronger his PC muscles got, the better control Steven developed over when he ejaculated. Within four weeks he was confident of lasting longer when he and Kath had sex. And this despite his resistance to anything having to do with his "energy." "I thought The Loop was some weird visualization, but when I tried it I could actually feel the energy going up to my head," he told me. He found the technique so powerful, in fact, that eventually he didn't need pressure on The Point anymore, but would just *think* about drawing energy up from his perineum to his head when he wanted to last longer.

15

Sex in Six

Six Weeks to Wanting Sex Again

The Sex in Six plan is focused on getting you comfortable with a core set of practices and exercises—and helping you fit them all into your life. By the end of the six weeks, you should have mastered the techniques you need to recharge your libido and your sex life—and feel confident you'll be able to draw on them as necessary going forward. No matter your age or the length of your dry spell.

Most of all, by the end of the sixth week, you should feel your own sexual energy again, your desire—and be ready, willing, and able to act on it. That's because these techniques sharpen your skills, expand your repertoire, improve sexual satisfaction, and deepen intimacy. With them, you can be sure that when you have sex, it will be good sex—and that you'll want to be having sex.

The best prep for success with Sex in Six is to have your own house in order before you begin this with your partner. If you've followed the advice in Chapter 5 as you read through this book, you should be good to go. If you want to, you can tackle this all at once, so after the standard Sex in Six plan, there's a "combination" plan that shows you how. Obviously, it's going to require a little more time and energy from you each week, but if you are up for a faster-paced, somewhat more advanced challenge, that's the path for you. There's also a bare-bones "Quick-Start" program if you feel you only need a little nudge to get things going again—or if you'd rather just go ahead and jump in the deep end first, get good and wet, and refine your strokes later.

You'll get your best, most complete results from finishing this program in six weeks. But of course life intervenes sometimes, and you'll take some time off because one of you is ill, or traveling, or because you don't want to have sex during your period, or you otherwise get sidetracked. And that's no big deal—just pick up again where you left off as soon as you can. You might also find that you just need some more time to complete everything that's called for in one week, and in that case it is far better to go ahead and take the time you need to fit in everything than it is to omit something. Finally, sometimes you may just feel you need longer to really get a handle on the week's activities, and then you should definitely keep at it until you're satisfied you're ready to move on to the next step.

Whether you run start to finish in six weeks flat or you need to revise the time frame to fit your life, do be sure to do *something* every day. If you've got the flu, or had to pull an all-nighter for work, you can still do the simplest things, like Take a Breath. In fact, you might really need Take a Breath in situations like that! If your partner's away at a conference, you can still be doing your own Loop, even if you're "scheduled" to be doing one together. Even if you never get a moment to yourself, literally, you can Think About It, or do the parts of The Squeeze that are acceptable in public—no one has to know but you.

Several parts of this plan you can tuck into your day wherever you can grab a spare moment—Take a Breath whenever you are stressed, Think About It while stuck in traffic, kiss your partner as you pass on the stairs, and so on. In fact, unpredictably sprinkling this stuff into your life is a good thing. But you should carve out a protected time each day to work this program, so you can be sure of doing what you have to do. If you schedule just five minutes a day—maybe first thing in the morning, or just before bed?—you'll be able to accomplish many of your assignments. And in most cases, five minutes twice a day should be enough to cover it. Some days, of course, you'll need longer, because I definitely do not want to hear of anyone completing a partner massage in a five-minute window! Should you end up with five minutes you've set aside for this but have no particular assignment, do something anyway. Maybe a new breathing exercise. Or try Exploring, but just one small area of your body (without neglecting a full-body version at some other time). Simply synchronize your breathing for a little while. Or offer your partner a minimassage—maybe just their hands, or neck?

One more note: You can/should keep having sex with your partner throughout this program. There's no need to abstain just because the week's plan does not call for sex. If you are not having sex often enough for this issue to have occurred to you, don't worry—follow the plan and you soon will be.

Three to Get Ready

A little preparation goes a long way when it comes to working the Sex in Six plan to full advantage. For most of the sexercises there are a few common elements to a successful experience. You need to prepare your body, your mind, and your surroundings. The particulars of how you do that will be up to you and your partner, keeping in mind three goals:

1. Get comfortable

2. Relax

3. Focus

The main idea is to create the best environment for creating connection. Whichever way you approach it, your ultimate goal is to get both partners centered, present in the moment, with an intention to fully share in the experience together. Both people need to be fully engaged, and ready to both give and receive. Holding your attention here, fostering the spirit of connection, focusing on yourselves *and* each other—that's what the getting ready is all about. Whether getting ready means tidying up, or shaving your legs, or leaving a little love note, or contemplating asking your partner to try this new thing . . .

The path to this state is formed of different bricks for different people—maybe putting on some soft music, or maybe arranging for sleepovers for the kids. Maybe putting away the laundry and taking a hot bath, maybe picking out some lingerie and taking an afternoon nap so you'll have energy for a late-night encounter. Maybe having wine with dinner, maybe stopping after one glass.

> ***Your ultimate goal is to get both partners centered, present in the moment, with an intention to fully share in the experience together.***

You need to eliminate distractions so no one's sidetracked by *It's too cold in here* or *How's my breath?* or *Geez, look at all that paperwork.* You also need to do the things you need to do to help you focus on what you are trying to do. Set yourself up for success: Schedule some time just for this, and don't make it for when either or both of you predictably has low energy. If you're not having sex because by the time you fall into bed at night you are totally exhausted . . . then perhaps it is time to figure out if you can manage a lunchtime rendezvous now and then, or experiment with setting the alarm back a little for some early morning action. If there are kids in your household, make whatever arrangements you need to ensure your time is undisturbed. Sitters who take the kids to their house are good. So are door locks, and firm early bedtimes for younger kids. And springing for movie tickets for older ones.

Taking care of your body may mean having extra pillows and bedding on hand, for temperature control and physical comfort and support as necessary. It definitely means good personal hygiene! It may mean eating lightly beforehand—you don't want to be distracted by feeling uncomfortably full, or by rumbling stomachs. Dinner dates are probably one of the most common mistakes people make when aiming for romance. Most of us do much better if we make sex the appetizer rather than the dessert!

You want to prepare mentally, too. A long-term goal for improving your sex life is to improve your mental and emotional health. You want to get yourself in a good frame of mind before you begin any of this stuff.

If you have emotions you need to recognize, or stress you need to diffuse, do it before you begin. Try a breathing exercise or relaxation technique or just taking a few slow, deep breaths. Perhaps do some physical exercise, or take a quick shower. Or talk it out with your partner—or another confidante before you meet up with your partner—or jot down your worries in a journal. Whatever will help you shift away from whatever might be weighing you down in the moment. Then combine that with some things to tap into your positive emotions and sexual energy. Pay your partner a compliment, or do something else nice for your partner (don't wait for when you want to get busy to do this—but an extra one when you're in the mood, or want to be, is always a good idea!). Spiff yourself up if you enjoy that (or think your partner would).

As with so many things in these chapters, the difference between success (connected sex) and failure (unconnected sex, or no sex) has a lot to do with your attitude and intention. Putting on a CD to spark shared memories, increase relaxation, bring a smile to your partner's face, or otherwise generally enhance the mood is a great idea. If your plan is to occupy yourself with something to listen to until this is over with—not so great. You can spend time "warming up" by ridding your body of all traces of hair not found atop your head, and if that makes you feel sexy and at home in your own body, or if you use the process to entertain thoughts of what is to come, you'll be on your way to good sex. If it's about answering a demand from your partner (actual or perceived), or motivated by a feeling that sex is "dirty" and can be cleaned up this way, or an attempt to live up to some Hollywood image, you're headed for trouble. The Taoists would say that where your mind goes, your qi (including your sexual qi) will follow. So send your mind where you want your energy to go.

Also remember that while marking the calendar, lighting candles, putting on perfume, and sending the kids to grandma's might be a great way to start off a roll in the hay with your partner, those same steps could create a nice space for you to practice a meditation, or have that long talk you've been meaning to have, or to give each other massages with nothing else on the menu this particular time. All those things will be good for your connection, your relationship, and your sex life, too.

The Sex in Six Program

WEEK 1

Kissing (page 188)
Synchronize Your Breathing (page 160)

- Start with Daily Kisses and Unexpected Kisses (also daily!), and when you are ready, incorporate whatever of the other kissing exercises or "tips and tricks" appeal to you both.
- Practice Synchronize Your Breathing at least once over the course of a week.

WEEK 2

The Loop, a variation for two (page 116)
The Squeeze, a variation for two (page 123)
Morning and Evening Meditation (page 165)

- Continue with kissing (daily) and Synchronize Your Breathing (at least once).
- Teach your partner The Loop and The Squeeze, if he hasn't already learned them on his own. Then practice each simultaneously at least once—or do them in combination, at the same time as your partner does. Or, try The Squeeze variation where your partner provides massage while you handle the squeezes—then switch roles. If you want to be really efficient: combine The Loop with Synchronize Your Breathing (variation 3 on The Loop, page 116).
- Also do Morning and Evening Meditation at least once. It also makes a nice combination with Synchronize Your Breathing, if you like. You'll knock off two assignments and also get more bang for your buck!

WEEK 3

Exploring (partner version) (page 131)
Partner Massage (page 132)

- Continue with kissing (daily), and a partners' Loop and full Squeeze (at least one time).

- Do the Exploring exercise together at least once with each of you guiding your partner. (Be sure to share what you've learned doing your own Exploring.)
- Do Partner Massage at least once, too, with each of you getting a chance to both give and receive. If you need to, take two weeks to accomplish both Exploring and Partner Massage for both of you—following this plan should never be allowed to create more stress. But if you can manage it, set aside the time—you'll have yourselves quite a weekend!

WEEK 4

Foreplay (page 194)
Nine and Nine (page 221)

- Continue kissing (daily).
- Your project this week is to have sex with your partner at least once—and good foreplay is mandatory. Use what you learned from Exploring and Partner Massage, or use any of the tips, techniques, or exercises from Chapter 11 that appeal to you both. Synchronized breathing makes a nice prelude to foreplay. Once you move on to intercourse, do Nine and Nine. Or save Nine and Nine for another encounter this week. Once again, the no-added-stress policy applies: If you need to, stretch this phase out for up to two weeks and have sex at least twice, once focusing on foreplay, and once incorporating Nine and Nine.

WEEK 5

The Squeeze and/or The Loop during sex (pages 117, 123, 162)
Try something new

- Continue kissing (daily).
- Your week's assignment is to use The Squeeze and The Loop during sex at least once. And also to try something new during sex. Yes, sex twice this week. Or, layer something else new on top of trying The Squeeze and The Loop during sex, if you think you won't have time for more than once. Remember, no stressing over following this plan. You could also stretch this phase out to two weeks. Your new thing doesn't have to be anything "out there," or anything you've *never* done before—something

that hasn't been in regular rotation would be fine. Perhaps something from the Top Ten list of positions, or oral sex, or To the Edge and Back during sex, or (if it qualifies as something out of the ordinary) a "quickie."

WEEK 6

Qi-exchanging exercise
Yin-nourishing exercise for two
Yang-boosting exercise for two

- Continue kissing (daily).
- And have sex again. At least twice. When you do, it should involve an activity specifically chosen to shore up the pair of you where you most need it. And everybody could always use a bit of shoring up, even in the strongest relationships. Yin/yang balance is a moving target in any case. And a little fine-tuning never hurt anyone—though *lack* of fine-tuning has! So consider the yin/yang balance in your relationship, and the state of your qi exchange, and choose a sexercise or two or three to target any weak spots. As always, take longer than a week if you need to.

Appendix 2 has a full list of exercises and what they are good for, but here are the main choices for couples during sex:

To Exchange Qi

Quickie (page 199)
Cunnilingus (giving) (page 209)
Fellatio (giving) (page 205)
The Top Ten (page 214)
Keep on Rocking (page 221)

To Nourish Yin

Cunnilingus (receiving) (page 207)
Dragon (for women) (page 214)
Monkey (for women) (page 215)
Cicada (for women) (page 215)
Phoenix (for women) (page 216)

Fish (for women) (page 216)
Mandarin Ducks Joined (for women) (page 217)
Keep on Rocking (page 221)
Open Wide (page 221)

To Boost Yang

Quickie (page 199)
Fellatio (receiving) (page 206)
Dragon (for women) (page 214)
Tiger (for women) (page 214)
Turtle (for women) (page 215)
Rabbit (for women) (page 216)
Fish (for women) (page 216)
Crane (for women) (page 217)
The Thigh Master (page 221)

Quick Start Plan

The absolute fastest way to begin recharging your libido is with the following five select practices. Done daily (well, maybe not *daily* in the case of foreplay), they will start reconnecting you to your sexual energy—feeling it within yourself, and feeling the desire to share it with your partner. You will improve your results and your technique with the full six-week program, but you don't have to wait until you are ready to commit to that whole thing before you give key strategies a try:

The Loop (page 61)
The Squeeze (page 85)
Think About It (page 34)
Kissing (Chapter 11)
Foreplay (Chapter 11)

Sex in Six Combination Plan

This schedule gets you up to speed with solo strategies and couples' assignments at the same time, if you are ready for that kind of stepped-up commitment and intensity.

Every week—every day, in fact—you should do Think About It (page 34) and Take a Breath (page 25), as well as Daily Kisses and Unexpected Kisses (page 193). Then layer in the other exercises as follows (some exercises have shifted to a new order in the interests of making the personal and couples' plans work together):

WEEK 1

2x/week: *Synchronize Your Breathing* (page 160)

WEEK 2

4x/week: *The Loop* OR *The Squeeze* OR *The Loop* AND *The Squeeze* (pages 61, 85, or 98)

1x/week: *Exploring (solo)* (page 129)
Synchronize Your Breathing (page 160)
Morning and Evening Meditation (page 165)

WEEK 3

3-4x/week: *The Loop for couples* (page 116)
OR *The Squeeze for couples* (page 123)
OR *a combination* (page 162)

1 -2x/week: *Choose your own solo exercise* (above)

1x/week: *Exploring (with partner)* (page 131)
Partner Massage (page 132)

WEEK 4

3x/week: *The Loop (solo or couple)* (page 61 or 116)
The Squeeze (solo or couple) (page 85 or 123)
Buddha Belly (page 78)
Opening the Senses (page 54)

1x/week: *Foreplay* (page 194)
Nine and Nine (page 221)

WEEK 5

1-2x/week: *Progressive Relaxation* (page 108)
The Loop (solo or couple) (page 61 or 116)
The Squeeze (solo or couple) (pages 85 or 123)

1x/week: *The Squeeze* AND/OR *The Loop during sex* (pages 117, 123, or 162)
Try something new

WEEK 6

1-2x/week: *Masturbate with The Squeeze, The Loop* AND/OR *To The Edge and Back* (pages 142, 146, or 228)
Choose your own couples exercise

FOR THE GUYS: The Yin and Yang of the Top Ten

The Top Ten, which all serve to move qi in anyone, tend to affect men and women differently when it comes to yin and yang. For men, here's one way to choose what you'd like to try out:

To Nourish Yin:	To Boost Yang:
Turtle	Dragon
Rabbit	Tiger
Fish	Monkey
Crane	Cicada
	Phoenix
	Mandarin Ducks Joined

part **four**

Troubleshooting

16

Health and Sexual Health

Physical Roadblocks to a Healthy Libido—and How to Get Around Them

This chapter covers two kinds of physical problems that can interfere with your sex life and libido. First up is problems that are specifically sexual—in medical jargon, sexual dysfunctions. In the second part of the chapter are the subtler issues—health problems that may cause sexual issues without you realizing it. You probably know if you have allergies or heart disease, for example, but you might not know those conditions may well be what's behind your difficulty getting aroused or having an orgasm.

No one needs to read every entry in this chapter. My recommendation is to look through for the topics that apply to you, and focus on those sections. Everybody, though, ought to read down the list of problematic medications (page 270) in case you recognize anything you are taking.

Overcoming Dysfunction

Low libido is often the result of basic sexual dysfunction—the inability to enjoy sex, usually due to physical or psychological factors that inhibit sexual responsiveness. The good news is that much of what falls into this category (like painful sex, lack of arousal, or lack of orgasm) can be handled at home. In some cases, you should also consult with a doctor and/or a Chinese medicine practitioner. Even then, however, the DIY stuff will still apply, and help you rebound that much more easily. The key is to aim to deal with any underlying issues, not just the symptoms. Pull it out by the roots!

You may also need a Plan B, however, if it is something you can't eliminate, and that plan is: Learn to manage it. In pretty much every instance, that is going to involve relying on a loving and trusting relationship, and good communication with your partner about what feels good and what doesn't, what works for you and what doesn't. It does *not* include not having sex. There is always a way. And often, when you find that way, you also find that having sex actually helps correct the original problem.

The following are some of the most common sexual issues.

DYSPAREUNIA, OR PAIN DURING SEX

In women, pain during sex is commonly caused by endometriosis or fibroids, infection, anatomical structure, vaginal dryness, or psychological factors. Chinese medicine usually considers dyspareunia to be a result of stagnant qi (and poor blood circulation) in the pelvic area, though it can also be associated with being yin deficient.

- **Treat any underlying conditions** (mentioned above).
- **Reduce vaginal dryness.** Following the advice in Chapter 3 about boosting yin will be helpful—especially the advice on lubricants—as well as the advice in that chapter and this one (Medications and Their Sexual Side Effects, page 270) on medications that cause vaginal dryness.
- **Follow the advice for moving qi** (page 42) if your pain is caused by anything other than vaginal dryness.
- **Consider Chinese medical treatment.** Acupuncture is good for pain relief in general, including pelvic pain of all types, and can address many of the underlying causes of dyspareunia. An herbal formula can be specially tailored to your condition as well.

- **Longer foreplay** helps stimulate your natural lubrication, and you may reduce or eliminate your pain by delaying penetration until you feel fully aroused.
- **Change position.** Being on top, where you have more control, is often the ticket.
- **Try desensitization therapy**—vaginal relaxation exercises that can decrease pain. A therapist who specializes in sexual dysfunction can provide pelvic floor exercises or other specific techniques to reduce pain during intercourse. This is a good option when the pain is of unknown origin and your doctor has ruled out specific physical problems.

VAGINISMUS

Vaginismus is a recurrent spasm of the outer vagina—an involuntary contraction of muscle near the entrance—that makes intercourse painful or even impossible. Western medicine considers some cases physiological and some psychological. Chinese medicine looks at all cases as a sign of qi stagnation in the vaginal area, or as yin deficiency causing inflammation in the vaginal area and/or in the body as a whole.

- **Seek professional help**—emotional therapy, sexual therapy, and/or medical treatment. The best choice depends on the cause of the vaginismus. Medical treatment is needed for vaginismus after gynecological surgery, for example. If the vaginismus is due to previous psychological trauma, talk therapy is appropriate.
- **Use a vaginal dilator** to help gradually and painlessly loosen the contraction, if your doctor recommends it. You can try something similar on your own, using your (or your partner's) fingers, and lube, after foreplay.

ANORGASMIA

Anorgasmia is the medical term describing a woman who has regular difficulty reaching orgasm after ample sexual stimulation, to an extent that it causes personal distress. In other words, if you are not having orgasms, or if it takes a lot of work to reach orgasm, *but you don't care,* you *don't* have anorgasmia. Inability to orgasm affects at least one in five women around the world. The cause may be psychological, neurological, vascular, or hormonal. It can also be caused by medications, recreational drugs, or alcohol. It may appear in a woman who can orgasm during masturbation but cannot do so with a partner.

- **Follow the advice for qi stagnation** in Chapter 2. From the Chinese medicine perspective, problems with orgasm occur when blood and qi aren't flowing.
- **Layer in the advice on improving your ability to orgasm** from Chapter 8.

FOR THE GUYS: Male Sexual Dysfunction

Men's experience of sexual dysfunction is distinctly male, as you might expect, given the difference between men's and women's anatomy.

DYSPAREUNIA

If you experience pain during sex, you can probably blame infection (like a UTI—urinary tract infection), inflammation (as from prostatitis), muscular problems (such as pelvic floor dysfunction), or anatomy (as with Peyronie's disease, or a tight foreskin). Or, yin deficiency or qi stagnation. There's a variation on the theme, too, known as post-ejaculatory pain syndrome, caused by stagnation or, in Western terms, by pelvic floor spasm.

- **Identify and treat any underlying condition,** like infection.
- **Consult your doctor about possible changes to medication** if you suspect something you are taking could be involved. (See page 270.)

- **Find a position that works for you.**
- **Delay penetration until your partner is fully aroused.**
- **Review advice for yin deficiency** (page 68) . . .
- **. . . and advice for qi stagnation** (page 38).
- **Consider Chinese medical treatment.**

DELAYED (OR INHIBITED) EJACULATION

Delayed (or inhibited) ejaculation, or DE, is a "condition" you have only if it is troubling you (or your partner): being unable to ejaculate with sexual stimulation with a partner—either in intercourse or manually. Or it's a problem only if you are taking longer to ejaculate than you or your partner would like. (The Taoists put much emphasis on achieving orgasm *without* ejaculating, so I want to be clear here that delayed ejaculation *is not the same thing.* Unless avoiding ejaculation is your primary intention and you are fully committed to the spiritual practices that will help you attain that, taking too long to ejaculate—or being unable to ejaculate—is a problem to be solved, not a goal.)

- **Consult your doctor about possible changes to medications.** The most common physical factor I see in DE is, in fact, a medication side effect. Usually the culprit is an SSRI or tricyclic antidepressant (see page 271), though antiseizure medications can cause it as well.
- **Stay in the moment.** Focus on giving and receiving pleasure, without worrying about whether or when you will ejaculate.
- **Consider abstaining from intercourse for a while,** gradually working on ejaculation through other types of stimulation before coming back around to intercourse.
- **Perform daily pelvic floor exercises** like The Squeeze to help with ejaculation by bringing blood to the area (page 124). But in this situation, do *not* do The Squeeze during sex.
- **Do The Twist** (page 259). Ironically, the same thing that can help premature ejaculation can help here, too. And for the

same reason: holding your focus. For men who have trouble reaching orgasm, distraction is usually part of the problem. Because this position is slightly awkward, it will help you keep your focus and prevent your mind from wandering.

- **Reflect on your attitude** toward sexuality to discover if you are harboring ideas about sex being shameful or sinful—they could be disrupting your sex life. You may be able to do this on your own, perhaps with the help of a journal, or a trusted friend, or you may benefit from seeing a therapist to talk this through.
- **Enhance your relationship** with your partner, and the emotional intimacy between you, and you may remove the roadblocks to satisfying sex. Focus on what attracts you about your partner (sexually and not), your history of satisfying sex, and the strengths of your relationship. Sometimes we get sidetracked looking at the things that rub us the wrong way, and it blinds us to what we love.
- **Follow the advice for yang deficiency** (page 88).
- **Follow the advice for stuck qi** (page 38).

ERECTILE DYSFUNCTION (ED)

Erectile dysfunction (ED) is difficulty achieving or maintaining an erection. It affects ten to fifteen million American men, and at least three-quarters of those men are under sixty-five. According to Chinese medicine, it takes yang energy to have and maintain an erection, so this is a problem that crops up in people with yang deficiency. Maintaining an erection also requires good blood flow, so ED often occurs in people with stuck qi.

Western medicine says many cases are primarily physiological in nature, most commonly coexisting with heart disease, atherosclerosis (clogged blood vessels), high blood pressure, diabetes, obesity, fatigue, Parkinson's, multiple sclerosis, low testosterone levels, Peyronie's disease, or development of scar tissue inside the penis. Treatments for prostate cancer or enlarged prostate may be culprits, as can any surgery or injury affecting the pelvic area or spinal cord. Certain prescription medications can cause it, as can use of tobacco in any form, or alcoholism or other substance abuse (see pages 270, 256, and 261).

ED that happens consistently, or comes out of the blue, is particularly likely to have a physical cause. In any case, your first step in handling it should be to consult with your doctor about it, to look for any physiological cause.

- **Don't stop!** Men experiencing ED often avoid sex to spare themselves embarrassment, but studies show that's only going to make the situation worse. The more sex you have, the more oxygen is available to reach the penis, resulting in firmer erections. You may have to rethink how you "do" sex, at least for a while, to focus on connection and giving and receiving pleasure in ways that don't require an erection.
- **Get good sleep.** And plan on having sex at a time when you are not tired. Fatigue makes ED worse.
- **Avoid alcohol,** especially before sex.
- **Limit your consumption** of animal fats, sugar, and junk food.
- **Lose weight** if you are overweight.
- **Take an essential fatty acid supplement** to support your nervous system and prostate and increase blood flow.
- **Balance your yin and yang.** See advice in Chapters 3 and 4.
- **Move your qi.** See advice in Chapter 2.
- **Practice The Squeeze and other "holdback" techniques** (see Chapter 14) to help draw qi and yang into your genitals.
- **Take time to "warm up" with nongenital stimulation.**
- **Work on expressing your emotions** if you have stuck qi.
- **Eliminate porn from your regular repertoire.** Regular use of porn can interfere with your ability to focus on connection with your partner. It also draws energy out—but none comes back in.

- **Consult your doctor about possible changes in medication.** Some men experience ED from taking statins to lower cholesterol levels. Less widespread is the same side effect from epilepsy medications.
- **Stop smoking.** Smoking impairs circulation, which impairs erections.
- **Practice one of the following three exercises every day:**
    1. **Underwater.** In a warm bath—alone—begin to masturbate, all the while being careful not to ejaculate. When the penis is fully erect, firmly hold, squeeze, and pull the testicles. Repeat this exercise as many times as you can while the water is still warm, and repeat the whole process regularly over time. The manipulation of the testicles stimulates hormone secretion (as well as sperm production, if you're interested in that), which boosts the strength and duration of erections. The water pressure lends a hand. You can try this in the shower as well, if you don't have time for a bath.
    2. **Back and Forth.** Stand, sit, or lie in a position that allows the testicles to hang freely. Rub the palms of your hands together to warm them, then cup the scrotum with one hand while rubbing the lower abdomen with the other. Rub back and forth at least a hundred times in total. As you are doing so, inhale deeply and then hold your breath. Contract your anus, perineum, and butt muscles. Release when you need to. Then rub your hands together again to generate more heat, and switch to using the other hand to rub with. This increases circulation and stimulates hormones—and, from a Chinese perspective, strengthens yang and moves qi in the pelvis. You can do this on your own, or with your partner.
    3. **Two-Hand Massage.** This is a variation on the above: Rub your palms together until hot, then press one hand firmly against the thigh where it meets the groin area, and press

the other hand against the lower abdomen on the same side, hard. Keeping both hands moving at the same time, rub from one thigh to the other, and massage the abdomen, all without touching or pressing against the genitals. Use enough force that the massage makes the penis move. Repeat for a total of twelve times. This increases the energy to the genitals, indirectly stimulates the prostate gland, and improves circulation.

- **Try acupuncture.** It can balance hormones, promote healthy circulation, reduce inflammation in the prostate and pelvic area, reduce stress, and mitigate the side effects of medications.
- **Consider Viagra only as a last resort.** You are better off trying other methods first to solve the root problem. You can use pharmaceuticals to treat the symptom if that fails—but you're likely not to have to.

If you have ED and your yang is low (see page 82)**:**
Consider adding some or all of these to the yang deficiency advice (Chapter 4):

- **Use the Chinese herbal formula Jin Gui Shen Qi Wan** (Rehmannia Eight), which is available over the counter, to boost yang energy.
- **Take L-carnitine supplements** (according to package instructions); research documents its effectiveness in treating ED.
- **Try zinc and vitamin C** supplements, both of which help boost testosterone levels.

If you have ED and your qi is stuck (see page 31):
Consider adding some or all of these on to the qi stagnation advice (Chapter 2):

- **Use the Chinese herbal formula Xiao Yao Wan** (Relaxed Wanderer) which is available over the counter, to help move qi.
- **Take L-arginine supplements** to help dilate blood vessels and increase blood flow, including to the penis.
- **Try ginkgo** supplements, particularly if you are experiencing ED as a side effect of taking antidepressants. Ginkgo enhances blood flow in the penis.
- **Use vitamin E** supplements to help increase blood circulation (but *not* if you are already taking some other blood thinner).

PREMATURE EJACULATION (PE)

Premature ejaculation (PE) is when a man ejaculates sooner than he, or his partner, would like—such as before intercourse begins, or shortly after it does. Chinese medicine ascribes most cases of PE to yin deficiency, though it is sometimes due to stuck qi. Ejaculation is very yang. But you need yin energy to help hold yang energy in the body. Without it, the yang won't stay contained—and ejaculating too quickly is one common way that happens. With qi stagnation, premature ejaculation happens when so much energy is pent up it is hard to contain, and any release will do.

Most often, PE is simply a habit that needs to be unlearned, not a true medical condition. One typical way this particular habit develops is from early sexual encounters that have to be quick and furtive—and speedy ejaculation is the way to go under those circumstances. It may take a little while to adopt a new habit, especially since we live in a culture that is, generally speaking, totally in favor of *speeding up.* Slowing down—at anything—may be a new skill. So be patient with yourself.

- **Ask for kelp.** As a food or as a supplement, kelp is a natural source of iodine, selenium, iron, calcium, vitamin A, niacin, phosphorous, and protein, all of which help prevent PE. All that, and it nourishes yin as well. What more could you ask of a sea vegetable?

- **Break the habit/learn a new habit.** If what you're dealing with is mainly a bad habit, you can fairly simply retrain yourself to take longer before ejaculating. The exercises here will help.
- **Follow the advice for yin deficiency** (page 71). It is especially important to avoid overwork and late nights, and to get sufficient sleep and to find time to rest and relax.
- **Don't squeeze your penis.** You may have heard or read that to foil PE, a man should withdraw when he feels he is near ejaculation, then squeeze (or have his partner squeeze) his penis at the point where the head meets the shaft for several seconds before picking up where he left off. But to my way of thinking, what you are mainly going to accomplish by stopping to perform a mini-Heimlich maneuver on the penis is to interrupt the intimacy and energetic connection that sex builds between partners, so I don't recommend it. You have much better options available to you. Such as:
- **Take some of the focus off intercourse.** Lessen the pressure of having sex by using oral and manual genital stimulation to give your partner pleasure. For many women, this is a more effective route to orgasm anyway—and you also may find that with more variety in your technique, you have a different perspective on whether or not you are in fact lasting long enough.
- **Do The Twist.** The woman lies on her side, then twists her hips and pelvis to face upward. The man penetrates from on top. Nine and Nine (see page 221) may be a useful addition. It is the slight awkwardness of this position that is helpful, because it encourages the man to keep his focus—an effect intensified by doing Nine and Nine. So if this exact position doesn't suit one of you—or if you don't happen to be working with a man/woman combination—choosing

something else a little bit tricky should accomplish essentially the same thing. Nine and Nine on its own, but in a more familiar position, might also be just the ticket.

- **Find The Point.** See page 233 for a full description, but here is the gist: When you begin to feel you may ejaculate, pause—but don't withdraw—and press firmly in the space between your scrotum and anus with your fore and middle fingers. Hold for a slow count of four. Take a deep breath while you are holding.
- **Practice the Three Locks.** This breathing exercise builds and moves qi, and practicing it regularly can help prevent PE. See pages 109 and 111.
- **Hold still.** One way to get used to being inside your partner without ejaculating is to simply be there, without any movement. Morning and Evening Meditation (page 165) is a great way to practice this while also promoting intimacy and connection. This would be a good time to also practice synchronizing your breathing with your partner's (see page 160). Think of Morning and Evening Meditation *not* as a prelude to intercourse but as a separate practice all its own. Save intercourse as you usually practice it for another time.
- **Consider acupuncture.** It has helped many of my patients with PE a lot. It nourishes yin and also helps restore flow of qi.
- **Try Chinese herbs.** Liu Wei Di Huang Wan (Rehmannia Six) nourishes yin. You can combine it with Wu Wei Zi (Schisandra), an herb that is good for both yin deficiency and stagnant qi and specifically helps PE. The herbal formula Zuo Gui Yin (Cyathula & Rehmannia) is another good option; it also nourishes yin.

General Health and Libido

Dealing with any specific sexual dysfunction is an important key step in reviving your sex life and reinvigorating your libido. But you also have to consider other physical health issues that have a more indirect effect on your sex drive. In fact, even if you are ready to get started with some of the solutions above, you should still scan through the rest of this chapter in case there's another layer to your situation. The reality is that if you are dealing with health problems, your libido may be hurting, too. But likely it doesn't have to be.

ALCOHOL AND DRUG USE

One drink might make you more amorous, but too much alcohol will spoil your sex drive. Alcohol is a depressant and causes your system to slow down—taking your libido right along with it. While it is notorious for interfering with strong erections, alcohol can cause just as much havoc with a woman's desire. The same is true of recreational drugs—including nicotine (smoking). Alcohol and drugs initially give energy, but then they draw more energy out than they put in. You're left with low energy—and a good chance that the next time you'll need more of whatever to get the same initial energy boost.

- **Don't abuse it.** One drink isn't likely to cause any disruption to your sex life; the problem is when you drink more, whether it's just one night, or a regular thing. And add sex to the long list of reasons you should not abuse alcohol or drugs, and seek treatment if you do have a problem.
- **Limit your intake before sex.** Even if you don't have a general problem with alcohol or drugs, it will behoove you to use them sparingly anytime you are hoping to have sex.

ANXIETY

In Western medicine, anxiety is about what's going on in your head, and the menu of recommended solutions is basically medications to address chemical imbalance in the brain, talk therapy, and/or stress management.

Chinese medicine understands anxiety not so much through the brain or mind as through the *chest.* Western medicine sees a lot of the symptoms in the chest—heart palpitations, shallow breathing, muscle tightness near the heart—but in Chinese medicine the chest is central in anxiety. Chinese medicine recognizes a few different types of anxiety.

Any anxiety related to qi stagnation, stressful events, repressed emotions, or loss will subconsciously cause us to tighten the muscles in our chests, restraining the flow of qi there, as well as to other organs. When this stagnation builds up, it causes a feeling of constraint or tightness in the chest. It can cause a feeling of agitation known as "heat in the heart." (In Western medicine this is a panic disorder or anxiety attack.) People with stuck qi can become preoccupied with their anxiety, and they are likely to have feelings of irritability or moodiness, poor appetite, hypochondriacal tightness or pain, muscle tension, fatigue, or alternating constipation and loose stools, too. They may also have low libido, and/or find it difficult to orgasm.

Yang deficiency anxiety, on the other hand, causes overthinking and worry. In people with this variety, anxiety tends to be chronic and recurring, and experienced as preoccupation, fear, or dread. They may struggle with a lack of sexual responsiveness.

In people with yin deficiency, anxiety shows up as restless mind, jumpiness, or fidgetiness. These are people who just can't settle down. When they are anxious, they tend to have a subjective sensation of heat—especially in the solar plexus, palms, and soles of the feet—night sweats, a general feeling of being hotter at night, or dry skin or mouth. Their restlessness may make it hard to focus on sex, which can cause various problems in their sex lives.

Treatment for anxiety can create its own sex problems. Antianxiety sedatives like Valium and Xanax may cause low libido, and make it difficult to become aroused.

- **Cry. Or laugh.** No matter what your type, the first step to getting rid of anxiety is to move qi in the chest. I tell my patients to try laughing or crying—either one can work—or even all-out wailing.
- **Breathe.** Breathing exercises like the ones in Chapter 6, or for any yogis out there, like pranayama, are another great way to release the chest and allow the free flow of qi.

- **Work out.** Exercise helps relieve anxiety. And it moves qi, which relieves anxiety. Boxing, or just about any upper-body exercise, like push-ups, is particularly good for moving qi in the chest, and therefore particularly good for relieving anxiety.
- **Get a massage** to help move qi, especially through the chest. A whole body massage helps qi to flow and can stop the anxious feeling of a knot in your chest.
- **Do yoga,** which is all about moving energy, even if the energy isn't going by the name of "qi."
- **Consult your doctor about possible changes to medication** (see page 270). You may be able to support changes in the way you use problematic medication with nonpharmaceutical strategies to alleviate stress and manage anxiety—such as meditation, biofeedback, yoga, acupuncture, herbs, and nutritional supplements.
- **Use an omega-3 fatty acid supplement.**
- **Try acupuncture** to move stagnant qi and relieve muscle spasms and tightness associated with anxiety. Acupuncture is also calming, and can induce a feeling of well-being (the opposite of anxiety!) that lasts even after the treatment ends. It can also help counter any side effects of anxiety medication (including low libido). Often my patients can lower the dose of medication they take, which can have many benefits, including eliminating side effects.
- **Take Suan Zao Ren (Ziziyphus)** to relieve anxiety.
- **OR take Tian Wang Bu Xin Dan (Emperor's Tea)** for yin deficiency anxiety.
- **OR try hops (humulus),** an herb that helps relax muscles, calm the mind, and improve sleep.
- **OR try skullcap and/or valerian root** to help prevent panic attacks.

FOR THE GUYS: Performance Anxiety

Anxiety is mostly the same no matter whether you have XX or XY chromosomes, but there is one aspect that is much more common in men's sex lives: performance anxiety. Women have the option of faking it in a way we just don't. Not that I recommend faking for anyone, but the truth is, we are just *out there,* every single time, and that can be a lot of pressure.

You might get performance anxiety in nonsexual as well as sexual ways—before a presentation at work, for example, or an important discussion with your kid. It's also likely that stresses from all aspects of your life can contribute to sexual performance anxiety. Pressure at work, spilling over to being moody, irritable, or withdrawn at home, fraying your relationship . . . this is a typical tale of performance anxiety.

You can relieve performance anxiety with the same advice as for anxiety in general (see page 261) (and, if it's a factor, with the advice for ED, see page 254). The Loop may be especially useful. The Squeeze may prove valuable because it helps focus energy and direct it, keeping your energy from being scattered, off balance—and anxiety provoking. It is also a good way to be present in your own body, which is a good way to feel your own sexual energy, and learn to trust it.

In addition to those things, you will probably find it useful to do something with your partner *other than* sex. Something where you won't feel pressure to perform, but where you two can feel your connection. One of my patients, for example, started cooking meals together with his wife. Bonus points for him for choosing an activity that is nourishing and sensual! Another good choice: teaching your partner any breathing or meditation exercise, and practicing it together.

CANCER AND CANCER TREATMENTS

The experience of having cancer can be as complicated psychologically as it is physically, which can be either the cause or the result of new complications in your sex life. Gynecological cancers are especially hard on sexuality. The side effects of many cancer treatments (pain, nausea, serious fatigue) don't do your desire any favors, either. You may experience changes in sensation (from radiation), contend with premature menopause (from some chemotherapy, especially for breast cancer), or struggle with body image issues related to disfigurement or scarring (from surgery) and/or hair loss (from chemo).

- **Consult with your doctor about potential changes to medications** and about managing sexual side effects like vaginal dryness and low libido. You could be having libido interference from treatments, or from many other things in your medicine cabinet, like antihistamines or antidepressants. (See page 270.)
- **Talk to your partner.** Sharing your worries can ease them enough for you to want to have sex even amid turbulent times.
- **Choose your position carefully.** If you have vaginal shortening as a result of cervical cancer or hysterectomy, using positions that allow only shallow penetration will be your best bet. (See Chapter 13 on positions).
- **Try acupuncture,** especially if you have depression (see following). Or hot flashes: A recent study established that it's better than medication at controlling hot flashes from breast cancer treatment.

DEPRESSION

Western medicine offers primarily therapy and pharmaceuticals to deal with depression, which is viewed as an imbalance in brain chemistry. Chinese medicine, on the other hand, sees depression as the result of stagnant emotional qi—meaning emotions do not move in and out of the body as they should.

East or West, one of the commonly recognized side effects of depression is low libido. In the Chinese view, this is because the stagnation that causes the depression also affects the flow of qi and blood to the genitals and pelvic area. Of course any negative emotions that are stuck in there aren't exactly going to help get your motor running, either. Depression can also be caused or exacerbated by serious problems in a relationship—the kind of problems that can affect not only your mood but also your sex life.

In the Western view, depression and lack of sexual interest are so closely associated that "inhibited sexual desire" is considered one of the symptoms of depression. On top of that, many of the drugs used to treat depression can cause dulled libido, or, as those long package inserts tend to put it: "reduced sexual performance."

Having sex is an almost surefire way to boost your mood, even if you are depressed, so it should be a component of any depression treatment plan. You don't even need a partner to reap most of the effects: At least one study has found an association between masturbation and decreases in depression. Count these as more reasons to *just do it*—and if you are not yet at a place where you can, the suggestions below can help get you there.

- **Talk to your doctor about possible medication adjustments.** (See page 271.). You may be able to facilitate effective medication changes by using nonpharmaceutical approaches to depression, like regular exercise, acupuncture, Chinese herbs, and B vitamins, even if you don't leave behind the Rx all together.
- **Plan sexual activity for just before you take your medication,** if you are taking a once-a-day dose. That's when side effects will be at their weakest.
- **Try acupuncture** to reduce symptoms of depression—it can have an effect significant enough that some people who get acupuncture no longer meet the official diagnosis for depression. Research has shown acupuncture alone can be as effective as other types of treatments, including therapy and drugs, and it is also useful in working alongside those treatments. Acupuncture can often counter the side effects of drug treatment.
- **Take He Huan Pi Cortex Albizzia Julibrissin (mimosa tree bark).** We call this mild treatment "herbal Prozac." It is good for depression, and also for the irritability and insomnia that may come with it. You

can usually take it along with actual Prozac or other prescriptions, but you should seek professional advice before you do so.

- **Or try Saint-John's-wort.** Do not take if you use prescription antidepressants or anticoagulants. It is also contraindicated with chemo and radiation, so people undergoing cancer treatment should not take it. It can increase sensitivity to the sun, making the use of sunscreen of prime importance.
- **Or take SAMe (S-Adenosyl-Methionine).** Do not use if you take prescription antidepressants, or have bipolar disorder.

DIABETES

When diet and medication are under control, most people with diabetes (type 1 or type 2) don't experience any effect on their sex lives. But when control is imperfect, many struggle with painful intercourse or problems with arousal. People with diabetes often have high levels of cholesterol in their blood, and that can diminish the flow of blood to the sex organs, which can interfere with sexual arousal and response.

In ancient China diabetes was known as wasting and thirsting disorder because of the overall dryness it causes, and many women with diabetes are bothered by vaginal dryness or lack of lubrication. Women may have chronic vaginal yeast infections and/or UTIs, resulting from high levels of glucose in vaginal mucus, which can make sex uncomfortable.

- **Prevent yeast infections** with a good probiotic supplement and by adding yogurt with active cultures to your daily diet. Consider taking a garlic supplement as well.
- **Prevent UTIs** by urinating before and after sex.
- **Use a vibrator with your partner** for extra stimulation if you develop neuropathy (nerve damage) that makes it difficult to orgasm.
- **Try the missionary position—with a twist.** The ancient texts suggest a variation on the missionary position for those with diabetes. They present it as a treatment, but I wouldn't rely on it alone. Still, if it appeals to you, why not try it? Here's how: In the

Dragon (missionary) position, the woman wraps her legs behind the man's thighs and rotates her pelvis alternately clockwise and counterclockwise, and the man limits himself to shallow penetration.

HEART DISEASE

Amid the (rightful) concern over high cholesterol, high blood pressure, blocked arteries, and the attendant increased risk of stroke and heart attack, the collateral damage to sex drive is often overlooked.

Women need good blood flow to and through the genitals to get sexually aroused, and to orgasm, for example. Many women with high blood pressure have difficulty becoming lubricated. On top of that, blood pressure medications may tamp down libido (see page 273).

For women with heart problems who are afraid sex isn't entirely safe, it can be very difficult to reach orgasm, even if they do brave a roll in the hay. Chinese medicine looks at heart health and the accompanying sexual issues as a matter of circulation of blood *and qi.* The sages would say this kind of fear causes stagnation—and an inability to let go.

Heart disease is hard on everyone's sex life in one more way, too: fear. Sexual arousal has a lot of the same signs as heart attack—rapid breathing, sweating, etc. Fear of this sort is a lousy reason to hold back on sex, however. Among other things, sex is a form of exercise, and a stress-buster to boot, so it's really good for the heart. The actual risk of heart attack during sex is vanishingly small. Check with your doctor, of course, but usually there is no reason *not* to have sex, even if you have a heart condition.

- **Choose a heart-healthy diet,** get regular aerobic exercise, include lots of garlic in your regular menus, and get lots of omega-3 oils via food and supplements. What is good for your heart will be good for your sex life as well.
- **Consult with your doctor about potential changes in medication** (see page 273). Lifestyle changes (losing weight, eating healthfully, exercising) can lower blood pressure all on their own, or allow you to reduce the dose of medication you take to the point

that it doesn't interfere with your sex life anymore. Acupuncture and Chinese herbs have been used effectively for centuries to treat high blood pressure, so that combination may be another option for you.

- **Spend plenty of time on foreplay,** allowing your heart rate to increase gradually.
- **Wait to have sex until at least three hours after eating**—digesting a meal can put a strain on your heart, and there's no sense in finding out the hard way if the combination could be too much.
- **Avoid receiving anal sex;** there is some evidence that stretching the nerves around the anus can cause an undesirable slowing of the heartbeat.
- **Explore alternatives to intercourse.** Sometimes when recovering from a heart attack it is necessary to abstain from intercourse for a while—check with your doctor to see if this applies to you. If it does, this will be a good time to explore other forms of intimate contact that may have more or less dropped out of your repertoire: kissing, massage, perhaps mutual masturbation.
- **Practice The Loop** (see page 61), which is particularly beneficial for people with cardiovascular issues.

HYPOTHYROID

Low levels of thyroid hormone is a fairly common condition. The sluggishness that is a typical symptom is quite enough to dampen sex drive all on its own. So is the weight gain, and the additional health and body image issues that come along with it. You'll have other biochemical challenges, too: In women low thyroid can lead to high levels of another hormone, prolactin, which can lead to low libido.

- **Get treatment** to raise thyroid levels if you test low. Your doctor might recommend pharmaceutical thyroid hormones like Synthroid. There are more natural (though still prescription) versions like Armour Thyroid or Nature-Throid that work better for some women because they more closely match the chemical structure of the thyroid hormone your body makes. You may want to work with an endocrinologist to fine-tune your treatment.

- **Be patient.** Whether you are using prescriptions or herbs, it will take a few weeks for libido to return.
- **Try Chinese medicine.** In mild cases of hypothyroidism, Chinese herbs may be enough to get you back on track. You may want to try Jin Gui Shen Qi Wan (Rehmannia Eight).

INSOMNIA

If you are having problems getting to sleep, or staying asleep, it is bound to affect your mood and your energy levels, thereby interfering with your libido as well. Furthermore, clinical research shows that genital blood flow (and therefore libido) is affected by REM sleep.

If you regularly suffer from insomnia, talk with your doctor about it. But please do not take sleep medications unless you have already made a serious effort to get good sleep using other means. At best, medications are an expensive, and short-term, strategy. For most people, good "sleep hygiene" will do the trick.

- **Reserve the bed for sleep (and sex) only.** That means no TV watching, no Web surfing, and so on. (Though I'm pleased to say reading is OK.) This is typical good-sleep advice. But it is also an excellent thing for your sex life!
- **Set aside some time at bedtime for sex.** It's a great way to unwind and help you get ready for sleep. And then, fortified by sound sleep, you'll be even more interested in sex in the future.

MEDICATIONS AND THEIR SEXUAL SIDE EFFECTS

Many prescription medications as well as common over-the-counter drugs come with a major side effect that far too often goes undiscussed: libido-killing. So if you are on a medication and your sex drive has gone missing, talk to your doctor about it. Ask about alternative medications, alternatives *to* medication, changing doses, or other ways to counter the side effects. Never stop taking a medication without consulting your doctor about it first. But it's just as big a mistake to keep on taking a medication that's giving you grief without talking to your doctor about *that.*

In many cases you can use nonpharmacological treatments to heal a condition, and even if that doesn't get you to where you quit meds altogether, it may allow you to take a lower dose that is both effective and without side effects. Acupuncture and Chinese herbs can often be used to treat conditions instead of drugs, or to improve performance of drugs at lower (non-side-effect) doses, or to treat side effects from drugs. Talk to a practitioner for your specific options and, just as with any medical professional, don't hold back about explaining any libido issues.

Following is a list of the most common culprits:

- **Antianxiety Medications** Sedatives like Valium and Xanax may cause low libido and make it difficult to become aroused.
- **Antidepressants** Antidepressants may be depressing your sex drive. **SSRIs** cause sexual side effects like low libido and failure to orgasm in many people. **Tricyclics** can cause low desire and fatigue.

SSRIs include:
citalopram (Celexa)
escitalopram (Lexapro)
fluoxetine (Prozac, Prozac Weekly)
paroxetine (Paxil, Paxil CR)
sertraline (Zoloft)

Tricyclics include:
Amitriptyline
Amoxapine
Desipramine (Norpramin)
Doxepin
Imipramine (Tofranil, Tofranil-PM)

Maprotiline
Nortriptyline (Pamelor)
Protriptyline (Vivactil)
Trimipramine (Surmontil)

Your doctor should be able to suggest some options. Among them:

Duloxetine (Cymbalta) may have less bothersome sexual side effects than other SSRIs.

Bupropion (Wellbutrin) generally has a lower risk of sexual side effects.

Adding an additional medication can sometimes help; taking buspirone (Buspar), for example, an antianxiety medication, may ease sexual side effects caused by an antidepressant.

- **Antihistamines** OTCs like Allegra, Zyrtec, Sudafed, Benadryl, and Claritin can dampen libido when they lead to vaginal dryness and fatigue. You might have better luck with a nasal spray such as the prescription Flonase, which acts locally and doesn't circulate through the entire body. You might also explore alternative methods of easing allergies, including herbs, homeopathy, acupuncture, and washing your nasal passages with a neti pot.
- **Birth Control Pills** It should come as no surprise that birth control pills, which shift a woman's sexual hormones, often wind up decreasing libido, lubrication, and sexual satisfaction. Putting people off sex is definitely one way to prevent conception, but somehow I don't think it's what anyone has in mind when they fill a prescription for "the Pill." Recent research suggests that not only do women using birth control pills have significantly lower levels of sexual desire than women not using them, but they also may struggle with that effect even after they've stopped taking the medication. So if hormonal birth control is hindering rather than helping your sex life, talk to your doctor about a low-dose pill, or other forms of contraception. (Nonhormonal birth control can

cause libido problems, too, so choose carefully and apply creatively. For example the diaphragm hinders spontaneity, and sometimes women would just rather skip the sex than deal with putting the diaphragm in. One idea is to teach your partner to put it in, and make insertion a part of foreplay.)

- **Blood Pressure Medication** Take a pill to lower high blood pressure, and you might just end up with a side order of low libido and poor sexual arousal, thanks to reduced blood flow. Fortunately there are several different categories of drugs used to control high blood pressure, and some have less effect on sexual function than others, so you may have an alternative open to you.
- **Cancer Treatments** In women, treatments for cancer of the bladder, breast, cervix, colon, ovaries, uterus, rectum, or vagina may cause loss of libido, vaginal dryness, and difficulty with orgasm. Radiation and surgery may be to blame (see page 264), but medications, especially medications with hormonal effects (which is many of them!), very often cause the trouble. The good news about sexual side effects linked to chemotherapy and radiation is that they are generally temporary—they'll stop when treatment stops. But if surgery causes a problem, it may be a permanent effect.

  When you are dealing with cancer and cancer treatments and struggling with your sex life as well, it is also important to consider if you are taking any other medications (not directly related to the cancer) that might be affecting your libido. (Antidepressants are often the most common culprits, as I've often seen with my patients.)
- **Epilepsy Medications** Antiepileptic drugs (AEDs) are so sedating (especially the barbiturates) that many of them have sexual side effects. Many AEDs are associated with significant shifts in hormones affecting sexual behavior and function. People taking AEDs may experience low libido, trouble getting aroused, and/or difficulty reaching orgasm.
- **Multiple Sclerosis Medications** Some medications used to treat MS can interfere with sexual arousal.

♂ FOR THE GUYS: Of Meds and Men

File under: Cure is worse than the disease. Well, maybe not worse, but sometimes even less sexy. Men should take a full look at the section about medications and their sexual side effects, but there are a few things of concern just to men:

Antidepressants, particularly those in the SSRI and tricyclic categories, can cause decreased sex drive and delayed ejaculation.

Cancer treatments for prostate, bladder, and rectal and colon cancer can lead to painful sex, ED, and/or low sex drive. The hormonal medications often used with prostate cancer, in particular, can affect both desire and ability to perform sexually. It may help to add a medication for sexual function, such as Viagra, so talk to your doctor.

Epilepsy medications can cause low libido, ED, and/or delayed ejaculation.

Cholesterol medications—statins—in men may decrease libido and sexual function right along with cholesterol levels. Some men experience ED while taking these medications.

MIGRAINE

Migraines can be triggered by orgasm, thanks to the rush of neurotransmitters—and/or the burst of yang energy. Fear of migraine is a surefire turnoff if ever there was one.

- **Choose a sexual position** that avoids arching the neck or back: It's the one simple way you can avoid the possibility of setting off a migraine during sex.

NEUROLOGICAL ISSUES

All kinds of things can impair your neurological system, and while they all present more obvious and immediate challenges, there's one common effect that is often overlooked: interference with your sex life.

Multiple sclerosis can come along with an erratic sexual response—sometimes you're fine, sometimes you have trouble getting aroused or trouble achieving orgasm. Muscle weakness and spasm don't make having sex easy, and nerve problems can mess with your pleasure when you *do* have sex, as they can decrease sensation in the genitals. Some of the medications used to treat MS can interfere with sexual arousal.

Seizure disorders including epilepsy can cause problems with arousal and lubrication. And most of my patients with epilepsy fear triggering an episode by having sex, which greatly reduces their desire. On top of that many antiseizure meds can cause low libido, trouble getting aroused, and/or difficulty reaching orgasm.

Spinal cord injuries are often devastating, and part of the reason why is that they can make you feel as if you will never be sexual again. Loss of sensation can certainly cause arousal problems, and loss of mobility definitely makes having sex the way you always used to have it more difficult or even impossible.

Stroke. If you've had a stroke, you may have muscle weakness, or loss of sensation, and, perhaps most disruptive of all, lack of confidence—for which your sex life is suffering.

Solutions to lack of sex when you have neurological issues may vary according to the particulars of your situation. But there are several underlying strategies common to most scenarios:

- **Communicate with your partner about your fears (and theirs).** Make a plan about what to do to minimize your chances of having any problems with sex, as well as what to do if you do run into trouble, as a way of helping you let go of your fear.
- **Consult with your doctor about possible medication changes.**
- **Create opportunities for extra stimulation** if you have diminished sensation in your genitals. For example, choose a position for intercourse that allows for the hands to be pressed into service at the same time. Or incorporate a vibrator into your sex life.
- **Have intercourse lying side by side, and front to back.** (see Mandarin Ducks Joined, page 217). This is a good one for allowing extra stimulation, as above, but it is also useful because it is less

strain on the body, and particularly helps in the case of muscle spasms.

- **Consider acupuncture,** which can help restore lost nerve sensation.
- **Consider Chinese medical treatment.** Some of my patients have successfully reduced their medications by having regular acupuncture and taking a specially tailored herbal formula. This approach requires close communication between acupuncturist, doctor, and patient.

POSTPARTUM

The first weeks and months after childbirth can take quite a toll on your sex drive. You may be flattened by fatigue, for one. Changes in your body may mean you can't get busy the same ways you always have—and that your body image may be taking some hits. And the stress involved in caring for a new baby can also contribute to the dulling of libido.

Breast-feeding may reduce desire, because it raises prolactin, which lowers libido and, double whammy, lowers estrogen levels, interfering with lubrication. And that's before you even get into the way many women think about their breasts and their sexuality—and how much more complicated it can get, thanks to nursing.

Some simple changes can help make sure you see some action as you find your "new normal":

- **Love your body.** Pregnancy changes your body in many ways that don't always change back once the baby is born, and it's common for women to get sucked into a negative self-image as a result. Be on the lookout for signs of that in yourself, and choose to embrace your "new normal" instead. You have after all just had an amazing experience of how powerful your body is and the incredible things it can do. Show it some love.
- **Stay hydrated** while you are breast-feeding. Start with the obvious: Drink plenty of water.

- **Get plenty of omega-3 fatty acids** (via diet or supplements or both) to help keep things moist.
- **Eat plenty of protein.**

FOR THE GUYS: Men's Health

Medical and health problems that impact libido—and their solutions—are much the same for men and women, save the obvious exceptions, like pregnancy. There are a few special issues or mechanisms for men, however:

CANCER TREATMENTS

Any cancer that strikes at sex organs can be especially hard on sexuality. And the treatments themselves for prostate, bladder, rectal, and colon cancer can lead to lowered testosterone, painful sex, ED, and/or low sex drive.

Herbs and acupuncture can help with side effects of treatment. Acupuncture is particularly helpful in treating the psychological effects and many stresses of cancer diagnosis and treatment. Acupuncture can prevent or relieve the stagnation that can be the result of—or that could lead to—low libido and ED.

DIABETES

Men who have diabetes have a likelihood of experiencing sexual problems (particularly ED) that is *three times* that of men who don't have diabetes, thanks to the way diabetes can impair nerves, blood vessels, and muscle tissue. In addition, high cholesterol, common in people with diabetes, can impede the flow of blood to the penis, causing trouble with erections. (And cholesterol medications can cause their own sexual side effects—see below, and page 82.)

HEART DISEASE

Heart health is crucial for a healthy sex life because you need good blood flow to and through the penis to be able to get and stay erect. If you haven't had problems yet, but you do have some artery-clogging processes under way in your body, trust me: You will. Take action. Your (sex) life is on the line.

The sexual side effects of some heart medications (see page 82) can provide good motivation to make a serious attempt at controlling cholesterol via diet and exercise. Even if you don't get your cholesterol all the way to a safe level that way, you are likely to be able to reduce the dose of medication, which may eliminate the side effects. If you want natural ways to supplement your efforts, research backs the use of these supplements to lower cholesterol levels: psyllium powder, apple pectin, Chinese red yeast rice extract, and artichoke leaf extract (Cynara scolymus). For improving the ratio of HDL to LDL, you could try chromium picolinate.

HYPOTHYROID

Low thyroid levels inhibit testosterone synthesis, and low testosterone can lead to low libido.

MIGRAINES

Migraines may also be triggered by ejaculation. Learning to ejaculate with less yang energy, as with the "holdback" techniques in Chapter 14, can avoid this risk.

NEUROLOGICAL ISSUES

The side effects of epilepsy medication can include ED and/or delayed ejaculation.

Appendix 1

Finding and Using Chinese Herbs

Throughout this book, I recommend herbs and herbal formulas available over the counter so you can use them on your own at home. If you went to see a practitioner of Chinese medicine, you would get prescribed combinations of herbs customized and adjusted precisely to your body and your situation (though probably based on the same formulas I'm writing about). Obviously I can't replicate that in a book, so if you have access to a practitioner you may want to optimize my recommendations with expert guidance. But the formulas I mention here are time-tested and very effective—and I've included only those that are very safe for independent use—so you can also get excellent results without seeing a practitioner.

You do have to make sure you get high-quality herbs from a good source, so you can be sure you are getting exactly what you want—nothing more, nothing less. You can buy them in Chinatown, if you live near one, but ordering online is probably what's most convenient. Either way the important thing is to go with a reliable brand. Brands I recommend to my patients include:

- **Golden Flower Chinese Herbs** and **Plum Flower** for pills
- **Kan Herbs** for tinctures (concentrated herbs in an alcohol extract)
- **KPC Herbs** for granules

I like herbs that come as granules, since they are effective and easy to use—just add hot water and drink like tea. Herbs also come in raw form, but they require cooking up daily into a kind of tea, which I think is too much bother for most people—and in any case requires professional guidance to manage.

You also need to work with a practitioner if you are thinking of taking herbs along with any other medication, including another herbal formula. You can take herbs when you are using other supplements—vitamins or fish oil or what have you—but my advice is simply to not start more than one new thing at a time. Introduce each additional thing slowly, so you have time to notice how your body is handling one before you complicate matters with something else.

If you do have a reaction to any herb or formula—a symptom you didn't have before—stop taking it and consult a practitioner.

Appendix 2

Exercises to Move Qi, Nourish Yin, and Boost Yang

For all-around energy promoting and balancing, learn all-purpose exercises that move qi, nourish yin, and/or boost yang:

The Loop (page 61)
The Squeeze (page 85)
Kissing: Use Your Hands (page 190)
Head to Toe (page 203)
Nine and Nine (page 221)

When you want to move qi, check out:

Take a Breath (page 25)
Synchronize Your Breathing (page 160)
Think About It (page 34)
Morning and Evening Meditation (page 165)
Mixing Bowl (page 127)
Breast Massage (page 125)
Exploring (page 129)
Partner Massage (page 132)
Kissing (page 188)
Kissing: Make Eye Contact (page 190)
Kissing: Heart to Heart (page 191)
G-spot (page 142)
A-spot (page 143)
Tease and Release (page 198)
Quickie (page 199)

Cunnilingus (giving) (page 209)
Fellatio (giving) (page 205)
The Top Ten (page 214)
Keep On Rocking (page 221)

For nourishing yin, try:

Inner Smile (page 112)
Opening the Senses (page 54)
Morning and Evening Meditation (page 165)
Breast Massage (page 125)
Partner Massage (page 132)
Kissing (page 188)
G-spot (page 142)
A-spot (page 143)
Tease and Release (page 198)
Cunnilingus (receiving) (page 207)
Dragon (page 214)
Monkey (page 215)
Cicada (page 215)
Phoenix (page 216)
Fish (page 216)
Mandarin Ducks Joined (page 217)

In order to boost yang, consider:

Belly Breath (page 96)
Energy Meditation (page 114)
Buddha Belly (page 78)
Mixing Bowl (page 127)
Tease and Release (page 198)
Quickie (page 199)
Fellatio (receiving) (page 206)
Dragon (page 214)
Tiger (page 214)
Turtle (page 215)

Rabbit (page 216)
Fish (page 216)
Crane (page 217)
The Thigh Master (page 221)

FOR THE GUYS: Exercises for Men

Almost all the exercises above move qi, nourish yin, or boost qi in the same ways for men and women. One for-men-only addition is Prostate Massage (page 144), which is good for yin deficiency or yang deficiency.

In addition, The Top Ten, which all serve to move qi in anyone, tend to affect men and women differently when it comes to yin and yang.

To nourish yin, choose:

Turtle (page 215)
Rabbit (page 216)
Fish (page 216)
Crane (page 217)

To boost yang, choose:

Dragon (page 214)
Tiger (page 214)
Monkey (page 215)
Cicada (page 215)
Phoenix (page 216)
Mandarin Ducks Joined (page 217)

Appendix 3

Resources

Products

For **high-quality vitamins,** try Premier Research Labs, Pure Encapsulations, and/or Metagenics.

Water-based lubricants are the only appropriate kind for use with latex condoms (and won't damage rubber or plastic in toys). **Sylk** is one I recommend. **Astroglide** also offers some good options. It is important to read labels: **Sliquid** Organics Silk Lubricant, for example, is certified organic, contains no glycerin, petroleum or parabens, and so is a good choice even before you know it also has green tea, hibiscus, flax and sunflower seed extracts.

Zestra arousal oil is available at Zestra.com.

Salivary hormone test available from Unikey Health:
http://www.unikeyhealth.com/product/Salivary_test/Parasite_Testing

Custom-compounded natural hormones available
with a prescription through: Women's International Pharmacy, www.womensinternational.com and The Healthy Choice Compounding Pharmacy, www.thehealthychoice.net

Good source for **toys** include: **Good Vibrations** (www.goodvibes.com) and **My Pleasure** (www.mypleasure.com), which also has some good articles on sex.

Books

To **learn more about Chinese medicine:**
The Web That Has No Weaver by Ted Kaptchuck
Between Heaven and Earth by Harriet Beinfield and Efrem Korngold

To **read more about Taoist sexology:**
The Tao of Sexology by Stephen Thomas Chang
Sexual Reflexology by Mantak Chia and William U. Wei

Taoist sexology for women:
Healing Love through the Tao: Cultivating Female Sexual Energy by Mantak Chia and Maneewan Chia

For the **full scoop on holdbacks** and other aspects of Taoist sexology for men I recommend:
The Multi-orgasmic Man by Mantak Chia and Douglas Abrams Arava

Good, non-Chinese takes on sex in long-term relationships include:
The Sex-Starved Marriage by Michele Weinter-Davis
Passionate Marriage by David Schnarch. This author, together with Dr. Ruth Morehouse, offers workshops and retreats. www.passionatemarriage.com.

Index

(Page references in **boldface** refer to instructions for the exercises.)

H

I

J

K

L

T

U

Z